Richard Lee Metcalfe, R. C Mindill

The Great Fight for Free Silver

Richard Lee Metcalfe, R. C Mindill

The Great Fight for Free Silver

ISBN/EAN: 9783744708265

Printed in Europe, USA, Canada, Australia, Japan

Cover: Foto ©ninafisch / pixelio.de

More available books at **www.hansebooks.com**

Hon. WILLIAM J. BRYAN,

THE GREAT FIGHT

.. FOR ..

FREE SILVER

An Interesting History of the first great struggle in which
the Fearless and Brilliant Leader of the People
championed the cause of humanity in the
memorable campaign of 1896.

It recounts his heroic and untiring efforts in the Halls of Congress, at
the Chicago Convention, and in his great campaign throughout
the country; his matchless oratory; the splendid
achievements won, and the brilliant outlook
for the future of Bi-Metalism, and
a Biographical sketch of
MRS. BRYAN

———

IT CONTAINS AN

AUTHORIZED BIOGRAPHY

OF HON. WM. JENNINGS BRYAN, PREPARED BY R. L. METCALF, ESQ.,
OF THE OMAHA WORLD-HERALD, ASSISTED IN OTHER PARTS BY
R. C. MINDILL, OF THE N. Y. JOURNAL.

———

PROFUSELY ILLUSTRATED

———

EDGEWOOD PUBLISHING COMPANY

AUTHOR'S PREFACE.

In the services to the nation of Abraham Lincoln, the rail-splitter; of James A. Garfield, the canal-boy; of James G. Blaine, the school-master; of the hosts of men, who have risen from poverty and obscurity to place and power, the splendid possibilities of American citizenship have been amply demonstrated.

It is with these possibilities that this little book has to do. For it no literary merit is claimed. It goes to the public as the simple and hastily-written life-history of one who, unaided by inherited wealth, or environment, other than that of the great common people with whom he has cast his lot, has risen from obscurity to world-wide fame.

This book deals with facts, not surmises or idle compliments. It is not intended as a feather in the plume of knighted hero, or banner upon the wall of moated castle. Its only purpose is to familiarize the people of to-day with one who, by force of ability, and unswerving honesty, has, like the martyr, Lincoln, won his way to fame.

Lincoln said that he knew that God loved the common people because He made so many of them. William Jennings Bryan has manfully fought their battles, undismayed by organized opposition, and unswerved by temptations of place and power. The honors that have come to him have come because the people have recognized in him the nearest approach to that high ideal of the Christian statesman, which was held up by the founders of the Republic to be the guide of future generations.

To the cause of popular government, represented by its ablest defender—William J. Bryan—this book is respectfully dedicated.

R. L. Metcalfe.

TABLE OF CONTENTS.

TABLE OF CONTENTS.

CHAPTER XXVI.

CHAPTER XXVII.

LIST OF ILLUSTRATIONS.

LIST OF ILLUSTRATIONS.

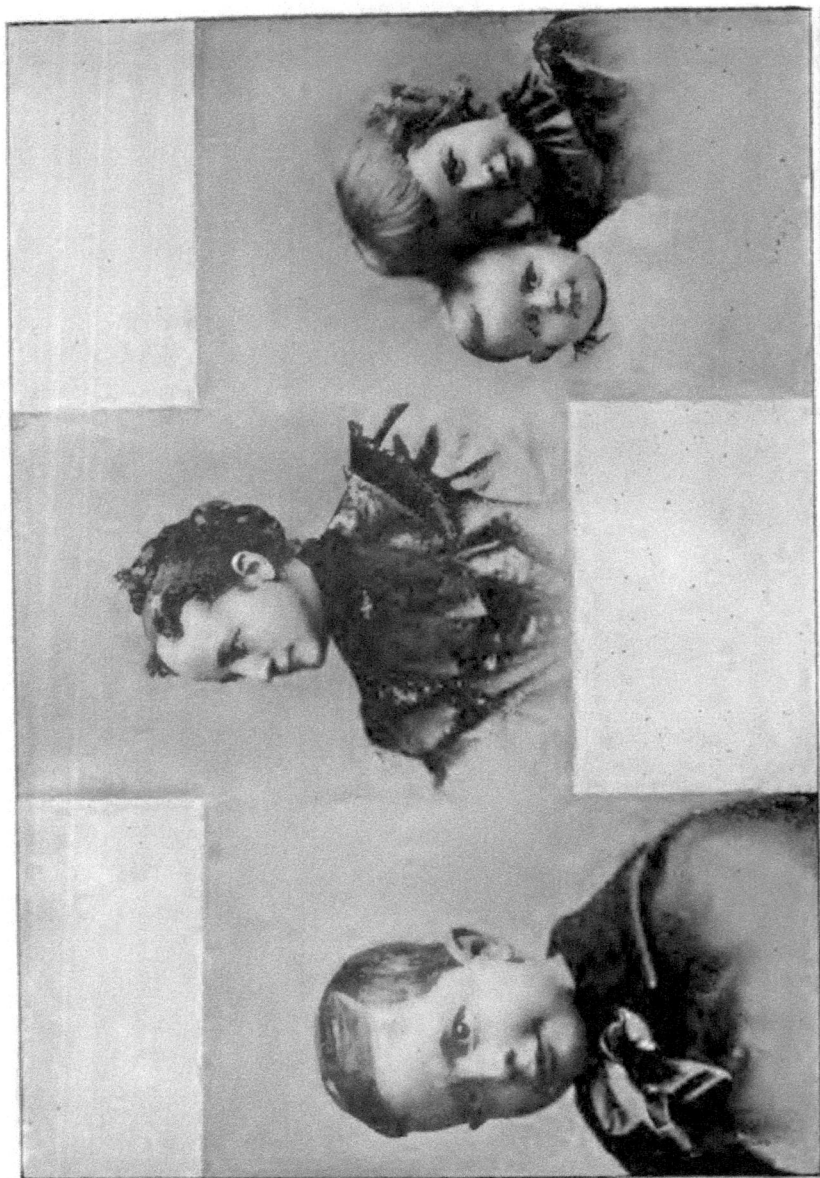

CHAPTER I.

BRYAN'S EARLY DAYS.

William Jennings Bryan, the Democratic nominee for President of the United States, was born in the town of Salem, Marion County, Illinois, March 19, 1860. He is the descendant of the Jennings and the Bryan families, whose men and women made the world better by their existence. None of these achieved national distinction, but each appears to have performed his or her part in life with strict fidelity to duty. Along all the branches of the very numerous family it is not difficult to observe the existence of a strong family pride. Not that pride which comprehends an aristocracy, nor, indeed, that which considers genius, but a pride that contemplates the ancestry of honest men and women, who provided well for their families, educated their children, bestowed charity where charity was deserved and contributed materially to society in their respective spheres.

The father of William Jennings Bryan was Silas Lillard Bryan, and his mother's maiden name was Mariah Elizabeth Jennings. The American history of the Bryan family begins in

Culpepper County, Virginia. A church still standing in that vicinity is known as the "Bryan Church," and the house in which Silas Lillard Bryan was born is also intact.

William Bryan, the great grandfather of the presidential nominee, the first of the family known to the descendants, lived in Culpepper County, Virginia. Five children were born to this couple. One of these was John Bryan, the grandfather of William J. Bryan. In 1807, John Bryan married Nancy Lillard. Miss Lillard was the daughter of one of the best families in Virginia, and she was a woman of unusual talent and strength of character. In 1828, John Bryan and wife moved to Cabal County, living there two years, finally locating in Mason County, Virginia, where they resided until their death. To this couple ten children were born. Of these children two are living to-day. One of these children was Silas Lillard Bryan, the father of the presidential candidate.

Silas Lillard Bryan was born near Sperryville, in what was then Culpepper County, Virginia, in 1822. He located in Illinois in 1842 and lived in Marion County until his death. Silas Lillard Bryan was purely a self-made man. He worked his way through McKendree College and obtained for himself an excellent education. For thirty years Silas Lillard Bryan was an honored member of the Marion County bar. He served eight years in the Illinois State Senate, and for twelve years—from 1860 to 1872—was circuit judge. Judge Bryan was a member of the convention of 1870, which framed the present State constitution of Illinois.

Silas Lillard Bryan married Mariah Elizabeth Jennings. Israel Jennings, a native of Connecticut, the founder of the Jennings family in Illinois, was married to Mary Warden, in Maysville, Kentucky, in 1800. In 1819, he removed, with his family, to Marion County, Illinois, settling near Walnut Hill. He was a member of the Illinois Legislature in 1827. The union of Israel and Mary Jennings was blessed with five children, one of whom, Charles W. Jennings, was the grandfather of the presidential candidate. Charles W. Jennings settled near his parents' home and was united in marriage to Mariah Davidson. Eight children were the fruit of this union. One of these was Mariah E., the mother of William Jennings Bryan.

Russell Bryan, the youngest brother of Judge Bryan, located in Salem, in 1841, and still lives in that vicinity. Elizabeth Bryan, Judge Bryan's youngest sister, married George Baltzell, and lives at Deer Ridge, Lewis County, Missouri.

Zadoc Jennings, brother, and Mrs. Harriett Marshall, Mrs. Nancy Davenport and Mrs. Docia Van Antwerp, sisters of Mrs. Judge Bryan, still survive. The descendants of the Jennings and

Bryan families are numerous, and they have contributed materially to good government and the welfare of society in Virginia, Kentucky, Illinois, Ohio, Arkansas and Missouri. Nine children were born to Judge and Mrs. Bryan. Of these, five are living. Frances, the eldest sister of the presidential candidate married James W. Baird. Mr. and Mrs. Baird reside at Salem, Illinois. Two other sisters, Miss Nanny Bryan and Miss Mary Bryan, also reside at Salem. Charles W., the only brother of the presidential candidate, is a citizen of Omaha. He is six years younger than William, and was married four years ago to Miss Bessie Brokaw. Judge Bryan, the father of the presidential nominee, died March 30, 1880. Mr. Bryan's mother died three weeks prior to the Chicago Convention.

A pathetic feature is found in the fact, that the mother had in recent years believed that a great future awaited her distinguished son, and whatever claims may be made and established concerning the "original Bryan man," there can be no question but that the devoted mother of the presidential candidate was the original Bryan woman. Bryan gets his even temper and his sunshine from his mother, who was one of the most lovable of women. He inherits his eloquence and his courage from his father, whose platform speeches and whose bravery yet live in the memory of the people of Salem. His high character comes from both parents, whose careers are full of good deeds and whose lives are those of consistent, earnest Christians. One of the oldest inhabitants of Salem, says : " Judge Bryan, William J. Bryan's father, had one weakness. He was not content with family prayers, morning and night, but he prayed at noon as regularly as the clock struck twelve. I have seen him adjourn court before twelve o'clock and then kneel at his seat in prayer. I saw him once about to mount his horse in the public square ; he took out his watch, observed that it was twelve o'clock, and kneeled beside his horse and prayed. Judge Bryan was a very devoted man, and observed what he considered to be his religious duty, as strictly as he did every official and personal duty.

It has been related that Judge Bryan had the habit of opening court with devotional exercises, but this tale is without foundation other than as related above. But Judge Bryan had a firm reliance in divine guidance and inculcated in the breasts of his children the same supreme faith in the Creator. The same Christian spirit dominated the life of Mrs. Bryan, mother of the presidential candidate. There are very many tender recollections among the people of Marion County of the practical and consistent Christianity practised by Judge and Mrs. Bryan. Their purses and their energies were always available for the advancement of the Christian religion, and their store-houses were always open for the relief of God's poor.

It is not surprising that such parents as these should have been able to rear up a son whose life is modeled after their own good careers, and whose public services are dedicated to the cause of popular government, as his private life is dedicated to the service of his parents' Master.

It is related of Judge Bryan that on one occasion his poultry house was broken open and a large number of prize hens were stolen. Certain indications led the Judge to suspect a certain worthless resident of the neighborhood. Several weeks afterward this worthless resident met the Judge while the latter was on his way to court. "Judge," said the worthless resident, "I understand you lost some chickens." "Sh! Sh!" replied the Judge, as he placed his hand upon the shoulder of the worthless scamp, "don't say a word about it, don't say a word about it, there is only three people that know anything about that, God, yourself and myself, and I don't want it to get out."

When William Jennings Bryan was six years old, his parents moved to a farm in the vicinity of the town of Salem. Until young Bryan was ten years of age his parents taught him at home, hoping to mould his young mind to better advantage under such circumstances, in his more tender years. At the age of ten, young Bryan entered the public school of Salem. There he attended until he was fifteen years of age, when in the fall of 1875 he entered Whipple Academy, Jacksonville, Illinois. Two years later, in 1877, he entered Illinois College at Jacksonville, and completed a classical course, being graduated in 1881, at the age of twenty-one, as valedictorian and class orator.

The graduation oration of William J. Bryan, with valedictory address, delivered at Illinois College, Jacksonville, Illinois, Thursday, June 2, 1881, was as follows:

"It is said of the ermine that it will suffer capture rather than allow pollution to touch its glossy coat, but take away that coat and the animal is worthless.

"We have ermines in higher life—those who love display. The desire to seem, rather than to be, is one of the faults which our age, as well as other ages, must deplore.

"Appearance too often takes the place of reality—the stamp of the coin is there, and the glitter of the gold, but, after all, it is but a worthless wash. Sham is carried into every department of life, and we are being corrupted by show and surface. We are too apt to judge people by what they have, rather than by what they are; we have too few Hamlets who are bold enough to proclaim, 'I know not seem!'

"The counterfeit, however, only proves the

value of the coin, and, although reputation may in some degree be taking the place of character, yet the latter has lost none of its worth, and, now, as of old, is a priceless gem, wherever found. Its absence and presence, alike, prove its value. Have you not conversed with those whose brilliant wit, pungent sarcasm and well-framed sentences failed to conceal a certain indescribable something which made you distrust every word they uttered? Have you not listened to those whose eloquence dazzled, whose pretended earnestness enkindled in you an enthusiasm equal to their own, and yet, have you not felt that behind all this there was lurking a monster that repelled the admiration which their genius attracted? Are there not those, whom like the Greeks we fear, even when they are bringing gifts? That something is want of character, or, to speak more truly, the possession of bad character, and it shows itself alike in nations and individuals.

"Eschines was talented: his oration against the crowning of Demosthenes was a masterly production, excellently arranged, elegantly written and effectively delivered; so extraordinary was its merits, that, when he afterwards, as an exile, delivered it before a Roadian audience, they expressed their astonishment that it had not won for him his cause, but it fell like a chilling blast upon his hearers at Athens, because he was the 'hireling of Philip.'

" Napoleon swept like a destroying angel over almost the entire eastern world, evincing a military genius unsurpassed, skill marvellous in its perfection, and a courage which savored almost of rashness, yet ever demonstrated the wisdom of its dictates. For a while he seemed to have robbed fortune of her secret, and bewildered nations gazed in silence while he turned the streams of success according to his vascillating whims.

"Although endowed with a perception keen enough to discern the hidden plans of opposing generals, he could but see one road to immortality—a path which led through battle-fields and marshes wet with human gore ; over rivers of blood and streams of tears that flowed from orphans eyes—a path along whose length the widow's wail made music for his marching hosts. But he is fallen, and over his tomb no mourner weeps. Talent, genius, power, these he had— character, he had none.

" But there are those who have both influence through life and unending praises after death ; there are those who have by their ability, inspired the admiration of the people and held it by the purity of their character. It is often remarked that some men have a name greater than their works will justify; the secret lies in the men themselves.

" It was his well-known character, not less than his eloquent words ; his deep convictions, not less than the fire of his utterance ; his own patriotism, not less than his invectives against the Macedonian that brought to the lips of the reanimated Greeks that memorable sentence, 'Let us go against Philip.'·

"Perhaps we could not find better illustrations of the power and worth of character, than are presented in the lives of two of our own country-men—names about which cluster in most sacred nearness the affections of the American people—honored dust over which have fallen the truest tears of sorrow ever shed by a nation for its heroes—the father and savior of their common country—the one, the appointed guardian of its birth ; the other, the preserver of its life.

" Both were reared by the hand of Providence for the work entrusted to their care ; both were led by nature along the rugged path of poverty ; both formed a character whose foundations were laid broad and deep in the purest truths of morality—a character which stood unshaken amid the terrors of war and the tranquillity of peace ; a character which allowed neither cowardice upon the battle-field nor tyranny in the presidential chair. Thus did they win the hearts of their countrymen and prepare for themselves a lasting place of rest in the tender memories of a grateful people.

"History but voices our own experience when it awards to true nobility of character the highest place among the enviable possessions of man.

" Nor is it the gift of fortune. In this, at least, we are not creatures of circumstances : talent, special genius may be the gift of nature ; position in society, the gift of birth ; respect may be bought with wealth ; but neither one nor all of these can give character. It is a slow but sure growth to which every thought and action lends its aid. To form character is to form grooves in which are to flow the purposes of our lives. It is to adopt principles which are to be the measure of our actions, the criteria of our deeds. This we are doing each day, either consciously or unconsciously ; there is character formed by our association with each friend, by every aspiration of the heart, by every object toward which our affections go out, yea, by every thought that flies on its lightning wing through the dark recesses of the brain.

"It is a law of mind that it acts most readily in familiar paths, hence, repetition forms habit, and almost before we are aware, we are chained to a certain routine of action from which it is difficult to free ourselves. We imitate that which we admire. If we revel in stories of blood, and are pleased with the sight of barbaric cruelty, we find it easy to become a Caligula or a Domitian ; we picture to ourselves scenes of cruelty in which we are actors, and soon await only the opportunity to vie in atrocity with the Neroes of the past.

"If we delight in gossip, and are not content

unless each neighbor is laid upon the dissecting table, we form a character unenviable indeed, and must be willing to bear the contempt of all the truly good, while we roll our bit of scandal as a sweet morsel under the tongue.

"But if each day we gather some new truths, plant ourselves more firmly upon principles which are eternal, guard every thought and action that they may be pure, and conform our lives more nearly to that Perfect Model, we shall form a character that will be a fit background on which to paint the noblest deeds and grandest intellectual and moral achievements; a character that cannot be concealed, but which will bring success in this life and form the best preparation for that which is beyond.

"The formation of character is a work which continues through life, but at no time is it so active as in youth and early manhood. At this time impressions are most easily made, and mistakes most easily corrected. It is the season for the sowing of the seed;—the springtime of life. There is no complaint in the natural world because each fruit and herb brings forth after its kind; there is no complaint if a neglected seed-time brings a harvest of want; there is no cry of injustice if thistles spring from thistle-seed sown. As little reason have we to murmur if in after-life we discover a character dwarfed and deformed by the evil thoughts and actions of to-day; as little reason have we to impeach the wisdom of God if our wild oats, as they are called in palliation, leave scars upon our manhood, which years of reform fail to wear away.

"Character is the entity, the individuality of the person, shining from every window of the soul, either as a beam of purity, or as a clouded ray that betrays the impurity within. The contest between light and darkness, right and wrong, goes on: day by day, hour by hour, moment by moment our characters are being formed, and this is the all-important question which comes to us in accents ever growing fainter as we journey from the cradle to the grave, 'Shall those characters be good or bad?'

"Beloved instructors, it is character not less than intellect that you have striven to develop. As we stand at the end of our college course, and turn our eyes toward the scenes forever past—as our memories linger on the words of wisdom which have fallen from your lips, we are more and more deeply impressed with the true conception of duty which you have ever shown. You have sought, not to trim the lamp of genius until the light of morality is paled by its dazzling brilliance, but to encourage and strengthen both. These days are over. No longer shall we listen to your warning voices, no more meet you in those familliar class-rooms, yet on our hearts 'deeply has sunk the lesson' you have 'given, and shall not soon depart.'

"We thank you for your kind and watchful care, and shall ever cherish your teachings with that devotion which sincere gratitude inspires.

"It is fitting that we express to you also, honored trustees, our gratitude for the privileges which you have permitted us to enjoy.

"The name of the institution whose interests you guard, will ever be dear to us as the schoolroom, to whose influence we shall trace whatever success coming years may bring.

"Dear class-mates, my lips refuse to bid you a last good-bye; we have so long been joined together in a community of aims and interests; so often met and mingled our thoughts in confidential friendship; so often planned and worked together, that it seems like rending asunder the very tissues of the heart to separate us now.

"But this long and happy association is at an end, and now as we go forth in sorrow, as each one must, to begin alone the work which lies before us, let us encourage each other with strengthening words.

"Success is brought by continued labor and continued watchfulness. We must struggle on, not for one moment hesitate, nor take one backward step; for in the language of the poet—

'The gates of hell are open night and day,
Smooth the descent and easy is the way;
But to return and view the cheerful skies,
In this, the task and mighty labor lies.'

"We launch our vessels upon the uncertain sea of life alone, yet, not alone, for around us are friends who anxiously and prayerfully watch our course. They will rejoice if we arrive safely at our respective havens, or weep with bitter tears, if, one by one, our weather-beaten barks are lost forever in the surges of the deep.

"We have esteemed each other, loved each other, and now must with each other part. God grant that we may all so live as to meet in the better world, where parting is unknown.

"Halls of learning, fond Alma Mater, farewell. We turn to take one 'last, long, lingering look' at thy receding walls. We leave thee now to be ushered out into the varied duties of an active life.

"However high our names may be inscribed upon the gilded scroll of fame, to thee we all the honor give, to thee all praises bring. And when, in after years, we're wearied by the bustle of a busy world, our hearts will often long to turn and seek repose beneath thy sheltering shade."

During his six years at Jacksonville, young Bryan made his home with a relative, Dr. H. K. Jones, a man of profound learning and high character. Mr. Bryan never loses an opportunity to express his gratitude for the good fortune which led him into the Jones family, and placed him under the influence of the learned doctor and his noble wife.

In the fall of 1881, young Bryan entered the

Union College of Law, at Chicago. During his attendance at this school his spare time was employed in the law office of the late Lyman Trumbull. Mr. Trumbull had an extensive library, and as he had taken quite a fancy to the young student, Mr. Trumbull gave him every possible advantage.

Mr. Bryan's expenses through law school, as well as through college, were defrayed by his parents. His independent spirit, however, would not permit all of the load to rest upon his family, and he scrubbed the floors of the Trumbull law office, cleaned windows and performed other little services during his spare moments for the purpose of obtaining odd wages and thus lessen his demands upon the family fund. Newspapers have been full of stories intending to show that Mr. Bryan worked his way through college and law school entirely by his own efforts, paying his expenses by dint of hard work. It is true that Mr. Bryan's education was not obtained with ease, and it is also true that he lost no opportunity to lighten the burden his good father had assumed in his behalf, but it is no less true that Mr. Bryan owes his education largely to his parents, who lost no opportunity to push their son to the front and to give to that son every possible advantage whereby his splendid manhood could be developed. No man was ever blessed with parents more devoted or more self-sacrificing in their

HOME OF HON. W. J. BRYAN, AT LINCOLN, NEB.

children's interests, and no parents ever reared a son more worthy of filial devotion than is William Jennings Bryan.

Mr. Bryan remained at Union College for two years, graduating there in June, 1883. He located at Jacksonville, July 4, 1883, and swung this shingle to the breeze:

```
W. J. BRYAN,
   LAWYER.
```

Mr. Bryan was married October 1, 1884, to Miss Mary Baird, of Perry, Ill. The young lawyer very soon built up a paying practice and he remained at Jacksonville until 1887, when, with his young wife and child, he removed to Nebraska.

Young Bryan early manifested a love for politics. In 1880, at the age of twenty years, he took the stump for Hancock, and delivered Democratic speeches at Salem, Centralia and two other points in Illinois. In the campaign of 1884 young Bryan, at the age of twenty-four, took the stump for Grover Cleveland. Mr. Bryan's first political speech was delivered in 1880, at the court house in Salem. But there is an interesting story about the first political speech that he did not deliver. Several weeks before the Salem speech young Bryan was working on the farm of

3

N. B. Morrison, of Odin, Illinois. A political
meeting was arranged for a grove several miles
away. Hand-bills were distributed, announcing
that two distinguished men, giving their names,
and " Mr. W. J. Bryan" would address the
"gathered hosts." When the day came young
Bryan and the distinguished orators drove to the
grove. When they arrived they found a man in
charge of the grove, one man with a wheel of fortune, and two men presiding over a lemonade
stand. With the exception of a few children
from the neighborhood that was the extent of the
" gathered hosts." The orators waited until late
in the evening and no one came to hear them.
Young Bryan returned home, possibly greatly
disappointed, but he was rewarded within a few
weeks by being able to deliver that speech before
a great gathering at Salem.

Bryan's boyhood is without sensational features.
If he ever robbed a melon patch, it is not a matter of record. If he was ever guilty of mischiev-
ous pranks, no one recalls the fact. He was a
light-hearted, good-natured lad, who, in his more
tender years, devoted himself to two things :
hard physical work, and earnest, persistent duty.

Bryan's splendid physical development, is due to
his out of door exercise, and work on the farm during his boyhood. His first employer was John
Odin, and in the days of his youth, John W. Patrick, now a railroad freight clerk, at Cincinnati,

finds considerable pride in the fact, that he was the second employer of William Jennings Bryan. Mr. Patrick several years ago lived in Salem, Ill. He was a neighbor of the Bryan's, and at one time purchased a field of hay from the elder Bryan. While the harvesting was in progress, young Bryan was employed by Mr. Patrick, to carry water to the farm hands.

Professor S. S. Hamill, of Decatur, Illinois, is the teacher under whom young Bryan studied elocution, while attending Illinois College at Jacksonville. Speaking of his pupil recently, Professor Hamill said: "He was a good student, and stood first in all his studies, but he was an awkward speaker. I had many pupils, but few that made the lasting impression on me that Bryan did. That was because of his intentness and earnestness in that particular study. There were not many who studied elocution long, but with Bryan, that seemed to be the one thing in which he desired to excel. He was not satisfied with the instruction in the class, but took a term in private, for which he paid me twenty dollars. While others were trying to beg off the pro-grammes of literary societies for orations, he took extra assignments and worked on all of them with the greatest earnestness. He made political speeches about Jacksonville in the following cam-paign, and made some reputation for himself. After that, he was often selected to represent the colleges in oratorical contests, and won honors for both the college and himself in them. I have rarely had a more determined or brilliant student. I recognized him then as a bright scholar, who was bound to make his mark, by reason of the determination with which he went at all he did."

Mrs. A. V. Beville, of St. Louis, was a Sabbath-school teacher of young Bryan. Concerning her pupil, Mrs. Beville recently said: "He attended my Sunday-school class for years and was a frequent visitor at our house. Mr. Bryan has never missed writing to me of his doings and of his progress. He is still to me one of my boys. He was a great favorite with all who knew him. He was always full of fun and dearly loved a joke. He could tell a capital story, and was moderately fond of out-door sports. Although he came to Sunday-school regularly, he was not by any means a meek boy. He was full of spirits and seemed to have a natural fund of goodness in him. He was always fond of reading. He was a good student as you can tell when reading of his record in college. However, his great application to his books did not render him either unhealthy or morbid. He was one of the heartiest, most wholesome of boys and the apparent contradiction of his studious bent and his jolly nature endeared him doubly to me. He was a very considerate fellow. I remember once when I was sick in bed and he and three other of my scholars

came to see me. They were told that they
could not see me, but I heard their voices,
and called down to say they might come
up if they did not stay long and did not do
any talking. They came and gazed at me as
though I was a dead person. William overcame
the situation by approaching the bed and asking
in a deep voice, 'Are you better?' The simple
question was very characteristic of him, and after
I had assured him that I was better, he went
away satisfied. One thing about Mr. Bryan I
think has, in a great measure, contributed to his success. He was always willing to listen to advice.
He used to give the most careful attention to
what others said. Even as a little boy this trait
was very marked. From his earliest childhood
he has been the soul of honor, honesty and truth.
I never heard of any unkind or unfair action of
his. His life seemed to have been cut from very
pure material. He inherits much of this rectitude
and beauty of character from his father, Judge
Bryan, who was noted for his piety and goodness.
William had set his heart on going to Oxford.
His father, also, who always took an active interest
in the boy's education, had likewise determined
that his son should attend the great English University when he finished his college course here.
It was supposed to be a settled fact, but Judge
Bryan's death changed everything, and William,
without a moment's hesitation, gave up all

thoughts of Oxford because the family could not spare the money. William never went to Oxford; so the credit of his cultivated intellect must remain on this side of the water. His oratorical powers are the result of his careful study of human nature. In his numerous letters to me he mentions getting ready for his examination days, the orations he had to study and all that.

"Whether speaking came naturally to him when he jumped into manhood, I cannot say, but I am sure he never would have succeeded in the way he has if it had not been for his untiring energy. He has not a lazy bone in his body, and he seems to be a stranger to fatigue. When we moved to St. Louis, William always stopped a day with us on his way home from the college at Jacksonville, and, I remember, we were reminding him one day of the agreement made between the Sunday-school boys to read the Bible through during the year. He replied that he had not forgotten, and that he and some of the fellows at college had agreed to read the Book of Proverbs through once a month for a year. He must have kept the agreement very well, for I don't know anyone fuller of proverbs than Mr. Bryan. He is also full of jokes and stories, and never seems to lack matter for conversation. Judge and Mrs. Bryan were Baptists, but William belonged to the Presbyterian Church. He is a religious man, and a moral man in every sense of the term, and while attending church with punctilious regularity, he never offends people with a parade of piety. The combination of natural goodness, wit, good humor and eloquence, topped by his cultivated and commanding intellect, render Mr. Bryan to-day the most remarkable man of my acquaintance. I remember, I told him one day that, when the capital was moved to St. Louis, when he was nominated for president, and when women could vote, I would be perfectly happy. He replied, with his charming and quizzical smile: 'Ah, you are looking far into the future.' While never indulging in extravagant apparel, Mr. Bryan was, nevertheless, always very carefully dressed. As a boy, he was neat, and paid careful attention to his linen and cravats. He was fond of society, and found time to indulge in social frolics with his many less studious friends. In short, you will see that Mr. Bryan's success is the result of application, earnest endeavor, and high resolves. He was reared upon a sure foundation. He had health to begin the race with, and intellect to enable him to forge ahead. The present glorious culmination of his career should be a shining ex-ample to all men. Mr. Bryan's life has not been marred or blotted by any vice. He is not addicted to the use of any stimulants, such as liquor or tobacco. His manners are easy and graceful in the extreme, and with his ringing voice and sparkling eyes, he represents a magnificent speci-men of manhood."

In closing her glowing description of Mr. Bryan, Mrs. Beville said: "I am not saying all this simply because I am fond of him, but because it is the conviction of all who know him. You can't say anything too good for William J. Bryan; and, oh, I hope he will be elected!"

This is the story of "Bryan's early life." There is to this portion of his career no romance, and little of more than ordinary interest. The greatest interest will, however, attach to his subsequent career, which has been remarkable in many respects.

CHAPTER II.

BRYAN'S POWER OVER MEN.

When William J. Bryan was nominated to be President of the United States by the Democratic National Convention at Chicago, his political opponents and newspapers whose editors were not in sympathy with the principles he has so gallantly represented confidently declared that his nomination was due entirely to his admirable speech upon that occasion. Many people who are not familiar with Mr. Bryan's remarkable record readily accepted this idea as a fact. It is true, however, that Mr. Bryan had already established a national reputation among the champions of bimetallism as an able advocate of the restoration of the coinage of the Constitution. When the Chicago Convention assembled, there were hundreds of delegates present who had closely watched Mr. Bryan's career, who had either read or heard delivered many of his splendid speeches upon the money question and who had learned that this young man had fought the battles of free coinage when his followers were few and weak and his opponents numerous and strong. They knew that his private character, no less than his public record, was entirely creditable. They knew

(45)

that he was a man conscientiously committed to the principles he had espoused. It is perhaps true that his splendid speech before that Convention turned the tide immediately in his favor, but it is no less true that the tide had already set in that direction among the people who were represented by the delegates to that Convention. The unprecedented public demonstrations which have been accorded Mr. Bryan since his nomination show that upon the hearthstones of the people the fires of enthusiasm in his behalf had been kindled by the grateful men and women who had carefully observed his career.

It is true that William J. Bryan is a great orator, perhaps one of the greatest this country has ever produced, but had he been only an orator, he would not occupy his present distinguised position. Behind the orator is the man, firm in his adherence to principle, devoted in his observation of the rules which guide the good citizen in private life. The mighty demonstration at Chicago which was produced by Mr. Bryan's speech was a strange sight to the world. But the people of Nebraska during the last eight years have often seen the same public demonstration, on a smaller scale it is true, but no less intense in character.

In 1888, on the occasion of Mr. Bryan's first public appearance in Nebraska, he drew men to him by the power of the orator, and held them

there in subsequent years by the virtues of the
man. Since that time he has undergone, as a
public speaker, a steady course of improvement.
It has been the privilege of the writer to hear
every important political speech made by Mr.
Bryan in Nebraska, and including his Congressional efforts, and to this writer perhaps this improvement has been more noticeable than to any
other of Mr. Bryan's auditors. As a newspaper
correspondent the writer has witnessed Mr.
Bryan's joint debates and observed his complete
triumphs over his opponents and his complete
capture of the hearts of his auditors.

Bryan's power over men was well demonstrated
in Nebraska, before the Chicago Convention was
called to order.

In 1890, when he accepted the nomination to
Congress in the First Nebraska District, he led
what seemed to be a forlorn hope against what
appeared to be an invincible foe. But Bryan
triumphed. He beat down an overwhelming opposition majority, because of his power over men.

Two years later, when his district had been re-
arranged, with a special view to his certain defeat,
and when money in unlimited sums was distributed
against him, Bryan won because of his power
over men.

In 1894, when he fought at the head of the loyal
Silver Democrats of Nebraska in the effort to
wrest the temple of Democracy of that State from

undemocratic hands, Bryan won because of his power over him.

In 1896, when he went to Chicago at the head of a delegation whose seat was contested, without right or reason it is true, but contested, nevertheless, when few men had any idea that Bryan would be the nominee of that Convention, Bryan was nominated because of his power over men.

It is undoubtedly true that this power is partially due to Bryan the orator, but the greater part of it is due to Bryan the man. The ability to meet and conquer the ablest of those who deny the correctness of his political principles is certainly a valuable talent. But the fact that the man who is able to draw men to him by the power of oratory is able to retain friendship or admiration by his undeviating traits of character is the greatest power that any man may possess. Bryan does that. He has done that in the city of Lincoln, his home. He has done that throughout the State of Nebraska. He has done that in the halls of Congress, where men are not readily influenced. He has done that among the trained newspaper men of the country, men whose keen eyes readily detect hypocrisy or insincerity. He has done that throughout the States of the Union, wherever he has made himself known, and he will do that in national life if the people triumph in November.

This estimate is placed upon Mr. Bryan's character by one who has met him and associated with

him under various circumstances and conditions.
When it is said that he is a gentle, manly man, it
is not with the purpose of flattery, but with the
desire to state an absolute fact. As a man he
would not do his humblest nor his greatest fellow-
man an injury or an injustice. As a lawyer he
would never knowingly plead a dishonest cause.
As an editor he would never knowingly advocate
a dishonest or an unpatriotic idea. As a member
of Congress he would not cast his vote upon any
proposition, great or small, against what he regarded the interest of the people whom he was
elected to serve. As President of the United
States he would be the people's executive, the
cleanest, the best and the bravest since the days
of Abraham Lincoln.

The most interesting feature of Mr. Bryan's
public career is the consistency of his political
principles. There is nothing that he represents
now that he has not represented in all of his public life. Every platform upon which he has accepted a nomination for office provided that no
caucus dictation should be permitted by a representative in Congress to interfere with his conscientious representation of his constituents.

No one wondered, when his party colleagues in
the House determined to unseat a Republican,
that Mr. Bryan refused to cast his vote in accord
with that decision. He said to the House that he
had investigated the circumstances and he be-

lieved the Republican was entitled to his seat and therefore proposed to vote for him, and his vote was recorded that way.

Every platform upon which he has accepted a nomination for office has protested against the giving of subsidies of any kind from the public treasury. He has maintained the integrity of that plank at every opportunity. The beet sugar interests have been an important political factor in Nebraska, but in the State Legislature, in 1891, when the State bounty on beet sugar was to be repealed, and a strong lobby was operating against the proposed repeal, Mr. Bryan visited the Legislature in person and gave to the Democrats and Populists of that body his good advice and vigorous encouragement. The result was that the bounty was repealed, only to be replaced by a subsequent Republican Legislature.

Mr. Bryan's platforms have favored an income tax, and his splendid fight in behalf of that measure is a matter of history.

Mr. Bryan's platforms advocated the election of Senators by the people, and he used his best efforts in Congress to carry that plank into execution.

Some people were surprised when immediately following the Chicago Convention Mr. Bryan announced that, if elected to be President, he would under no circumstances accept a second term, on the ground that a President should be free from

possible motive to work for renomination, and
thus be able to discharge the duties of his high
office for the greatest good to the greatest number. But when we look back over Mr. Bryan's
political history in Nebraska, we find that in two
of his platforms almost the identical words used
in this announcement are embodied in the planks
of those platforms.

Bryan's political platforms have advocated rigid
economy in public expenditures, and his record in
Congress shows that he has lost no opportunity
to carry that principle into execution.

Bryan's home life is that of the ideal American.
He is the companion of his wife and children as
well as the devoted husband and father.

Bryan's public interest in the people who suffer
under heavy public burdens is not assumed. It
is characteristic of the man who has a tender
sympathy for every personal woe. Having no
vices, he is not extravagant in his public expenditures, while he is methodical in his personal affairs,
and jealously provides that his expenditures shall
never exceed his income. At the same time he
has a warm, generous heart and his limited purse
has, only too often, been at the disposal of those
in distress.

One of Mr. Bryan's most striking characteristics
is his mildness. It may be difficult for those who
have seen him on the platform, hurling defiance
eloquently at the enemies of popular government,

to imagine that this is a man who was never known
to lose his temper. He is temperate in all things.
He is open to reason and is entirely considerate
of the opinions of others. He is true to his friends
and no man would go further than he to accommodate a worthy acquaintance.

Because Mr. Bryan is a brilliant leader of men,
it has in some quarters been assumed that he is
hasty and unstable, if not erratic. Nothing could
be further from the truth. His whole private life
and his entire public career prove that Mr. Bryan
is as deliberate as a philosopher in forming his
opinions and that he is firm as rock in standing
by his convictions.

Few men at fifty are as mature in judgment
as Mr. Bryan is at thirty-six. Few men at fifty
have devoted so much time to the arduous study
of the science of Government as Bryan has at
thirty-six. Pitt was prime minister of England
before he was thirty; Napolean was crowned
Emperor of France at thirty-five; Alexander
Hamilton had attained world-wide fame as a statesman at thirty-three; Thomas Jefferson wrote the
Declaration of Independence before he became
thirty-four. Time will show that Mr. Bryan is entitled to rank among these extraordinary men, not
simply as a brilliant leader, but also as a profound
student. His powers as an orator are naturally
the first to secure public recognition, but it is his
intellectual force and firmness of character which

HON. W. J. BRYAN, AT AGE OF 30.

hen he was first elected to Congress. Picture taken at close of a joint debate when he was
presented with floral pieces shown.

HON. B. R. TILLMAN,
U. S. Senator from South Carolina.

will in the end win for him the lasting glory which
is accorded to men truly great. He has all of
Jefferson's devotion to the interests of the people,
and all of Jackson's courage in defending them.
These two statesmen are his models, and in him
they may almost be said to live again.

One of the tender features of Mr. Bryan's
private life is his associations with the boys' class
in the Presbyterian Sunday School in Lincoln.
For a number of years Mr. Bryan has been the
teacher of this class, and the depth of the affection on the part of the pupils to their distinguished
teacher could not but be gratifying to any one
upon whom that affection was bestowed.

On the Sabbath following Mr. Bryan's nomina-
tion the Rev. W. K. Williams, clergyman of the
M. E. Church, filled the pulpit of the Presbyterian
Church of which Mr. Bryan is a member.

In the course of his sermon Mr. Williams said:
"We are told in the twenty-sixth verse, twelfth
chapter, of First Corinthians, that if one member
suffers, all the members suffer with it, and that
if one member is honored, all the members
rejoice. One of your members has been highly
honored by the people; he has been honored by
God, and I rejoice that a fellow-citizen and a
member in Christ has been thus highly honored.
I also rejoice in the purity of his life, in the
nobility of his thought, in the vigor of his young
manhood, in the majesty and grandeur of his im-

4

passioned eloquence, and in the fearless manner
in which he proclaims to the world the principles
that lie deep within his heart. I shall continue to
pray that God will keep him pure and make him
a yet mightier force for good in this nation, and
that Christ shall be his leader always."

In writing of Mr. Bryan, Hon. Champ Clark, of
Missouri, gave this admirable description of him:

"Bryan is a collegiate, and has stowed away in
his capacious cranium much of the golden grain
of wisdom and little of the husks, and it is all
there for use, either as argument or embellish-
ment. Some men are so ugly and ungainly that
it is a positive disadvantage to them as public
speakers. Some are so handsome and graceful
that they are on good terms with the audience
before they open their lips. Of the latter class
Bryan is a shining example. His appearance is a
passport to the affections of his fellow-men which
all can read. He is the picture of health, mental,
moral and physical. He stands about 5 feet 10,
weighs about 170, is a pronounced brunette, has a
massive head, a clean-shaven face, an aquiline
nose, large under jaw, square chin, a broad chest,
large, lustrous dark eyes, mouth extending almost
from ear to ear, teeth white as pearls, and hair—
what there is left of it—black as midnight.
Beneath his eyes is the protuberant flesh which
physiognomists tell us is indicative of fluency of

language and which was one of the most striking features in the face of James G. Blaine.

"Bryan neglects none of the accessories of oratory. Nature richly endowed him with rare grace. He is happy in attitude and pose. His gestures are on Hogarth's line of beauty. Mellifluous is the one word that aptly describes his voice. It is strong enough to be heard by thousands. It is sweet enough to charm those the least inclined to music. It is so modulated as not to vex the ear with monotony and can be stern and pathetic, fierce or gentle, serious or humorous, with the varying emotions of its master. In his youth Bryan must have had a skilful teacher in elocution and must have been a docile pupil. He adorns his speeches with illustrations from the classics or from the common occurrences of everyday life with equal felicity and facility. Some passages from his orations are gems and are being used as declamations by boys at school —the ultimate tribute to American eloquence.

"But his crowning gift as an orator is his evident sincerity. He is candor incarnate, and, thoroughly believing what he says himself, it is no marvel that he makes others believe."

One of the closest friends of Mr. Bryan in Lincoln, who is himself a lawyer, relates an incident which occurred several years after the arrival of Bryan in Nebraska. This was in 1890, when the young men of the Democratic party in the First

Nebraska Congressional district were urging Mr.
Bryan to make the race for Congress. Without
money and comparatively a new man in the State,
it did not seem to his more cautious friends that
there was much chance of his success in a district
which had gone Republican two years before by
a majority of 3400. The Republican member,
W. J. Connell, was a candidate for re-election and
it was he who in the previous contest had defeated
J. Sterling Morton, one of the Democratic pioneers of Nebraska. These cautious friends en-
deavored to show to Bryan that he had but little
to hope for in the unequal fight for the seat in
Congress. One of these, Judge C. L. Hall, a
Republican, but a warm friend of Bryan, advised
him to let the nomination for Congress go to anyone who would take it and turn his attention to
an endeavor to get the office of county attorney
of Lancaster county, where there was a reason-
ably good show for his election. Mr. Bryan
looked serious for a moment and then replied to
Judge Hall's suggestion by saying, with a decision
that could not be shaken, "What you say is possibly true, but I had rather be a defeated candidate for Congress than a successful candidate for
county attorney."

This subordination of certain pecuniary profit
and professional advancement to the desire to put
before the people his opinions on public questions
has been characteristic of Mr. Bryan since he

grew to manhood, and was as well known among his acquaintances in Illinois, when he had his office with the law firm of Brown & Kirky at Jacksonville, as it afterwards became in Nebraska.

Little things tell even in the lives of great men. Mr. Charles C. Moore, of Carlyle, Ill., relates an incident that happened in the city of St. Louis during the Republican National Convention. Mr. Moore says:

"Myself and friend were on our way to the Auditorium from the Planters' Hotel and had reached Twelfth street. We were walking along chatting together, not noticing anyone in particular. A one-armed bicyclist attracted our attention for a few moments, and I remarked then that he was in a dangerous vicinity, as there were many vehicles on the street. The bicyclist was not given further thought until we had proceeded on our journey a block and a half, when we observed the one-armed man and bicycle piled up in one promiscuous heap. A man was observed to emerge from the surging mass of people and proceed to render assistance to the unfortunate wheelman.

"We stopped and watched the pair. The man who had so kindly gone forward and offered help was busily engaged in assisting the bicyclist replace his tire, which had left the rim, and otherwise straighten the injured machine. When matters had been satisfactorily adjusted, the kind gentleman, with greasy hands and soiled linen, made dirty by the work, returned to the sidewalk. Upon closer investigation it was found that the man was none other than W. J. Bryan."

Mr. Bryan is quick at repartee. On one occasion in a public speech, Mr. Bryan said something about silver falling like manna from heaven. In a public interview J. Sterling Morton remarked that Bryan could not be well posted on the Scriptures. He reminded Bryan that the streets of Paradise and the harps and crowns were all golden, and he pointed with some pride to the fact that the gold standard prevailed in heaven. When these suggestions reached Mr. Bryan he said that that was a severe thrust at Mr. Cleveland's idea of international bimetallism to come from a member of the Cabinet. "For how," inquired Mr. Bryan, "can international bimetallism be right if they have a gold standard in heaven?"

Mr. Bryan added: "I have been told that some of the members of the Cabinet wear diamonds. If they are so anxious to be in accord with heavenly custom they should put pearls on their shirt fronts, for we read in verse 21, chapter xxi., of Revelation, that "each gate of the New Jerusalem was a pearl."

Mr. Bryan does not parade his Christianity, but he adheres strictly to it in every walk of life. He

is fond of quoting the last verse of Bryant's lines
" To a Waterfowl : "

" He who from zone to zone
   Guides through the boundless sky thy certain flight,
In the long way that I must tread alone
   Will lead my steps aright."

In a eulogy on a dead colleague in Congress,
Mr. Bryan used these eloquent words, full of the
beautiful faith which has been his guide in his
public and private life :

" I shall not believe that even now his light is
extinguished. If the Father deigns to touch with
divine power the cold and pulseless heart of the
buried acorn, and make it to burst forth from its
prison walls, will He leave neglected in the earth
the soul of man, who was made in the image of
his Creator ? If He stoops to give to the rose-
bush, whose withered blossoms float upon the
breeze, the sweet assurance of another springtime, will He withhold the words of hope from the
sons of men when the frosts of winter come ? If
matter, mute and inanimate, though changed by
the forces of Nature into a multitude of forms, can
never die, will the imperial spirit of man suffer
annihilation after it has paid a brief visit, like a
royal guest, to this tenement of clay ?

" Rather let us believe that He who, in His apparent prodigality, wastes not the raindrop, the
blade of grass, or the evening's sighing zephyr,

but makes them all to carry out His eternal plans, has given immortality to the mortal, and gathered to Himself the generous spirit of our friend."

Mr. Bryan is one of the bravest of men. He never yet dodged a question concerning his attitude upon any public affair. He never held back because the hill which it was his duty to climb seemed too steep for a human being to ascend. He never indulged in personalities, but in a contest of principles he has been relentless and has shown no mercy to his foe. He has never asked for quarter in any contest where duty called him. He has never evaded a political fight and has demonstrated a perfect willingness to lead his forces to battle upon the enemy's territory. Those who are best acquainted with him were not surprised when he suggested Madison Square, New York, as the place where he would meet the notification committee. That is right in the heart of the territory claimed by the enemy as its own, and that was the very point suggested by the courage and determination characteristic of Mr. Bryan's entire career.

One of Mr. Bryan's marked characteristics has been his absolute confidence that the principles he has advocated will ultimately triumph. The writer has seen Mr. Bryan fresh from a hard-earned victory at the polls, when every politician, as well as the people, was anxious to pay him homage; and he has seen Bryan in defeat. In both instances it was the same Bryan. True, in the presence of victory the heart was lighter, but it could not be said that in defeat that heart was heavy. There is no room within Bryan's great make-up for despondency. Every defeat he regarded as being of temporary importance. His friends, who monopolized the despondency of the occasion, were reassured by the young statesman's confident declaration, "Our principles are right and they will ultimately prevail. Victory will be all the greater because a few battles have been lost before Appomattox has been reached."

Commenting upon Mr. Bryan's nomination at Chicago, the Washington City *Post* said:

"We do not wonder that on the following day, still palpitating under the spell of Bryan's wondrous eloquence, the convention turned to him as a needle to a magnet. It may not be capable of analysis, it may not be coldly and accurately demonstrable. The fact remains, Bryan swept the floor of the convention as the fire sweeps the autumn prairie. The delegates went to him in a strange passion of desire. Nothing could check the fury of their bent. He was nominated—slowly at first, swiftly next and at last, in a wild crescendo of enthusiasm, he was lifted on a white-cap of unanimity and thrown high and dry on the beach of his surpassing triumph.

"The country at large knows little of this extraordinary young man. He has been in Congress. He delivered a speech upon the tariff that enchanted and enchained the House. He has spoken many times since with reference to the tariff, and always he has held his audience as the sirens held the fated crew that sailed with Ulysses from the shore of Troy. He is a minstrel, a form of grace, a thing of beauty. What he is beyond that, who knows?

" He has no record in statesmanship. He was too young to assert his patriotism thirty-five years ago. What schemes of government, what social theories occupy his brain, no human being can disclose. He is young, he is ardent, he is ambitious, he is gifted with the power to sway men's minds, he is a born leader, an attractive figure on the stage, and that is all we know. Whether the American people, after four months of solid deliberation, will confide their destinies to his untried hands, we do not undertake to prophesy. What we do know is that William Jennings Bryan is the most dramatic product of our National politics, the most sensational and picturesque creation of our age."

William J. Bryan cannot be said to be an "untried man." It is true so far as the White House is concerned he is "untried," much as Abraham Lincoln was "untried." But from the beginning of Mr. Bryan's career, from boyhood to manhood, from Lyman Trumbull's office in Chicago to the Democratic nomination to be President of the

United States, William J. Bryan has met and discharged every duty as it arose and discharged
that duty with credit to himself. Like Lincoln he
was tried and found "not wanting" in small
things, and like Lincoln, if he shall be tried, he
will be found "not wanting" in great things.
Like Lincoln he had the confidence and the love
of all men who knew him well, and like Lincoln
he will, if given the opportunity, extend that confidence and that affection until it embraces the
people of the entire Union.

Mr. Bryan's career will not be regarded as
meteoric by one who analyzes that career carefully. He has developed as political conditions
have developed. He has grown in public estima-
tion steadily and strongly, first in the hearts of
the citizens of his own home, then of his own
State, and finally into the broader national field
which he entered in the discharge of his duty as
an eloquent advocate of popular government.

In his work on "Abraham Lincoln and Men of
War Times," Col. A. K. McClure says, "It was
the unexpected that happened in Chicago on that
fateful 18th of May, 1860, when Abraham Lincoln was nominated for President of the United
States. It was wholly unexpected by the friends
of Seward. The campaign in Pennsylvania was
really the decisive battle of the contest. A party
had to be created out of inharmonious elements
and the commercial and financial interests of that
State were almost solidly against us. I cannot

recall a commercial man of prominence in the city of Philadelphia to whom I could have gone to solicit a subscription to the Lincoln campaign with reasonable expectation that it would not be refused. Of all our prominent financial men I recall only Anthony J. Drexel, who actively sympathized with the Republican cause."

That condition, in some respects, at least, may be similar to the conditions of 1896. But in spite of all obstacles Lincoln was elected, because he represented principles dear to the hearts of the people; because in his public and private life he had so lived as to win for himself the love and the esteem of his fellow-citizens.

It is said of Abraham Lincoln, that he never shirked a duty; that he was a man who knew his countrymen well and sympathized with them thoroughly; that he was equal to every emergency with which he was confronted. The same may be said with equal truth of William J. Bryan. If Mr. Bryan shall be elected to the Presidency, the fathers and mothers of America may point with pride to the fact that the White House is occupied by a man whose public service is dedicated entirely to his people's interest, and whose private life is without a flaw. The ideal President of an ideal Nation he will be; one whose ear will be "tuned to listen to the heartbeat of humanity," one who will regard his office as a sacred trust to be discharged in the hope of accomplishing the greatest good for the greatest number.

CHAPTER III.

BRYAN IN NEBRASKA.

Mr. Bryan located in Lincoln, Nebraska, in October, 1887. From his Illinois home he had gone to Lincoln on law business, and while there he had met his old schoolmate, A. R. Talbot, Esq. Mr. Bryan was so captivated with the little city that he entered a law partnership with his old schoolmate, under the firm name of Talbot & Bryan. Returning to his Illinois home he closed up his affairs there and with his family removed to Lincoln, where he has since resided. At that time Lincoln was what is known as a "Republican stronghold." The few Democrats in Lincoln soon discovered that a man of more than ordinary ability had come among them, while the men of other political parties learned that their new fellow-citizen was one capable of gracing any community. Mr. Bryan devoted himself to the practice of his profession, and he soon became a favorite in all circles. Invitations to address literary societies, college associations, town meetings, and political gatherings came fast, and Mr. Bryan soon established for himself a local reputation, not so much as an orator as for a logician. It did not require long for this reputation to spread over the

State, and when Mr. Bryan was elected as a delegate from Lancaster County to the Democratic State Convention, in 1888, he was in great demand. Newspaper reports of that convention contain the following paragraph: "The youngest voter in the convention was Mr. Bryan, a bright young Democrat from Lancaster County. Mr. Bryan was rocked in a cradle made of hickory, and while he never cast a vote for 'Old Hickory,' he has, since his majority, never cast a ballot for any presidential candidate who did not represent the principles of true and tried Democracy." The same report contents itself with this reference to Mr. Bryan's first convention speech in Nebraska: "Mr. Bryan of Lancaster County was then called. He came forward and delivered a spirited address in the course of which he said, that, if the platform laid down by the President in his message upon the tariff question was carried out and vigorously fought upon in the State, it would, in the course of a short time, give Nebraska to the Democracy. He thought that if the Democrats went out to the farmers and people who lived in Nebraska, and showed them the iniquity of the tariff system, they would rally around the cause which their noble leader, Grover Cleveland, had championed."

The limited newspaper reference to Mr. Bryan's speech on this occasion did not do justice to either the effort or the manner in which it was received

by his auditors. As a matter of fact it created
the greatest amount of enthusiasm, and the young
orator impressed his personality indelibly upon the
public mind of his adopted State. Mr. C. V. Gallagher, then Postmaster of Omaha, approached Mr.
Bryan, and complimenting him upon his effort
said: "Young man we will send you to Congress." Although Mr. Gallagher did not pretend
to speak with authority, his words were in the
nature of a prophecy, and the Democrats of the
First Congressional District did send William J.
Bryan to Congress two years later.

At that time the great leaders of Nebraska
Democracy were Dr. George L. Miller, the
founder of the Omaha *Herald*, and now Collector
of Customs for Omaha, James E. Boyd, who
subsequently became Governor of the State, and
J. Sterling Morton, now the Secretary of Agriculture. The Nebraska Democracy had for many
years been split into factions by what was known in
common parlance as the "slaughter-house" and
the "packing-house" Democracy. On one side
Mr. Morton and his followers were arrayed, while
Dr. Miller and Mr. Boyd were the leaders of the
other faction. The rank and file of the party,
while true in the factional contests to their leaders,
had become weary of the discord and turmoil
within their own party ranks, and for this reason
perhaps, they turned more readily to the new man
who had come among them. At that time no one

had any thought of the great prominence which
this young man would attain in political affairs.
But at that time no one had foretold the great
public emergencies that would arise. And right
here it is worthy of observation, that as these
public emergencies developed, William J. Bryan
developed with them.

In 1888 the First Congressional District of
Nebraska comprised eleven of the most populous
counties of the State. The cities of Omaha and
Lincoln were in this district. In that year J.
Sterling Morton, the present Secretary of Agriculture, was nominated by the Democrats; the
Republicans had nominated W. J. Connell, one of
the ablest lawyers of the State. Mr. Connell was
elected over Morton by a plurality of 3,400 votes.

As the campaign of 1890 approached, a few
Democrats, who had come to appreciate Mr.
Bryan's real ability, believed that with him as the
nominee, the Republicans could be defeated.
But these confident gentlemen were pointed out
as mere enthusiasts; so when the Democratic Congressional Convention met at Lincoln, July 31, 1890,
the nomination was not sought by any man. One
gentleman, it is true, announced his willingness
to accept the honor, but he only received a few
votes from his own county. A few scattering
votes were distributed to favorite sons, but Mr.
Bryan was nominated on the first formal, by a
majority of 115, out of a total vote of 159.

There were a few gentlemen who came out of that convention who entertained and expressed some hope that Bryan would be able to overcome the overwhelming Republican majority. But their predictions were simply laughed at, even by many of their own party associates.

The platform upon which Mr. Bryan was first nominated for Congress declared for tariff for revenue only, condemned the giving of subsidies and bounties of every kind "as a perversion of the taxing power," favored liberal pensions to the disabled veterans, favored an amendment to the Constitution, providing for the election of United States senators by the people, declared for the Australian ballot system, declared against trusts in all their forms. That platform also contained these two planks: "We demand the free coinage of silver on equal terms with gold, and denounce the efforts of the Republican party to serve the interest of Wall Street as against the rights of the people." Also: "Believing that the duty of the representative is to represent the will and interests of his constituents, we denounce as undemocratic, any attempt by caucus dictation to prevent a congressman from voicing the sentiment of his people upon every vital question."

These two planks serve as an index to Mr. Bryan's subsequent political course. Unswerving in his devotion to the first plank, he has preached the doctrine of bimetallism from the stump in

5

every State and from his seat in Congress. Always mindful that the people have no voice in legislation, except through the vote and voice of their representative, he has hewn strictly to the line of his people's interest as he learned their interests, and has refused to surrender any principle in which he believed those popular interests to be involved. Mr. Bryan's speech, in accepting his first congressional nomination, inspired great hope in the breasts of his "enthusiasts." On that occasion Mr. Bryan said in part: —

"Mr. Chairman, Ladies and Gentlemen :—

"I scarcely know in what words to express my high appreciation of the honor which you have conferred, and my deep sense of the responsibility which the nomination imposes upon me. I shall cherish in grateful remembrance your kindness, which has resulted in this nomination. I accept from your hands and at your command the standard for this district, and, whether I carry it to victory, or, as our President has gracefully expressed it, fall 'Fighting just outside of the breastworks,' it shall not suffer dishonor. You have nominated me knowing that I have neither the means nor the inclination to win an election by corrupt influences. If I am elected it will be because the electors of this district, by their free and voluntary choice, have chosen me for their service. I have read your platform. If elected

I shall consider its conscientious execution as my
first duty, and I can follow its directions the more
cheerfully because the sentiments therein expressed have my unqualified approval. In matters not covered by the platform I shall feel free
to act for the best interests of my constituents
and of my country, according to the best light
that I have. I cannot promise my course will be
free from mistake, but I will promise that every
duty devolving on me, whether great or small, as
your representative upon the floor or in the execution of the details of the office, will be discharged as my judgment shall dictate and to the
best of my ability, so help me God.

"This is the first canvass, I may say, that I
have ever been called upon to make, and I lack
the experience which frequent contests, whether
successful or unsuccessful, would give. I must
rely, therefore, largely upon the wisdom of the
committee which you select. If it is their wish, I
am ready to meet in joint debate, in every county
in my district, the champion of high taxes, who-
ever he may be, and I shall go forth to the conflict as David went to meet the giant of the
Philistines, not relying upon my own strength but
trusting to the righteousness of my cause. ·

"Your platform says that the object of Government is to protect every citizen in the enjoyment of life, liberty and the pursuit of happiness,
unaided by public contribution and unburdened

by oppressive exactions. That is, indeed, the criterion by which every law should be judged, and it is only when that rule is disregarded that laws become unequal. Government is perverted and its instrumentalities turned to private ends. It is only when that rule is disregarded that class legislation springs up in its multiplied form, and robbery in the form and under the sanction of law begins its work of enriching the rich and impoverishing the poor. To the disregard of that rule can be traced every evil that flows from bad government, and by its wise application can be remedied every wrong which we now suffer. You have condemned the McKinley bill, and well you may ; for of all the wolves that in the clothing of sheep have sought their unsuspecting victims, that wolf is the most ravenous that we have known. Well has the Chicago *Tribune* likened the effect of the McKinley bill upon the farmer to the treatment of Amasa by his friend Joab. 'And Joab said, art thou in health, my brother? And Joab took Amasa by the beard to kiss him, and Amasa took no notice of the sword that was in Joab's hand, so Joab thrust him in the fifth rib therewith, and he died.' May we not hope that Amasa—the farmer—sees the sword in Joab's hand and will escape ?

"You have demanded the election of United States senators by the people. However wise the founders of our Government may have been

Hon. DAVID TURPIE,
U. S. Senator from Indiana.

Hon. SAMUEL PASCO,
U. S. Senator from Florida.

in making provision for the election of United States senators by the legislatures of the various States, we believe the time has come for a change. A seat in the United States Senate, the highest legislative body known among men, should be given as the reward for labor done in behalf of the people. It should not be an honor sold at auction to the man who is able to purchase it.

" You have condemned the caucus. Upon no plank do I stand with more firmness than upon this. And I am glad that our party, the representative of the principles of free government, has taken a position against any caucus dictation that will prevent a congressman from representing freely, fully and fearlessly the interests of his constituents upon every question. But this is no time for speech-making. It is not needed for encouragement. You who have stood by your party in the hours of adversity, when you found virtue its own and often only reward, could not be aided by any words of mine. Nor is it needed for instruction. For we have it upon good authority that the sick and not the whole need a physician. Let us prepare for the work which lies before us. When this convention has adjourned I desire to meet every delegate. And if time permits I will visit you in your homes. I will call upon you upon your farms and help you make hay while the sun shines, and I shall expect you to help me make votes all the time. It is no small task to shake hands with 70,000 voters and learn the names and ages of twice that number of children, but with your help I will try to accomplish it. Let us fight shoulder to shoulder, and carry on the battle all along the line, fighting for good government and the interests of our fellow-men. We are inspired by the noblest instinct that can inspire to deeds of bravery, and if you can work half as earnestly and bravely for the success of this ticket as your candidate does, your representative in Congress for the next two years will bear the name which my parents thirty years ago last March gave to me."

The people generally did not receive the news of Mr. Bryan's nomination with any very serious thought. It was generally believed that the overwhelming Republican majority could not be overcome. And yet the Democratic party was congratulated, even by its opponents, upon having selected a clean and able man as its standard-bearer. Gen. Van Wyck, who was supposed to be thoroughly acquainted with Nebraska politics, and whose sympathies with reform measures were well established, said Connell's election was assured, and that Bryan stood "not a ghost of a chance."

The Omaha *World-Herald*, which newspaper had been Mr. Bryan's consistent champion, took a more hopeful view of the situation and said editorially:

"The action of the Democratic convention of the First Congressional District in nominating William J. Bryan, of Lincoln, for Congress ensures a lively campaign for tariff reform and probably a victory also.

"Young, eloquent, earnest and able, Bryan is the very best standard-bearer who could have been chosen to lead the recently-aroused masses against the fortifications behind which the favored classes are entrenched. He not only fully understands the methods by which the people of the West have been despoiled, but he has a happy faculty of discussing the tariff issues so that even 'the way-faring man, though a fool,' can understand the evils of the present Republican policy on the great national issue.

"Mr. Bryan is as popular as he is able, and his integrity is as acknowledged as his ability. Exemplary and studious in his habits, he has always taken a keen interest in politics—not as the politician does, but rather as the statesman should. Upon the national issues, past and present, Bryan will prove himself to be thoroughly informed. His convictions are deep and his manner earnest. He is poor and he has stated in advance that he had nothing to contribute towards the campaign except his own services; but the *World-Herald* believes that in the thorough canvass of the district, which Mr. Bryan will make, an influence more potent in winning votes will be found than the gold of a boodle candidate.

"The people of the big First may expect to find Mr. Bryan often on the stump for tariff reform, but never up the stump."

The Republican newspapers of the district thought to cripple the Democratic nominee by ridicule. They applied to him the designation "Young Mr. Bryan." The Democratic newspapers accepted the challenge, and pleading guilty to the charge that their candidate was not old, declared "Young Mr. Bryan would be a credit to Nebraska in the lower house of Congress."

At the Democratic State Convention for Nebraska, held in 1890, the name of Bryan was on every tongue, and he stirred that convention to great enthusiasm by an eloquent speech from which these extracts are taken:

"We have declared in favor of free silver. We demand that the white metal and the yellow metal shall be treated exactly alike. For two hundred years before the Republican party demonetized silver, the ratio between silver and gold remained almost the same. In the seventeen years since demonetization, gold has risen from 1 to 16 to 1 to 22, and values have been shrinking in proportion.

"We have demanded the election of the United States senators by the people and no answer can be made to our demand that does not deny the right of self-government.

"We denounce the McKinley bill, which under

the guise of protection to American industries, seeks to increase the load of an already over-burdened people. What is a protective tariff? A tax levied upon the many for the benefit of a few. (Applause.) What does it mean? It means that when a man has labored for six days to provide the necessaries for his family, he has given four days for what he buys and two days for the tax. It means that four months out of a year are given for tribute—that a third of his life is wasted. It is strange that, under such conditions, so many are unable to lay aside in life's summer enough to support them in life's decline. (Applause.) Some have grown enormously rich, while the many have become extremely poor. Dives has prospered and Lazarus still sits waiting for the crumbs that fall from the table. (Applause.) The mass of Republicans in this State are as earnest in their desire for tariff reform as we are, but they have hoped for their own party. They have deluded themselves with the belief that the Republican party was only flirting with organized wealth, and that it would finally wed the poor man, but the marriage between the grand old party and monopoly has been consummated, and 'what God has joined together let no man put asunder.' (Laughter and applause.)

"When Ulysses, returning home, approached the island of the sirens he put wax in the ears of his sailors and had himself tied to the ship's mast so he could not turn aside. We have no sirens singing to-day, but there is a voice of moaning coming up from the agricultural classes—a great wail of distress, and the commanders of the Republican ship have stopped the ears of their sailors and made them deaf to the cry of the people, while they themselves are so tied to the protected interests by ante-election promises that hearing they cannot heed. (Long-continued applause.)

" Let us bring light to those that sit in darkness. As honest men to honest men present the iniquities of the robber tariff and success will come. How long will our farmers worship at the shrine of a high tariff?

" In Australia they have a tree called the cannibal tree. Its leaves, like great arms, reach out until they touch the ground, and on the top of the tree there is a cup containing a mysterious kind of honey. Some of the tribes worship this tree, and on their great days surround it, dancing and shouting. Then one of their number is selected as a victim, and at the point of spears is driven upon the tree. He tastes of the fluid and the cup and he is overcome by a strange intoxication. Then those great arms, as if instinct with life, rise up and, encircling him in their powerful folds, crush out his life while his companions look on with shouts of joy. (Applause.) Have we not seen a like picture in Nebraska? Farmer after farmer has been crushed to death in the arms of an oppressive tariff, and yet farmers have been found who, within sight of their unfortunate companions, have shouted their praise of the great American system.

"Let us hope that we are on the eve of a brighter day when equal laws will lighten the burden of the toiling masses. (Long-continued applause and cheers.)

Mr. Bryan immediately took the stump in his district, and drew men to him, on a smaller scale it is true, but in the same way as he drew men to him at Chicago, and as he has always drawn men to him wherever he has appeared in public.

The Omaha *World-Herald* sounded the first note of genuine hope to the Democrats of the First Nebraska District, when, in an editorial two months before the election, that newspaper announced: "Mr. Bryan is tearing Mr. Connell's fences into pieces, and if Wm. J. Bryan could personally meet one-half of the voters of the First district, the election of the young orator, by an overwhelming majority, would be assured. But Mr. Bryan will make a thorough canvass of the district, and wherever Bryan goes he wins earnest champions to his cause."

Mr. Bryan's remarkable campaign was well described in the following editorial in the *World-Herald :*

"The campaign which Mr. W. J. Bryan is

making in the First Congressional District is as
strong and vigorous as it is clean and honorable,
and that is saying much.

"He is speaking five or six times a week, and
it is noticeable that he draws large audiences and
makes good impressions. He handles the great
tariff question in so fair and candid a way and
discusses it in such plain and simple language
that a child can understand the points and follow
the argument. He wastes no time on oratorical
flights or glittering generalities, but he talks directly to the point, discussing the question with
the earnestness of strong convictions and the
eloquence of honest words.

"If Bryan is not a great orator he is, at least,
a convincing speaker, and he deals with his facts
so frankly and ably that he wins votes everywhere.

"He is, moreover, not a dodger. On everything he is outspoken and explicit. He never
fails to announce that he is against prohibition.
He tells this to small groups of farmers where
prohibition may be in favor as readily as he tells
it to city audiences where it is not. In short,
Bryan is a strong character as well as a clean one,
and he is making a campaign on principle.

"He is a tower of strength to the cause of
democracy and of the people, not only because he
is a popular candidate, but because he never fails
in his addresses to dwell upon the importance of

Hon. H. M. TELLER,
U. S. Senator from Colorado.

Hon. RICHARD P. BLAND,
Ex-Congressman from Missouri.

electing Mr. Boyd and his ticket over Mr. Rich-
ards and his.

" Bryan, as a campaigner, is a success. He will
be a congressman."

Mr. Bryan invaded Omaha, the home of Mr.
Connell, and he addressed a great gathering of
Omaha people, impressing upon his auditors his
earnestness, his eloquence and his ability.

Republican leaders had by this time become
thoroughly alarmed. They realized that a strong
man had been pitted against them.

In that year the Prohibition question was before
the people of Nebraska, and in the hope of injuring Mr. Bryan, one distinguished Republican
orator charged him with being a Prohibitionist. It
was charged that at a banquet given by the members of the bar, in Lincoln, Mr. Bryan opposed
the use of liquor on the banquet table. Mr. Bryan
met the charge promptly, as he has met every
question submitted to him. In a public speech he
said: " The use of wine at the Lincoln banquet was
abandoned for two reasons. First: Some of the
expected guests were known to have a weakness
for the flowing bowl which would result in their
intoxication. Second: It was a question of having the banquet without wine or without women.
Many of the guests at that banquet could do
without wine, but none of them could do without
the refining influence of woman, so wine was
abandoned and woman triumphed. If this be

treason, make the most of it." It is unnecessary to say that the Republicans were very ready to drop the Prohibition charge against Mr. Bryan.

Mr. Bryan's committee challenged his opponent to joint debate. His opponent called a conference of his friends, and Mr. Connell was urged to accept the challenge. He was assured that Mr. Bryan was a "one-speech man," and while Mr. Connell might be a little worse for the wear after the first meeting, he would grind his young opponent to powder in the subsequent contests. The Chairman of the Republican Congressional Committee struck upon a happy scheme of obtaining expert opinion on this subject, and selected a committee of three young lawyers and charged them with the duty of listening to Mr. Bryan and informing his opponent as to whether the challenge to joint debate might be safely accepted. These "experts" reported that Mr. Bryan was certainly a "one-speech man," and that his opponent would have easy sailing after the first week.

A series of eleven meetings were arranged at different points in the district. The opening was had at Lincoln, Mr. Bryan's home. Three thousand people gathered to hear the orators and while Mr. Bryan electrified the gathering by his eloquence and his logic, the friends of Mr. Connell congratulated themselves and their candidate that he escaped the ordeal with breath in his body, and they promised that in the next meeting, in Omaha, there would be nothing left to tell the tale of the young candidate from Lincoln.

One of the greatest gatherings that ever assembled, in the history of Omaha, attended the Bryan-Connell debate in that city. The audience was made up, for the most part, of the men one sees in courts, in business circles and among the manufactories. Mechanics from the shops, and attorneys fresh from conventions jostled one another. Capitalists were neighbors of laboring men, and the throbbing voice of the politician reached out to exercise itself. It was an interested and an interesting throng. Nobody was there to loiter ; one could readily see that by the attention given to every minor preliminary detail. A few ladies enlivened the monotonous *melange* of men, but the masculine side had the majority so extensively that they quite overshadowed. By eight o'clock the house was without standing room, and 1500 people, it was estimated, were turned away from the door. Mr. Connell learned then that expert testimony may not always with safety be relied upon. He learned that his opponent was not a "one-speech man." He learned that he was an orator, eloquent and powerful, a logician strong and accurate, and that in *repartee* he was without a superior. In spite of the fact that Mr. Connell defended his cause better than any other man could have done, he was com-

pletely overpowered by his young opponent. At
the conclusion of the debate men climbed over
one another to shake the hand of the young
orator. Thousands of people vainly struggled to
secure a foothold on the stage. From that moment it was evident that the Republican candidate
would be defeated, unless unusual efforts should
be put forth.

At subsequent appointments Mr. Bryan won
similar triumphs. The people flocked from all
parts of the State to hear the young orator and
witness his magnificent victories.

During the progress of these debates the
Omaha *World-Herald* contained an editorial
which is interesting at this time, not only because
of its description of Bryan's marvellous power,
but as well for it prophetic utterances.

BRYAN ON THE STUMP.

"It is very seldom in these days that oratory is
met with, for the reason that oratory is something
composed at once of eloquence, simplicity and
magnetism, and that while eloquence and even
magnetism are frequently met with among
Americans, simplicity is not. Mr. W. J. Bryan,
the Democratic candidate for Congress from the
First district, has this quality. He is, without
doubt, one of the most impressive men who have
ever been on the western hustings. To begin
with, he is no diplomat, and in one sense of the

word he does not possess adroitness. That is, he appears to be doing nothing for effect. His remarks are direct. They are unqualified, and they always have the effect of being spontaneous.

"He is not an apologetic speaker, but a commanding one. He does not sue for attention. He takes it for granted that he will receive it. He delights in his audience, and inspires in them a sense of exhilaration such as he apparently feels himself. He is enamored with his cause, and, believing fully in it, forces his listeners to do the same. So impregnated is he with the idea that his cause is righteous that he is without fear, relying on the truth to meet the subtlest argument that may be adduced by his opponents. Then he has a pleasant wit, and even a spirit of mischief, and at times that broad and responsive smile points a paragraph as no spoken words can do, and lays his opponent open to the ridicule which Bryan himself refrains from inflicting. This quality is contagious. And it kills rancor. For it is impossible to feel any anger toward an adversary at whom one laughs.

"Nature has gifted Mr. Bryan with a remarkable face—such a face as could be carved on a coin and not be out of place. He has a physical vigor which makes his unstudied gestures forcible and emphatic. He has an eye which is by turns commanding and humorous. And he has a voice which is equally adapted to tenderness or to de-

6

nunciation. All these natural gifts has William J. Bryan and to them is added a talent for research, a genius for accuracy, and a nature of truth. There are not many men cast in such mold in these days of sycophants, weaklings and time-servers.

"Let Nebraska congratulate herself on the fact that she has an orator who possesses the physical and mental qualities to make him a remarkable man in the history of this nation. And if the *World-Herald* reads the stars aright, the time will come when W. J. Bryan will have a reputation which will reach far beyond Nebraska—and it will be a reputation for the performance of good and disinterested deeds."

Mr. Bryan's opponents circulated the charge that he belonged to an Anti-Catholic Society. A telegraphic inquiry brought this response:

WEEPING WATER, NEB., October 18, 1890.
To the Editor World-Herald:

"Your despatch just received. I belong to the Presbyterian Church, but do not belong to any Anti-Catholic Society. I respect every man's right to worship God according to his own conscience." W. J. BRYAN.

The Bryan-Connell debates were concluded at Syracuse. In spite of the pronounced victory of one of the participants, there had grown up between the two contestants a strong personal friendship, which, by the way, has matured during succeeding years. A great crowd had gathered to witness the closing scenes of that debate. Preparations had been made by the farmers of the vicinity to avail themselves of the opportunity to hear and see the acknowledged champion of their cause. Badges bearing Bryan's name were numerous among the throng. Cheer after cheer greeted his appearance. Hundreds flocked around to shake his hand and to assure him of their personal intention to vote for him. Special trains from the capital city brought down a throng of interested friends. In that debate, Mr. Bryan had the closing, and when he had concluded his argument he turned to his opponent and presented him with a handsomely-bound volume of " Gray's Elegy" in the following words :

"Mr. Connell, we now bring to a close this series of debates which was arranged by our committees. I am glad that we have been able to conduct these discussions in a courteous and friendly manner. If I have, in any way, offended you in word or deed I offer apology and regret, and as freely forgive. I desire to present to you in remembrance of these pleasant meetings this little volume, because it contains "Gray's Elegy," in perusing which I trust you will find as much pleasure and profit as I have found. It is one of the most beautiful and touching tributes to humble life that literature contains. Grand in its sentiment, sublime in its simplicity, we may both find in it a solace in victory or defeat. If success should crown your efforts in this campaign, and it should be your lot 'The applause of listening senates to command,' and I am left

'A youth to fortune and to fame unknown,'

"Forget not us who in the common walks of life perform our part, but in the hour of your triumph recall the verse:

'Let not ambition mock their useful toil,
    Their homely joys and destiny obscure;
Nor grandeur hear, with disdainful smile,
    The short and simple annals of the poor.'

"If, on the other hand, by the verdict of my countrymen, I shall be made your successor, let it not be said of you:

'And melancholy marked him for her own.'

"But find sweet consolation in the thought:

'Full many a gem of purest ray serene,
    The dark unfathomed caves of ocean bear;
Full many a flower was born to blush unseen,
    And waste its sweetness on the desert air.'

"But whether the palm of victory is given to you or to me, let us remember those of whom the poet says:

'Far from the madding crowd's ignoble strife
    Their sober wishes never learned to stray,
Along the cool sequestered vales of life
    They keep the noiseless tenor of their way'

These are the ones most likely to be forgotten by the Government. When the poor and weak cry

Hon. JOHN. W. DANIEL,
U. S. Senator from Virginia.

Hon. J. C. S. BLACKBURN,
U. S. Senator from Kentucky.

out for relief they too often hear no answer but 'the echo of their cry,' while the rich, the strong, the powerful are given an attentive ear. For this reason is class legislation dangerous and deadly. It takes from the least able to give to those who are least in need. The safety of our farmers and our laborers is not in special legislation, but in equal and just laws that bear alike on every man. The great masses of our people are interested, not in getting their hands into other people's pockets, but in keeping the hands of other people out of their pockets. Let me, in parting, express the hope that you and I may be instrumental in bringing our Government back to better laws which will treat every man in all our land without regard to creed or condition. I bid you a friendly farewell."

Mr. Connell accepted the book, saying that it illustrated the bible truth, "It is more blessed to give than to receive," and he received it in the same friendly spirit in which it was given. Mr. Bryan then proposed three cheers for his opponent, "the able and gallant defender of a lost cause." Mr. Connell returned the compliment.

At this point a young man stepped out from the audience bearing two large floral designs. One was a great shield faced with Marcheil Neil roses of pure white, with a band of white carnations, on which was inscribed the word "Truth." The other floral design was a sword with a blade of white carnations with the word "Eloquence" in purple extending from hilt to point. The hilt was covered with red carnations all fringed with and set in a body of smilax. In presenting the floral tribute the young man said : "In behalf of the Democrats of the First district of Nebraska, I desire to say to Mr. Bryan that we have watched with interest your manly course and your courage upon eleven intellectual battlefields and I am commissioned by them to discharge the pleasant duty of presenting these two emblems. They show our respect, admiration and honor for the brightest and purest advocate of our cause in Nebraska. I present this shield of truth as emblematic of that which has protected you through the series of debates from the arrows of your able adversary. I present this sword as indicative of the predominating faculty of your nature, that of eloquence. Accept them as a tribute from a loyal party to its bravest defender." And then as the emblems were handed to the young orator the vast audience stood up and waved handkerchiefs and hats and cheered until Mr. Bryan beckoned them to be still. He then gracefully responded, thanking his friends for their kindness, and when the great session was over 2,500 people followed him to the train, giving him a royal ovation all along the line.

Mr. Bryan closed his remarkable campaign at the city of Lincoln. He was elected by a plurality of 6,700 in a district which two years before had given a Republican plurality of 3,400. It might be worthy of observation right here that Grover Cleveland's Secretary of Agriculture was defeated for Congress in 1888 by 3,400 plurality in the same district which William J. Bryan carried two years later by a plurality of 6,700.

Following the election the Omaha *World-Herald* editorially announced "Bryan is elected and he wins at the end of one of the fairest and most brilliant campaigns ever fought. He will become at once one of the most prominent members of the Lower House, from the West. His election is a triumph for principle and a victory for brains."

CHAPTER IV.

BRYAN ENTERS CONGRESS.

When Mr. Bryan entered Congress he immediately attracted attention, and his splendid personality drew men to him in Washington exactly as it had drawn men to him in Nebraska. Although it was unprecedented to give to a first-term member a position on the all-important Ways and Means Committee, Speaker Crisp conferred that unprecedented honor upon Bryan, of Nebraska. There was criticism at this exception on the Speaker's part. The St. Louis *Republic*, commenting upon the *personelle* of it, said: "William J. Bryan, of Nebraska, is a very amiable and a very enthusiastic young man who, it is said, has made some reputation on the stump out in Nebraska; but, having no service in the House heretofore, his knowledge of the details of the tariff is necessarily limited." But it was not long before the St. Louis *Republic*, as well as all others who took the trouble to observe, learned that Bryan's knowledge of the tariff was about as complete as any man's could be.

One of the first bills which Mr. Bryan introduced provided for the election of senators by the people, at the option of each State. The

people by constitutional enactment to provide the
manner in which senators were to be chosen.
The bill attracted considerable attention, although
it failed of final passage.

During Mr. Bryan's first session he received
many invitations to address gatherings in the
East. Among his first speeches of this character
was one delivered before the Philadelphia Young
Men's Association, where he responded to the
toast, "The Democracy of the West," on January 8, 1892. On that occasion he uttered these
prophetic words : " Prosperity to the great West!
Yesterday, the citadel of Republicanism ; to-day,
the battle-ground of the nation ; to-morrow, and
thereafter, the home of the Democracy."

Mr. Bryan was one of the most active members
of the Ways and Means Committee. Thomas B.
Reed was a member of that committee, and he is
exceedingly graceful at *repartee.* But Mr. Reed
occasionally finds his match. An interesting incident occurred at one meeting of the Ways and
Means Committee at which Mr. Bryan neatly
turned the tables on Mr. Reed. The committee
was in session when the bell rang indicating the
convening of the House. Mr. Reed arose pon-
derously from his seat and making an elaborate
bow to the committee, the majority of which, by
the way, were Democrats, expressed his regret at
being compelled to desert his colleagues in order
to take his seat in the House to listen to the

chaplain's prayer. "I trust" said he, with a touch
of sarcasm, "that I do not break the committee
quorum." "Oh, do not worry about that," quickly
retorted Mr. Bryan. "You can leave your hat
here and we will count it to make the quorum."
Chairman Springer's dignity was quite upset by
the roar of laughter which greeted this sally, and
Mr. Reed, very red in the face but chuckling,
made his way to the House.

On March 16, 1892 Mr. Bryan made his great
tariff speech in the House. And by that strong
and eloquent speech he made himself a national
figure. It will be many a day before such a
scene is re-enacted. At 2.30 o'clock Bryan arose
to address the House on the tariff question, and
at 5.30 closed a speech which will stand con-
spicuously in the recollections of thousands of
representatives. It was such a speech as no one
there expected, but just such a speech as Bryan's
friends knew he would deliver. Hardly that
either, for Bryan, with all his good record on the
stump, never before delivered such a masterly
combination of argument and rhetoric. No
speech delivered in the House attracted one-
tenth of the interest, either on the floor or in the
gallery. No speech delivered in any recent Congress awoke so much comment. For three full
hours the members on the floor and great crowds
in the gallery listened intently to every word, and
at the close of the speech tendered the young

orator an ovation. When Bryan closed, the
Democratic members arose *en masse*, even before
the House had adjourned, and rushed around
the young exponent of tariff reform, each running
over the other to shake his hand. From every
gallery and from every quarter came exclama-
tions of admiration. From the people as they
crowded each other from the gallery, came continued and earnest expressions complimentary to
the gentleman from Nebraska, and after the
House had adjourned, great crowds stood at the
doorways eager to catch a glimpse of the new
orator.

When the doors were opened many filed
through, and a long line passed Bryan, each man
taking him by the hand and congratulating him.
It was a long time before Bryan, weary with his
great effort, could tear himself away and find
refuge in the committee-room.

Those who have attended regularly the congressional sessions for years declared that at no
time could they remember when a speech received such generous attention and a speaker
such a splendid ovation. It was a great audience,
and it grew as Bryan proceeded with his speech.
Within an hour the galleries were packed and
crowded with people whose interest was clearly
manifested. As a rule, members sleep or attend
to their correspondence while a tariff speech is
being made ; but not so in this instance. Every-

body woke up. Even the press gallery was crowded, and when this is the case the attraction must be great.

Early in the afternoon two women sat in the gallery adjoining the press. One of these turned to the other and asked: "Who speaks on the tariff to-day?"

"Bryan, of Nebraska," was the reply.

"Umph, I never heard of him," said the first woman.

"This is his first term," said the second woman. "But I have Republican friends in Nebraska who say that Mr. Bryan thinks he can make a speech. I've come to see."

And these women sat there. Both were interested listeners to the speech, and when Mr. Bryan had finished, C. W. Sherman, Editor of the Plattsmouth, Neb. *Journal*, climbed over the gallery seats, and, touching the second woman on the arm, said: "Beg pardon, madam, but can you tell me who that was who spoke?"

"That, sir," replied the woman, "is Mr. Bryan, of Nebraska, and he has made a good speech, a very good speech, indeed." Then turning to her lady friend, the woman remarked: "I shall tell my Nebraska friends that I quite agree with Mr. Bryan. I, too, think he can make a speech."

Early in the afternoon a man who had fooled the people of Massachusetts in sending him to Congress twice, slapped another member on the

Hon. JAS. K. JONES,
U. S. Senator from Arkansas.

Hon. F. M. COCKRELL,
U. S. Senator from Missouri.

shoulder at the House entrance and said: "Come in; a new member is going to speak. Let's go in and see our boys have fun with him."

They went in; they saw the fun; but they were mistaken in the victim. "Our boys" started to have their usual amount of fun, but they were glad to retire into the corridor. For a long time Mr. Bryan proceeded without interruption. Then there was a whispered consultation among the Republican leaders, and one by one questions were fired at the Nebraskan. In each and every instance Bryan's retort brought him out on top. Of the probable fifty interruptions to which he was subjected his quick wit and ready logic were brought into play in such a manner as to win the respect of the members and stir up the enthusiasm of the galleries.

Not once did the interest decrease. At 3.30 when the time had expired, unanimous consent was given to prolong the treat. Several times when the speaker essayed to close his address he was urged by his colleagues on the floor to continue. It was an off-hand speech. It could not have been otherwise under the circumstances. It was replete with the argument for tariff reform, and the points made by the speaker were illustrated by new and charming features, which brought down the House. The peroration was superb, and when he said that time would come when legislation would be enacted exclusively in the people's interest and declared "in that day Democracy will be king—long live the king!" it was with an eloquence that proved a fitting climax. Then from every corner of the great room from floor to gallery came demonstrations of applause, while the novel sight was witnessed of over 200 members rushing around a colleague to show their appreciation of real ability.

Kilgore, of Texas, as he took Bryan's hand, declared: "This is the first time I ever left my seat to congratulate a member; but it is the first time I ever had such great cause to break the record."

Burrows, of Michigan, said: "I am free to say that Bryan made the best tariff-reform speech I ever heard."

Beside the Congressman sat his pretty little daughter, Ruth. Mrs. Bryan was in the gallery, and it would be strange if she were not at that moment the proudest woman in the world. It was, too, a proud moment for the several Nebraskans there. Editor Sherman, of Plattsmouth, represented the sentiment of all. In the corridor the great crowd was waiting to catch a glimpse of the orator of the day. Somebody asked:

"How old is Bryan?"

"Thirty-five," replied Sherman.

"Well, he has certainly a future before him," said the first speaker.

"It's the best speech I ever heard in the House," said another.

When several similar compliments had been uttered, Sherman held his head a little bit higher as he declared:

"Gentlemen, I live in Nebraska. We have wanted a man to send to Congress and we sent him. I want to tell you now, that when Nebraska Democrats pick out a man as worthy to represent them here they know what they are doing."

"You certainly made no mistake this time," said a by-stander.

The great newspapers of the country were full of compliments for "the new orator." Bryan became famous in a day.

The New York *World* had the following headlines :—

"Bryan Downed Them All."

"Nebraska's Young Congressman Scores a Triumph in the House."

"His Maiden Speech a Brilliant Plea for Tariff Reform."

"Mr. Raines, of New York, and Messrs. McKenna and Lind Interrupt Him with Questions and are Silenced by Sharp Replies."

"Party Leaders Enthusiastically Applaud the Orator, and His Speech is the Talk of Washington."

Then the *World* said: "When Speaker Crisp appointed Mr. Bryan, of Nebraska, one of the committee on Ways and Means, some criticism was made on the ground that he was a new

member and inexperienced in tariff legislation.
But Mr. Bryan, to-day, in a three-hours' speech,
made the biggest hit of the debate and confirmed
the Speaker's judgment of his ability. No more
dramatic speech has been delivered at this session. Mr. Bryan has the clear-cut features of the
Randall type. He spoke without notes, and his
barytone voice made the chamber ring. The Republicans sought to take advantage of his inex-
perience in Congress by interrupting him with
questions, which would have puzzled much older
heads. But Mr. Bryan brightened under this
friction and forced one Republican after another
into his seat. Old campaigners of the Reed
school, like Raines, of New York, and McKenna,
of California, found the young Nebraskan more
than their match. A lawyer by profession, Mr.
Bryan argued his case with a direct dramatic
directness that aroused not only the enthusiasm of
the Democrats, but won the applause of the galleries.

"When Mr. Bryan finished, the galleries ap-
plauded for fully five minutes, and Democrats
and Republicans gathered about him and shook
his hand warmly. This speech has been a revolution. No new member has received such an
ovation in years. Mr. Bryan's speech was the
talk of the town to-night."

The Washington *Post* said: "If, like Byron,
Congressman Bryan, of Nebraska, does not wake

this morning and find himself famous, then all the eulogies that were being passed on him in hotel corridors were meaningless. There was hardly anything else talked about, except the wonderfully brilliant speech of the young Nebraskan of the House."

The New York *Sun* said: "William Jennings Bryan, the young Democratic leader from Nebraska, whom Speaker Crisp placed on the Ways and Means Committee against the protest of a large element in the House, distinguished himself to-day by making the 'star' speech of the present session on the tariff question. Mr. Bryan astonished his associates and the occupants of the crowded galleries by an exhibition of finished oratory seldom witnessed in the halls of Congress. He is only thirty years old, is tall and well built, with a clean-shaven face and jet black hair. Charley O'Neil, the father of the House, as he is called, says Mr. Bryan looks something as the late Samuel Jackson Randall looked twenty-five years ago. An hour was given Mr. Bryan to speak, but when that time elapsed there was a general chorus of 'Go on,' 'Go on,' from both sides of the House. Members lingered in their seats and the spectators remained in the galleries till 5.12 o'clock, so intent were they in hearing the young orator from the West. Not only was he logical, but he was practical, and won for himself a place among the house orators beside the silver-toned Breckinridge of Kentucky, or the calm-voiced Henderson of Iowa."

The New York *Herald* said: "As Mr. Bryan took his seat he was the recipient of hearty congratulations from his party colleagues. Although this was his maiden speech, he showed every quality of a fine orator. No member who has addressed the House thus far upon the tariff question has received the same attention which was accorded to the young Nebraskan."

The New York *Times* had this to-day: "For most of the time since the tariff battle in the House began the Democrats have been attacking the Republicans' position largely with oratorical fire crackers. Some of these explosives made a merry crackling, but not enough of it fully to wake up the deliberate body, and certainly not enough fully to arrest the attention of many persons out of the House. To-day, almost with the effect of an ambuscade, the Democrats uncovered a ten-inch gun, and for two hours shelled the surprised enemy so effectively, that the protectionist batteries, at first manned with spirit, but supplied with very light guns, were silenced, Gunner Raines (Republican, New York), coming out of the engagement with a badly-battered muzzle, and with the conviction, probably, that he would be compelled next time to put in more powder and employ newer and more modern projectiles.

"The man who to-day ceased to be a new and

young unknown member, and jumped at once into the position of the best tariff speaker in ten years was Representative Bryan, Democrat, of Nebraska. To be a representative from Nebraska implies a condition of revolution in that State; but it also means something more in the case of Mr. Bryan that was not suspected before by those who are not familiar with his reputation at home. Some of the men who supported Mills were in doubt at the time of the caucus about his soundness generally, as he was one of the four Springer men who stuck to Springer after 'the last button was off his coat,' and when the votes of the four would have elected Mills instead of Crisp. After his speech of to-day there can be no doubt about where he stands on the tariff question. There can be no doubt about this power of oratory and argument, and Mr. Raines, who is apt at a certain shallow sort of sophistical cross-questioning, will probably admit that Mr. Bryan is able to hold his own with a veteran in the black-horse cavalry. For two hours and a half Mr. Bryan held the floor and his audience, being urged to go on after his hour had expired, and being inspired to still further continue by shouts of 'Go on,' 'Go on,' when he indicated a modest desire to bring his long speech to a close.

"Having a graceful figure, a little above the average height, Mr. Bryan is not unlike Carlisle in feature, but not so spare. His face is smooth shaved and the features are strong and well marked. His voice is clear and strong, his language plain but not lacking in grace. He uses illustrations effectively, and he employs humor and sarcasm with admirable facility. The applause that greeted him was as spontaneous as it was genuine."

On April 5, 1892, Mr. Springer, Chairman of the Ways and Means Committee, was to address the House on the tariff bill. Mr. Springer had been seriously ill and was admonished by his physician not to make the effort. He came to the House on that day, however, and paid Mr. Bryan the compliment of inviting him to read his, Mr. Springer's, address on the tariff question.

In the spring of 1892, evidences of the hostile silver sentiment had begun to manifest themselves among certain leaders of the Nebraska Democracy. The State Convention to elect delegates to the National Democratic Convention had been called for April 15, 1892. Mr. Bryan announced from Washington that he would attend that convention for the purpose of introducing a free-silver plank into the platform. It was evident that this act would create considerable trouble, and Mr. Bryan was urged by many Democrats not to do it. He refused to be dissuaded, however, from what he regarded as his plain duty, when he went to Omaha. That convention marked the beginning of Bryan's determined efforts to place the

Nebraska Democracy right on the money question. He introduced his plank favoring the free coinage of silver and was opposed by most of the old-time leaders of the party in Nebraska. It was a bitter contest. Bryan presented his cause with that eloquence and spirit that has made him famous; and during the entire day the battle raged. In speaking upon this plank, Mr. Bryan said among other things:

"I am here on a painful duty. I came to agree with all that has been said and to ask the adoption of the principle which has been a part of our platform heretofore, and I do not believe it is good policy to drop now as a Democratic tenet.

"Gentlemen," said Mr. Bryan, "I do not believe it is noble to dodge any issue. It was dodging that defeated Republicanism in Nebraska. If, as has been indicated, this may have an effect on my campaign, then no bridegroom went with gladder heart to greet his bride than I shall welcome defeat. It has been said that God hates a coward, and I believe it is true. Vote this down if you do not approve it, but do not dodge it, for that is not democratic."

The first vote on Bryan's minority report was announced: 267 for, 237 against. It was a clean-cut victory for bimetallism.

And that convention went mad—absolutely insane. Mr. Bryan tried to soothe things. It was impossible. At last it was decided to call another vote.

Governor Boyd opposed a recount. Congressman Bryan asked for it, and the Chairman, who had already proposed it, found a sentiment almost unanimous in favor of it.

The recount was taken amid much excitement, and the Chairman finally announced its result :

"Two hundred and twenty-nine, yes."

"Two hundred and forty-seven, no."

The majority report on platform was then duly adopted and the rejected free-silver plank laid carefully aside.

But Bryan's silver plank had been "counted out."

From that moment Mr. Bryan had incurred the hostility of the Cleveland administration, and from that moment that administration showed him no mercy, and no quarter. But it was characteristic of Mr. Bryan that he asked no mercy and accepted no quarter.

On June 17, 1892, Mr. Bryan addressed the students of Ann Harbor, in reply to a speech made there by Mr. McKinley, one month previous. The question was the tariff, and it was generally conceded that Mr. Bryan's effort more than matched that of his distinguished opponent.

On June 20, 1892, at Nebraska City, Mr. Bryan was re-nominated for Congress by acclamation.

Mr. Bryan's platform on that occasion denounced "unjust tariff laws and oppressive financial policy;" declared for tariff for revenue only; favored an income tax; condemned bounties and subsidies of every kind; declared in favor of the double standard of gold and silver money; denounced the demonetization of silver in 1873; advocated the re-establishment of silver to its honored place of free coinage, occupied by it from the beginning of the Government up to 1873. That platform favored the election of senators by the people; favored liberal pensions to disabled veterans; reiterated the plank in the platform on which Mr. Bryan was first nominated, that plank opposing caucus dictation.

In the meantime the Legislature had re-districted the congressional districts of the State. Omaha was taken out of Bryan's district and his new district was so arranged that under ordinary circumstances the Republicans would have an overwhelming majority. It was believed by Republican leaders that with this re-apportionment, Bryan's defeat could be accomplished.

The Republican party nominated Allen W. Field, then Judge of the District Court, and a resident of the city of Lincoln.

A series of debates were arranged between the contestants. This was probably the most interesting series of debates in the history of Nebraska. Although Mr. Field was a strong man and defended his cause well, the contest was one triumphal march for Bryan. At every meeting place people went wild in their demonstrations in behalf of the young orator. At Auburn, for instance, when the contest was concluded a crowd of Republicans rushed to the platform to shake Mr. Field's hand. And they shook it heartily. But right here is where the differenee was to be noticed. The crowd around Mr. Field numbered perhaps fifty men. At the front of the platform a great scene was being enacted. There was Bryan stooping with outstretched hands to grasp the hands of at least 2,000 people who were crowding over each other to greet him. The farmers and their wives, the laborers and their sisters and their cousins and their aunts all pressed forward to shake the hand of the man who will succeed himself as their representative. Children were raised up to clasp the hand of the man, who, by his great ability and courage, had become enshrined in the hearts of the masses in his district. It was a glorious reception to a public servant.

At Nebraska City 5,000 people had assembled on the Court House Square to hear the debate. Bryan's close was a mighty speech. It was as clean cut a talk as was ever heard. When he concluded, the greatest demonstration ever witnessed in Nebraska was seen. The audience seemed to rise *en masse* and rush to the platform. The great scene enacted at Auburn was repeated, only it was nine times greater. Farmers and laboring men cheered themselves hoarse. Half a hundred women stood upon chairs and waved their handkerchiefs. Three cheers were given Bryan and repeated fifty times. For half an hour he stood on the platform and shook hands with his delighted constituents.

The people refused to leave the grounds until, weary and exhausted, Mr. Bryan left the place, followed by a great crowd of people. The scenes were simply indescribable. It was the best ovation ever received ; the greatest triumph ever won by a public man. The scene will never be forgotten in Nebraska City and must long be remembered by Bryan as among the most valuable tributes in his career. A great crowd followed Bryan to his hotel, cheering him all the way.

At Weeping Water, when Bryan closed, the scene in Nebraska City was in part repeated. In this instance probably fifty people came forward to shake Mr. Field by the hand, but it seemed that the entire audience arose to greet Mr. Bryan. The town people and the farmers crowded over each other to shake the young congressman's hand. At first Bryan stood upon the platform, and bending down grasped the many hundreds of hands advanced to him.

But the great throng of his admirers increased and the young orator was literally dragged from the platform and for thirty yards he was crowded here and there, surged by the crowd, every member of which seemed anxious to shake his hand.

The ovation extended to Bryan was so marked that many deeply sympathized with Mr. Field. At every step from the grove Bryan was heartily cheered, and though this was a Republican precinct Bryan fairly captured everything in sight. At the start the crowd seemed to be against Bryan. At the close of the debate Bryan owned the earth, and had he desired a fence to be built around it, it was but necessary for him to say the word.

At all other points similar scenes were enacted. At the city of Lincoln, October 12, 1892, Bryan won another distinct triumph, and at the close of the debate a handful of people grasped the hand of Judge Field, but it required half an hour for Bryan to half complete the task of greeting his friends. A handsome floral piece was on the stand, the design being a pair of scales. It was the tribute of the young congressman's Lincoln friends.

The closing session of the debate was an overwhelming triumph for Bryan, in perfect keeping with his splendid victory in every previous meeting with his opponent.

The Republicans made desperate efforts to accomplish Bryan's defeat. Speakers of national renown poured into the district and large sums of money were expended against Bryan in all counties in the district. But in spite of all these efforts in the district, which had been arranged to give a Republican candidate from 4,000 to 5,000 majority, Mr. Bryan was re-elected by a majority of 152.

Commenting upon this triumph the Omaha *World-Herald* said editorially :—

" The more one thinks of Bryan's re-election the more wonderful it seems.

" In the face of overwhelming opposition, which was aided by such speakers as McKinley, Foraker and Thurston ; in spite of a district, not one county of which was or went Democratic—a district in which Harrison had more votes than Cleveland and Weaver combined, and which was on a congressional fight several thousand Republican ; in spite of boodle freely spent by the Republicans, and in spite of a third candidate running as a decoy duck for his principal opponent, Bryan is a victor by a majority of 140.

" He deserved and got the votes of both Independents and Republicans, and his election is a splendid tribute to the qualities which caused his selection both times for congressional honors, and which in one Washington session made him the most prominent man on the floor of the House of Representatives.

"Looking over the whole November fight, there is no more remarkable or brilliant victory than that won in the First Nebraska District."

CHAPTER V.

BRYAN AS "BLAND'S LIEUTENANT."

When Mr. Bryan entered upon his second term in Congress the money question had come to be recognized generally as the great question of the day. It was known that the Hon. Richard P. Bland, of Missouri, who for twenty years had fought the battles of bimetallism, would lead the fight in the then coming contest. It was also announced that Mr. Bryan would be one of Mr. Bland's lieutenants.

Mr. Bryan was a delegate to the National Silver Conference, held in Chicago, August 1, 1893, and addressed that gathering August 16, 1893.

Mr. Bryan addressed the House in opposition to the bill to repeal the purchasing clause of the Sherman Act. From that great speech, which was recognized as one of the strongest ever delivered in the House, the following extracts are taken :

" MR. SPEAKER: I shall accomplish my full purpose if I am able to impress upon the members of the House the far-reaching consequences which may follow our action and quicken their appreciation of the grave responsibility which presses upon us. Historians tell us that the victory of Charles Martel at Tours determined the history of all Europe for centuries. It was a contest 'between the Crescent and the Cross,' and when, on that fateful day, the Frankish prince drove back the followers of Abderrahman, he rescued the West from 'the all-destroying grasp of Islam,' and saved Europe its Christian civilization. A greater than Tours is here! In my humble judgment the vote of this House on the subject under consideration may bring to the people of the West and South, to the people of the United States, and to all mankind, weal or woe beyond the power of language to describe or imagination to conceive.

"In the princely palace and in the humblest hamlet; by the financier and by the poorest toiler; here, in Europe and everywhere, the proceedings of this Congress upon this problem will be read and studied; and as our actions bless or blight we shall be commended or condemned. *   *

"Rollin tells us that the third Punic war was declared by the Romans and that a messenger was sent to Carthage to announce the declaration after the army had started on its way. The Carthaginians at once sent representatives to treat for peace. The Romans first demanded the delivery of three hundred hostages before they would enter into negotiations. When three hundred sons of the nobles had been given into their hands they demanded the surrender of all the arms and implements of war before announcing the terms of the treaty. The conditions were sorrowfully but promptly complied with, and the people who boasted of a Hannibal and Hamilcar gave up to their ancient enemies every weapon of offense and defense. Then the Roman consul, rising up before the humiliated representatives of Carthage, said:

"'I cannot but commend you for the readiness with which you have obeyed every order. The decree of the Roman Senate is that Carthage shall be destroyed.'

"Sirs, what will be the answer of the people whom you represent, who are wedded to the 'gold and silver coinage of the Constitution,' if you vote for unconditional repeal and return to tell them that you were commended for the readiness with which you obeyed every order, but that Congress has decreed that one-half of the people's metallic money shall be destroyed? [Applause.]

"They demand unconditional surrender, do they? Why, sirs, we are the ones to grant terms. Standing by the pledges of all the parties in this country, backed by the history of a hundred years, sustained by the most sacred interests of humanity itself, we demand an unconditional surrender of the principle of gold monometallism as the first condition of peace. [Applause.] You demand surrender! Ay, sirs, you may cry 'Peace,

peace,' but there is no peace. Just so long as there are people here who would chain this country to a single gold standard, there is war—eternal war; and it might just as well be known now! [Loud applause on the Democratic side.] I have said that we stand by the pledges of all platforms. Let me quote them:

"The Populist platform adopted by the national convention in 1892 contained these words:

"'We demand free and unlimited coinage of silver and gold at the present legal ratio of 16 to 1.'

"As the members of that party, both in the Senate and in the House, stand ready to carry out the pledge there made, no appeal to them is necessary.

"The Republican national platform adopted in 1888 contains this plank:

"'The Republican party is in favor of the use of both gold and silver as money and condemns the policy of the Democratic administration in its effort to demonetize silver.'

"The same party in 1892 adopted a platform containing the following language:

"'The American people from tradition and interest favor bimetallism, and the Republican party demands the use of both gold and silver as standard money, such restrictions to be determined by contemplation of values of the two metals, so that the purchasing and debt-paying power of the dollar, whether of silver, gold, or paper, shall be equal at all times.

"'The interests of the producers of the country, its farmers and its workingmen, demand that every dollar, paper or gold, issued by the Government, shall be as good as any other. We commend the wise and patriotic steps already taken by our Government to secure an international parity of value between gold and silver for use as money throughout the world.'

"Are the Republican members of this House ready to abandon the system which the American people favor 'from tradition and interest?' Having won a Presidential election upon a platform which condemned 'the policy of the Democratic administration in its efforts to demonetize silver,' are they ready to join in that demonetization? Having advocated the Sherman law because it gave an increased use of silver, are they ready to repeal it and make no provisions for silver at all? Are they willing to go before the country confessing that they secured the present law by sharp practice, and only adopted it as an ingenious device for preventing free coinage, to be repealed as soon as the hour of danger was passed?

"The Democratic platform of 1880 contained these words:

"'Honest money, consisting of gold and silver, and paper convertible into coin on demand.'

"It would seem that at that time silver was honest money, although the bullion value was considerably below the coinage value.

"In 1884 the Democratic platform contained this plank:

"'We believe in honest money, the gold and silver coinage of the Constitution, and a circuating medium convertible into such money without loss.'

"It would seem that at that time silver was considered honest money.

"In 1888 the Democratic party did not express itself on the money question except by saying:

"'It renewed the pledge of its fidelity to Democratic faith, and reaffirms the platform adopted by its representatives in the convention of 1884.'

"Since the platform of 1884 commended silver as an honest money, we must assume that the reaffirming of that platform declared anew that silver was honest money as late as 1888, although at that time its bullion value had fallen still more.

"The last utterance of a Democratic national convention upon this subject is contained in the platform adopted at Chicago in 1892. It is as follows:

"'We denounce the Republican legislation known as the Sherman act of 1890 as a cowardly makeshift, fraught with possibilities of danger in the future, which should make all of its supporters, as well as its author, anxious for its speedy repeal. We hold to the use of both gold and silver as

8

the standard money of the country, and to the coinage of both gold and silver without discrimination against either metal or charge for mintage, but the dollar unit of coinage of both metals must be of equal intrinsic and exchangeable value or be adjusted through international agreement, or by such safeguards of legislation as shall insure the maintenance of the parity of the two metals, and the equal power of every dollar at all times in the markets and in the payment of debts; and we demand that all paper currency shall be kept at par with and redeemable in such coin. We insist upon this policy as especially necessary for the protection of the farmers and laboring classes, the first and most defenseless victims of unstable money and a fluctuating currency.'

"Thus it will be seen that gold and silver have been indissolubly linked together in our platforms. Never in the history of the party has it taken a position in favor of a gold standard. On every vote taken in the House and Senate a majority of the party have been recorded not only in favor of bimetallism, but for the free and unlimited coinage of gold and silver at the ratio of 16 to 1.

"The last platform pledges us to the use of both metals as standard money and to the free coinage of both metals at a fixed ratio. Does any one believe that Mr. Cleveland could have been elected President upon a platform declaring in favor of the unconditional repeal of the Sherman law?

Can we go back to our people and tell them that, after denouncing for twenty years the crime of 1873, we have at last accepted it as a blessing? Shall bimetallism receive its deathblow in the house of its friends, and in the very hall where innumerable vows have been registered in its defense? What faith can be placed in platforms if their pledges can be violated with impunity? Is it right to rise above the power which created us? Is it patriotic to refuse that legislation in favor of gold and silver which a majority of the people have always demanded? Is it necessary to betray all parties in order to treat this subject in a 'nonpartisan' way?

"The President has recommended unconditional repeal. It is not sufficient to say that he is honest —so were the mothers, who, with misguided zeal, threw their children into the Ganges. The question is not "Is he honest?" but "Is he right?" He won the confidence of the toilers of this country because he taught that 'public office is a public trust,' and because he convinced them of his courage and his sincerity. But are they willing to say, in the language of Job, 'Though He slay me, yet will I trust Him?' Whence comes this irresistible demand for unconditional repeal? Are not the representatives here as near to the people and as apt to know their wishes? Whence comes the demand? Not from the workshop and the farm, not from the workingmen of this country, who create its wealth in time of peace and protect its flag in time of war, but from the middlemen, from what are termed the 'business interests,' and largely from that class which can force Congress to let it issue money at a pecuniary profit to itself if silver is abandoned. The President has been deceived. He can no more judge the wishes of the great mass of our people by the expressions of these men than he can measure the ocean's silent depths by the foam upon its waves.

"Mr. Powderly, who spoke at Chicago a few days ago in favor of the free coinage of silver at the present ratio and against the unconditional repeal of the Sherman law, voiced the sentiment of more laboring men than have ever addressed the President or this House in favor of repeal. Go among the agricultural classes ; go among the poor, whose little is as precious to them as the rich man's fortune is to him, and whose families are as dear, and you will not find the haste to destroy the issue of money or the unfriendliness to silver which is manifested in money centers.

"This question can not be settled by typewritten recommendations and suggestions made by boards of trade and sent broadcast over the United States. It can only be settled by the great mass of the voters of this country who stand like the Rock of Gibraltar for the use of both gold and silver. (Applause.)

"There are thousands, yes, tens of thousands, aye, even millions, who have not yet 'bowed the knee to Baal.' Let the President take courage. Muehlbach relates an incident in the life of the great military hero of France. At Marengo the Man of Destiny, sad and disheartened, thought the battle lost. He called to a drummer boy and ordered him to beat a retreat. The lad replied:

"'Sire, I do not know how: Dessaix has never taught me retreat, but I can beat a charge. Oh, I can beat a charge that would make the dead fall into line! I beat that charge at the Bridge of Lodi; I beat it at Mount Tabor; I beat it at the Pyramids. Oh, may I beat it here?'

"The charge was ordered, the battle won, and Marengo was added to the victories of Napoleon. Oh, let our gallant leader draw inspiration from the street gamin of Paris. In the face of an enemy proud and confident the President has wavered. Engaged in the battle royal between the 'money power and the common people' he has ordered a retreat. Let him not be dismayed.

"He has won greater victories than Napoleon, for he is a warrior who has conquered without a sword. He restored fidelity in the public service; he converted Democratic hope into realization; he took up the banner of tariff reform and carried it to triumph. Let him continue that greater fight for the 'gold and silver coinage of the Constitution,' to which three national platforms have pledged him. Let his clarion voice call the party hosts to arms; let him but speak the language of the Senator from Texas, in reply to those who would destroy the use of silver:

"'In this hour fraught with peril to the whole country, I appeal to the unpurchased representatives of the American people to meet this bold and insolent demand like men. Let us stand in the breach and call the battle on and never leave the field until the people's money shall be restored to the mints on equal terms with gold, as it was years ago.'

"Let this command be given, and the air will resound with the tramp of men scarred in a score of battles for the people's rights. Let this command be given and this Marengo will be our glory and not our shame. [Applause on the floor and in the galleries.]

"Well has it been said by the Senator from Missouri [Mr. Vest] that we have come to the parting of the ways. To-day the Democratic party stands between two great forces, each inviting its support. On the one side stand the corporate interests of the nation, its moneyed institutions, its aggregations of wealth and capital, imperious, arrogant, compassionless. They demand special legislation, favors, privileges and immunities. They can subscribe magnificently to campaign funds; they can strike down opposition with their all-pervading influence, and, to those

who fawn and flatter, bring ease and plenty.
They demand that the Democratic party shall become their agent to execute their merciless decrees.

"On the other side stands that unnumbered throng which gave a name to the Democratic party and for which it has assumed to speak. Work-worn and dust-begrimed, they make their sad appeal. They *hear* of *average* wealth increased on every side and *feel* the *inequality* of its distribution. They see an over-production of everything desired, because of the under-production of the ability to buy. They can not pay for loyalty except with their suffrages, and can only punish betrayal with their condemnation. Although the ones who most deserve the fostering care of government, their cries for help too often beat in vain against the outer wall, while others less deserving find ready access to legislative halls.

"This army, vast and daily vaster growing, begs the party to be its champion in the present conflict. It cannot press its claims 'mid sounds of revelry. Its phalanxes do not form in grand parade, nor has it gaudy banners floating on the breeze. Its battle hymn is "Home, Sweet Home," its war cry "Equality before the law." To the Democratic party, standing between these two irreconcilable forces, uncertain to which side to turn, and conscious that upon its choice its fate depends, come the words of Israel's second law-giver: 'Choose you this day whom ye will serve.' What will the answer be? Let me invoke the memory of him whose dust made sacred the soil of Monticello when he joined

> "'The dead but sceptered sovereigns who still rule
> Our spirits from their urns.'

"He was called a demagogue and his followers a mob, but the immortal Jefferson dared to follow the best promptings of his heart. He placed man above matter, humanity above property, and, spurning the bribes of wealth and power, pleaded the cause of the common people. It was this devotion to their interests which made his party invincible while he lived, and will make his name revered while history endures. And what message comes to us from the Hermitage? When a crisis like the present arose and the national bank of his day sought to control the politics of the nation, God raised up an Andrew Jackson, who had the courage to grapple with that great enemy, and, by overthrowing it, he made himself the idol of the people and reinstated the Democratic party in public confidence. What will the decision be to day? The democratic party has won the greatest success in its history. Standing upon this victory-crowned summit, will it turn its face to the rising or the setting sun? Will it choose blessings or cursings—life or death—which?

Which?" [Prolonged applause on the floor and in the galleries, and cries of "Vote!" "Vote!"]

Copies of Mr. Bryan's speech on this occasion were in great demand. Senator Stewart circulated 5,000 copies, and other bimetallists distributed large numbers of them; the circulation aggregating, it has been estimated, very near one million.

All the great newspapers were filled with comments complimenting Mr. Bryan's great speech on this occasion. The *New York World* termed it "The most remarkable yet heard on the propositions now before the House." The *New York Tribune* said: "The speech was a success of which Mr. Bryan may well be proud." The *Atlanta Constitution* contained this reference:

"This afternoon young Mr. Bryan of Nebraska delivered the most remarkable speech heard upon the floor of the House in many years. It was upon the silver question. He advocated free coinage. For two hours and fifty minutes the young Nebraska orator held the close attention of a full house and crowded galleries. Instead of members leaving the hall as is usual, they crowded in, and every man who could, listened to the entire speech. There are few other men in Congress who could have held such an audience for so long a time. Certainly in the last ten years no man has performed such a feat. It was generally known that Mr. Bryan was to speak, but no one expected him to sustain the great repu-

tation made by his tariff speech delivered last year.
That speech made him famous. His speech of
to-day will perpetuate his fame. No such speech
has been heard on either side since the debate
opened. His delivery was perfect. His argument exceedingly strong. Every possible argument in favor of free coinage he placed before his
hearers in the most forcible style. He did not
repeat himself. Though without a note before
him, he went through every argument in language
that riveted his hearers to their seats. Occasionally
a single standard man would interrupt, but none
did it without subsequent regret. He knows his
case, so to speak. At repartee he is brilliant.
His handsome smooth face always broadened into
smiles when a question was propounded to him.
With the confidence and ease of a fencing master
he would clip the wings of his interrupters. He
drove every one to a seat who exhibited the temerity to face him, and he did it with the apparent ease
of the experienced matador. He pierced their
argument and called for others as the matador
would for a new bull. The speech was indeed
grand. No other kind would have received such
attention. Hardly a man left his seat even for a
moment. There is something inspiring about
Mr. Bryan's delivery. He is but 32 years of age,
with a smooth face of the Sam Randall type,
erect in his bearing, perfect in his gesticulation,
a manly man to look upon. He is pleasing to
the eye. His language is choice, smooth and

eloquent. He uses no surplus words. Every word fits just where he puts it. His voice is splendid, his utterances pleasing to the ear, his argument strong. The speech has established him as the greatest orator in the House. When he finished, great applause and cheers of Vote! vote! rent the air. Silver and anti-silver men, Democrats and Republicans alike, crowded over to congratulate him. He simply had electrified the House. Tom Reed and Joe Cannon grasped his hand, and told him it was the greatest speech ever delivered on his side of the silver question. Bourke Cochran and William L. Wilson declared it was the greatest silver speech ever made upon the floor of the House. Bland, Culbertson, Bankhead and all the silver men demonstrated enthusiasm of the most intense order. For full ten minutes the House business stopped to allow for the congratulations. Not a member failed to congratulate him. Speaker Crisp says since he has been in Congress he has never known another man to hold such an audience for two hours and fifty minutes. He had never seen such close attention. Such interest in a speech. The silver men are happy over it to-night. They know that it has strengthened the cause. Some of them claim it may change many votes. There are those who say since that speech the silver men have a chance of winning in the House. No definite idea of such a speech can be given in brief synopsis."

CHAPTER VI.

BRYAN'S DETERMINED FIGHT.

With the approach of the Nebraska Democratic State Convention of 1893 the interest in the money question increased. Friends of the administration determined that the Nebraska platform should contain no plank favorable to silver. On September 26, 1893, Mr. Bryan gave out for publication from Washington an interview in which he announced that he would return to Nebraska to serve as a delegate to the State Convention from Lancaster county, and to assist in giving expression to the sentiment of the party on the paramount question of the day. In the interview Mr. Bryan said: "I shall attend the State Convention, not to secure personal endorsement, but in the discharge of what I regard as a public duty. No one will assert that the President has the exclusive right to construe the platform upon so vital a question. Every Democrat is entitled to his opinion. The Democrats of the East have met and endorsed the President's construction. If our people agree with that construction, they ought to say so. They owe it to the President. If they do not concur in the President's construction, they owe it to the rest of the country to express dissent. The President is not infallible any more than any other man. If he is mistaken, we can better show our devotion to Democratic principles by dissenting, rather than by servile acquiescence. I may, as has been suggested, have few to stand with me in the fight. But if I stand alone I shall make the fight. I would be ungrateful for the honors the party has bestowed upon me if I deserted it in this hour of party danger, and I shall make any sacrifice necessary in its behalf."

This announcement created the greatest activity on the part of the administration in Nebraska, and their forces were organized for the defeat of the young Congressman in his effort to place the Nebraska Democracy once more in line for bimetallism. It was given out from high administration authority, that after this announcement Mr. Bryan need not expect any favors at the hands of the administration; that all patronage would be withheld from him. He was warned that if he persisted in his course, no man whom he recommended for office could obtain an office, and that his endorsement of an application would be an insurance of the applicant's defeat. The warning and threats did not deter Mr. Bryan from his course. But it may be remarked right here, that the administration kept its word. From that time on, Mr. Bryan's recommendation at the

White House was not worth the paper on which
it was written.

The State Convention met at Lincoln, October
4, 1893. True to his word, Mr. Bryan was on
hand, and he found himself confronted with the
greatest aggregation of federal office-holders that
ever assembled in one convention hall. It may be
said that in point of dramatic interest that convention was the most interesting of any ever held
in Nebraska. Mr. Bryan had an almighty big
fight on his hands, and while he came out of the
contest defeated for the moment he emerged
stronger in the hearts and the affections of the
people of his adopted State.

In that convention Bryan was not only sat upon,
but not the slightest mercy was shown him. Even
the ordinary parliamentary courtesies were ignored, and the young Congressman was not permitted to obtain the slightest advantage.

For several days it had been known that the
administration had scored a triumph in the election of delegates to this convention, but it was
presumed by many that with so pronounced a
victory the majority would at least be merciful.
There was no quarter, however. The administration element forced the fighting, and the Bryan
wing seemed to invite the slaughter by its motions
and demands for roll-call, which placed on record
every delegate in the convention. The first contest came upon the election of temporary chair-

man, and the administration won by an overwelming majority. The administration organized the convention permanently by the same decisive vote. Then when it came to selecting a committee on resolutions one of the delegates moved that Mr. Bryan be made a member of the committee. This brought on the fight in earnest, and the convention went wild. The administration men were determined that not even a personal compliment should be paid to the young Congressman. Although eight members of that committee were to be gold men, they were not willing that Mr. Bryan should be the ninth man. It was a different question from endorsing his financial policy. It was a personal question. But, as results indicated, there was no mercy in that convention. The chairman of one delegation, in casting his vote, said his delegation did not come to instruct the Chair in his duty. He voted "No." He was willing that the Chair should do his duty as he realized it. Everything seemed to be against Bryan until Douglas county, in which Omaha is located, was reached. When that county was called there was a dramatic scene. The chairman of the Douglas delegation arose and announced, "Douglas county casts 103 votes 'No.'" Be it remembered that this "103 votes 'No'" meant that the personal compliment should not be extended to Bryan of placing him as one man out of nine on the resolutions committee.

There was a deathlike stillness. G. V. Gallagher, of Douglas, arose and levelling his good
right arm at the Chair said, " Mr. Chairman."

" The gentleman from Douglas," said the
chairman.

In every quarter of the hall men stood upon
their tiptoes. Every eye was directed toward
Gallagher.

" Mr. Chairman," said he, " in order to set myself right before this convention I desire to say
that the unit rule has been adopted in the Douglas
delegation. As a Democrat I submit to the rule,
but I want to say here and now that if it were not.
for loyalty to the majority rule of my delegation,
my vote could never be recorded against paying
a deserved tribute to the Chevalier Bayard of the
Democratic party in Nebraska."

This broke the camel's back. The Bryan men
arose in their seats and yelled themselves hoarse.
The galleries added their chorus to the tumult.
The noise had not died away when C. J. Smyth,
of Douglas, who is now chairman of the Democratic State Committee, arose and declared :
" Mr. Chairman, I challenge the vote of Douglas
county. It has not been polled. No attempt has
even been made to poll the vote. I protest
against this system of ' gag ' rule. I demand
that the Douglas delegation be polled."

Then the entire convention arose ; everybody
yelled at the same time. Bryan alone sat in his

seat with that familiar set smile upon his face.
The Bryan men cheered until the tears rolled
down some of their faces. They waved um-
brellas, hats, newspapers, and everything available. The crowds in the galleries and in the lobby
seemed to be with Bryan and joined in the popular acclaim.

In the midst of all this tumult, the goldbug
chairman of the Douglas delegation, and who, by
the way, has since been rewarded by appointment
as postmaster at Omaha, like Casabianca on the
burning deck, stood with arms folded and a determined expression upon his face. He calmly
awaited the quiet which did not come until the
chairman declared that this was a Democratic
convention and every man should have a hearing.

Then the Douglas chairman said that he had
canvassed the vote " sufficiently to know how the
majority votes were." At this the Bryan men
hissed and the administration men cheered. One
gold delegate said that Mr. Smyth was the only
man that proposed to vote for Bryan, but at this
moment Ed. P. Smith, an Omaha lawyer, jumped
to his feet, and waving his umbrella yelled: "No,
he isn't. I want to say, Mr. Chairman, that if no
other vote is cast for W. J. Bryan I want my vote
cast in order that the Democratic party of Nebraska may accord him a slight tribute for his
great work. I am for Bryan as a member of the
Resolutions Committee."

9

Again the convention went wild. But the big body was against Bryan and nothing could stem the tide. After a poll of the Douglas delegation the chairman announced "103 votes 'No,'" and that settled it. The motion to instruct the Chair to appoint Bryan a member of the Resolutions Committee was defeated by a vote of 122 yeas to 373 nays. Everybody thought that in spite of this vote the Chair would appoint Bryan as a member of the committee, tying his hands with eight other members who were against him. But the chair wasn't built that way. He omitted Bryan from the committee.

When the committee was appointed, a motion to take a recess until 7 o'clock was adopted.

As Bryan moved from the convention hall he was surrounded by a great gathering of men. From there to the sidewalk he was kept busy shaking hands. When he reached the street a crowd of workingmen and citizens of all classes gathered around him and climbed over one another to grasp his hand. It was one of the most peculiar public ovations ever witnessed. Here was a man who had just been sat down on by an overwhelming majority of his own party convention, who was being congratulated on every hand —for what? For defending Democratic principles.

Let it suffice, however, to state that no man engaged upon a great triumphal march after a mighty conquest ever received such a splendid popular ovation as did Bryan after a mighty defeat.

While the convention was awaiting the arrival of the chairman of the Credentials Committee the crowd filled in the time at the evening session by yelling for Bryan. The calls for the young Congressman became so strong and earnest that the entire assemblage took up the refrain. The delay was becoming more than embarrassing. The crowd was an impatient one, and in the midst of all this one old delegate took a position in the center of the aisle and went through the pantomime of a speech, but it was all pantomime.

Not a word could be heard. It was simply ludicrous to see an old, bald-headed man standing up in a vast assemblage, and at one yell of the crowd the old man's arms would go down and at the next they would go up, and this pantomime was kept up until the crowd was weary. The assemblage was desperate by this time and called for "After the Ball." At 9.40 o'clock the chairman called the convention to order. The Resolutions Committee reported with a goldbug platform, and upon this report Mr. Bryan was permitted to speak. The federal officials who had packed the convention found that they had undertaken a difficult task in endeavoring to completely bury the young Congressman. He asked no quarter. He mounted the platform and hurled defiance at his enemies.

Mr. Bryan spoke as follows:

"Gentlemen of the Convention: We have to meet to-night as important a question as ever came before the Democrats of the State of Nebraska. It is not a personal question; it is a question that rises above individuals. So far as I am personally concerned it matters not that (snapping his fingers) whether you vote this amendment up or down; it matters not to me whether you pass resolutions censuring my course or indorsing it, and if I am wrong in the position I have taken I will fall, though you heap your praises upon me; if I am right in the position I have taken—and in my heart, so help me God, I believe I am—(applause)—if I am right I will triumph yet, although you downed me in your convention a hundred times. (Applause.)

"Gentlemen of this convention, satisfied with what I have done, you are playing in the basement of politics. Why, you think you can pass resolutions censuring a man, and that you can humiliate him. I want to tell you that I am exiled with no more joy than the delegates who come here and drown their sentiments for fear they will not get office.

"Gentlemen, if you represent your constituents in what you have done, and will do—because I do not entertain the fond hope that any of you men

Hon. CHARLES F. CRISP.

Hon. ROBERT E. PATTISON,
Ex-Governor of Pennsylvania.

who have voted as you have to-day will change it
upon this vote; I have no such idea, but I want to
say to you that if the delegates who came here
properly reflect the sentiments of the Democratic
party which sent them here; if the resolutions
which you have proposed here, and which you will
adopt; if they reflect the sentiments of the Democratic party of this State, and this party declares
in favor of a gold standard; if you declare in
favor of the impoverishment of the people of
Nebraska, if you intend to make more galling
than the slavery of the black, the slavery of the
debtors of this country; if the Democratic party
after you go home indorses your action and this
becomes your sentiment, I want to promise you
that I will go out and serve my country and my
God under some other name, if I go alone.
(Applause. Voice from convention: 'The people
of Nebraska will take care of you, Mr. Bryan.')

"Gentlemen, I want to express it as my humble
opinion that the Democratic party of Nebraska
will never ratify what you have done here in this
convention. My friends, in this city, when we had
our primaries, there were banks that called their
claquers in and told them to vote, but thank God,
there are many men in Nebraska who cannot be
driven and compelled to vote as somebody
dictates. (Applause.) The Democratic party
was founded by Thomas Jefferson, and Thomas
Jefferson dared to defy the wealth and power of

his day and plead the cause of the common people, and if the Democratic party lives it will still plead the cause of the man who wears a colored shirt as well as the man who wears the linen shirt. (Applause.)

"You have got to-day to choose what kind of Democracy you want. For thirty years the Democratic party has denounced the demonetization of silver; for twenty years it has proclaimed it the "crime of the age;" it has heaped upon the Republican party all the opprobrium that language could express. If you are ready to go down on your knees and apologize for what you have said, you will go without me. (Applause.)

"On the 14th day of July, 1892, John Sherman of Ohio introduced in the Senate of the United States a bill substantially like that which has passed the house known as the Wilson Bill. That bill was introduced in the Senate by the premier of the Republican party, by the leader of the financial system of the Republican party, and you come into this convention and attempt to thrust it down the throats of the Democrats as a Democratic measure. (Laughter.)

"There sits in Columbus, in the State of Ohio, a Democrat, once known as 'the noblest Roman of them all.' He has won and held the affection of the American people as few citizens have. He sits now crowned with the honors of a nation's gratitude. He sits waiting there for the summons to come that will call him home, where I know there is a reward for men who sacrifice themselves for their country's good, and from the solitude of his retreat Allen G. Thurman says he is opposed to unconditional repeal, and when I must choose between John Sherman of Ohio and Allen G. Thurman of Ohio I take my Democracy from the latter source. (Applause.)

"Do you say this is Democracy? Was it in the platform? Read the national platform; you can't find authority for unconditional repeal there. You find a demand for repeal, but you find a declaration that you shall coin both metals without discrimination, and without charge for mintage, and are you going to snatch away a little of the platform and thrust it down the throats of Democrats and turn your back upon the declaration which has been in their platform for the last twenty years. The Democratic party in Congress has on many occasions expressed itself, and until this year there was never a time but what a majority of the Democrats voted in the House and Senate for the free coinage of silver at 16 to 1, and in this Congress, when the question came up in the lower house, a majority of the Democrats voted to substitute the Bland law for the Sherman law, showing they were not in favor of unconditional repeal. Take the vote and see where it comes from.

"This platform says we know no section.

Well, my friends, we do not know as much as
some other people in other parts of the country
if we know no section. (Applause.) You take
the six New England States, the States of New
York, Pennsylvania, New Jersey and the two
southern States that are really eastern—Maryland
and Delaware, that cast 103 votes—101 were in
favor of repeal. (Voice from convention, 'Douglas county cast 103 votes.') I might suggest
this: That to get the 103 votes they do not have
to go back three years to find a convention.
(Laughter.) How did the South vote? You take
that section of the country which I have called
Democratic—I have mentioned—Maryland and
Delaware—and the vote of those southern States,
notwithstanding more influence was brought to
bear, perhaps, than was ever brought to bear
before, notwithstanding that, in those southern
states sixty-eight Democrats voted against unconditional repeal and forty-nine Democrats voted for
unconditional repeal.

"Take the States west of the Mississippi river
—and there were 29 votes against repeal and 95
for repeal—(applause)—and out of the 95 for
repeal one came from Douglas county, and was a
Republican, and I do not know whether my friends
from Douglas are indorsing him because they
elected him in a Democratic district or not. Then,
gentlemen of the convention, you will find there
were sectional lines in that vote. The great

country west of the Mississippi river was almost
to a vote against unconditional repeal ; the great
country south, to which we look for our Democratic majority, was, a majority of it, against unconditional repeal. Do you tell me those men don't
know what Democracy is? Out of thirteen
Democrats from Missouri twelve voted against
unconditional repeal. Take the Democrats of
Texas, and they rolled up their tremendous
Democratic majority, and yet a majority of them
were against unconditional repeal. You take the
men who have been preaching the gospel of
Democracy—take John W. Daniel of Virginia,
whose magnificent speech in defense of a constitutional money has not been answered, and will
not be answered by any man—(applause)—you
take Senator Morgan of Alabama ; take Senators
Vest of Missouri and Pugh of Alabama ; take
Harris and Beck of Tennessee, Vance of North
Carolina, Butler of South Carolina, George of
Mississippi—and they have stood up and said they
were Democrats ; they stood upon the national
platform, and they were opposed to the repeal of
the Sherman law unless you give something else in
the place of the Sherman law that provided for
the use of silver. (Applause.)

" These gentlemen are Democrats. Nobody has
dared to impeach their Democracy. And yet I
was read out of the Democratic party by a gentle-

man who could not be elected a delegate for the fifth ward. (Laughter and applause.)

" Now, gentlemen, there is a division in the Democratic party on this question. The platform declared for repeal, and it also declared for the use of both metals without cost for mintage. The President of the United States has construed that platform. Is there a man here so lost to hero-worship that he will declare that the President has the right to construe that platform for him? (Hisses.) Does anybody say that because a man is President it gives him the right to take from the platform what he desires and discard what he does not want, and bind that upon the conscience of the Democratic party?

" My friends, I believe that every Democrat in the United States, whether he be rich or poor, whether he be a common laborer or whether he be able to go as ambassador to Italy because of his wealth—(laughter and hisses)—I believe every Democrat has the right to construe the Democratic platform and to express that opinion. (Voices, 'We do.') And I am glad that you have had the courage—those who differ from me —instead of straddling the question, to come out squarely and state that the President is right in saying, after we have declared for free coinage, that we cannot have it unless foreign nations help us. Read the letter sent by the President to Governor Northen. In that letter he says: 'I am

opposed to free and unlimited coinage by this
country alone and independently.'

"I challenge you to find in any Democratic platform made by a national convention, or expressed
by any vote of the Democratic party in the Senate
or House, a declaration that sustains the President.

"The President has written a new platform, and
it must be endorsed by the Democracy of the
country before it is binding on any man. (A
voice, 'You are right.') If you believe the President is right in running his pen through our platform and declaring that the aid of foreign nations
is necessary to enable Congress to make laws for
our people, express it in your resolution ; but, if
you believe with me that this nation is great
enough, strong enough and grand enough to legislate for its own people, regardless of the entreaties and the threats of foreign Powers, then
vote for the minority report. (Applause.)

"Pass that bill through the Senate and where is
your hope for silver? Do you believe in the use
of gold and silver? Why, read what the platform
said in 1880 and 1884. In 1880 we said 'honest
money, consisting of gold and silver and paper
convertible into coin.' Silver was honest money
then. When did it become dishonest? In 1884
we believed in honest money, the gold and silver
coinage of the Constitution, and a circulating medium convertible into such coin without loss. In

1884 silver was honest money, and no Democrat in a national convention dared to denounce silver as cheap, nasty or dishonest. In 1888 we reaffirmed the platform of 1884, so that in 1888 silver was honest money. In 1892 we declared for the coinage of both metals without discrimination and without cost for mintage. Aye, silver was honest then, and until some national convention declares as the voice of the Democratic party of the nation that silver is dishonest money, I deny the right of any man, elected to any office, to denounce and ostracise silver as dishonest money; I care not what his position or what his rank. (Hisses.)

"Mr. Gladstone said the other day that England was opposed to silver, was opposed to bimetallism, because England was a creditor nation, and because she gained by the appreciation of the dollar caused by the rise in gold, and because of that selfish interest that England would not be in favor of bimetallism because she wanted to get the dollar fatter every day in payment for the debts we owe. I want to ask you if it is to the interest of the American people to give her that dollar that grows fatter at the expense of the toilers of the United States. (Cries of 'No,' 'No.')

"In these United States there are $132,000,000 upon farm mortgages. They tell us we must not speak of indebtedness. No, it is better to suffer from it than to mention it and to correct

Hon. HORACE CHILTON,
U. S. Senator from Texas.

Hon. E. C. WALTHALL,
U. S. Senator from Mississippi.

the wrong. They call us calamity howlers because we dare to suggest that that is a large debt. You make that dollar larger by appreciation; run it up until a gold ounce will exchange for twice as much as it will to-day and by legislation you fix upon this people a debt of $132,000,000 that they never contracted; you fix it to their disadvantage and to the advantage of the man that holds the note. You tell me it is not a sectional question; but, my friends, when a gentleman from Connecticut stands upon the floor of Congress and says, 'I want gold because my people loan money and I am interested in their getting as good a dollar as I can,' I tell you I will be sectional enough to stand upon the floor and say that my people owe money and you will never collect a bigger dollar than we borrowed if I can help it, so help me God! (Applause.) I will not detain you longer —(Cries of 'Go on' 'Go on!')—I will not detain you longer and enter into a discussion of this question which would go over the whole merits of it. It would require more time than you have to give. But, my friends, you know what the arguments are; you have heard them day by day, and you know that if we would put it to vote in the State of Nebraska and let every man write upon his ballot whether he wanted to use gold and silver, or wanted to repeal the Sherman law to aid some foreign nation in the use of a single standard, you know and I know that not only the

Democratic party, but all parties, would vote nine to one in favor of the free coinage of silver. You know it.

"If, knowing that fact, you dare to place the Democratic party on record against the interests of the people, you alone are answerable for the consequences which will follow.

"Why, my friends, why shall we appeal to the people for votes? Do you go to a man and say, 'Vote the Democratic ticket because you will get a postoffice?' No. The State Committee may send out letters to the candidates and tell them to come as delegates to the convention in order to get a postoffice, but you don't tell that to the people when you ask them for their votes. You say to them 'the Democratic party is the best instrument by which you serve your country;' you try to tell them that by the application of Democratic principles of government you will bring equality before the law; that you will bring equal rights to the people, and you have taught them that you will give equal rights to all, and no special privileges to any. That is what you say when you go before the people. You must have something to plead for; you must have something to show them.

"What are you doing, my friends? In 1890 you put in your platform a plank declaring for the free coinage of silver, and for the first time in the history of this State you elected a Democratic

governor.. Free coinage didn't drive people away
from the Democratic party. The next year you
met, and for fear of embarrassing your Eastern
brothers, you decided not to say anything at all
until after the national convention ; and after the
national convention you decided you could not say
anything then because the national convention had
spoken. (Laughter.) And we had a campaign
of eloquence and ability that cannot be overmatched, and as a result the Democratic party
that carried the State in 1890 was beaten by
34,000 by the Republicans, and 24,000 by the
Independents.

"Now go a little further: when you were bold
and declared for free coinage you carried the
State ; when you were afraid to express yourself
you fell down to nearly one-half your size ; and
now you bow as willing worshippers at the feet
of the golden calf. When you cry to the men
who have robbed you by taxation, and you
pleaded, and pleaded in vain for relief; when
they have robbed you by taxation and then loaned
the money that they took from you back to you
on interest, and now try to get back from you a
bigger dollar than the dollar which they loaned
you—now you say that you are in favor of it.
Say that instead of standing by the men who have
stood by the Democratic party in the hours of its
needs, instead of standing by the great producing
sections of the South and West, whose interests

are identical and who suffered from common burdens, say that instead of standing by those who
have stood by you in your efforts for tariff reduction, that in the hours of their need and yours
you will desert the history of the Democratic
party, you will turn a deaf ear to the pleadings of
its greatest senators, its greatest lights, and turn
and say to the people who have smitten you:
'We are ready to lick the hands that smite.' Say
that and call it Democracy, but I shall not call it
Democracy until the Democratic party of this
State has expressed itself upon the subject."
(Applause.)

Bryan's speech was greeted with a mighty
demonstration. The convention's refusal to even
place the young Congressman on the Resolutions
Committee was met with most severe criticism.
It was one of the best tributes that could be paid
to Bryan that his enemies were afraid to place
him upon the Resolutions Committee with eight
men on the same committee against him. But
that action was most severely criticised because it
was a violation of all parliamentary precedent,
which has been to treat the minority with decency.
Simply in keeping with the facts, it must be stated
that the Bryan men were not accorded the most
common courtesy due to a conquered foe. The
administration men plainly showed that they were
afraid of the prowess of the young Congressman,

and they did not propose to give him the slightest opportunity to exert his influence among his fellow-Democrats. The convention stood three to one against Bryan. The majority could have well afforded to place him on the Resolutions Committee with eight men against him, but it chose not to do so. They acted very much like men who had an antagonist down and who did not propose to let him up. The entire action, so far as Bryan was concerned, was impolitic and unwise.

The young Congressman in the convention met with a defeat which some of the delegates called "ignominious," but if it was to be judged by the popular ovation which was extended to Bryan on every hand, he might have said on that day, in the language of Daniel Webster: "I still live." And from the indications, W. J. Bryan, though he was disowned and dishonored by the State convention of his own party, was the biggest and most conspicuous Democrat west of the Mississippi river.

When the news of Bryan's defeat was carried to Washington the entire Cleveland Cabinet went wild with delight. It was proudly claimed by the Federal office-holders that Bryan was dead and that they had buried him politically forever. But subsequent events not far removed from that date showed that William J. Bryan was able to lay aside his grave-clothes and his shroud.

The parting of the ways with the young Con-

10

gressman and the so-called Democratic administration, however, had been reached, and no effort
was spared on the part of Mr. Cleveland and his
agents to humiliate the young man who dared to
have his own opinion and to express that opinion
even though it differed radically from the Chief
Magistrate of the nation. But Mr. Bryan was not a
man to be humiliated by the cheap tactics of the
Cleveland administration.

While the Secretary of Agriculture was loading
down the wires with long-winded interviews
denunciatory of Mr. Bryan, the young Congressman, true to his nature, had no word of personal
retort, but adhered strictly to the line of public
duty which he had marked out; and he grew
stronger and stronger each succeeding day with
the people, who had learned to appreciate his
splendid purpose.

CHAPTER VII.

"THE GRAVE GIVES UP ITS DEAD."

The administration forces at Washington and in Nebraska were considerably disappointed when they found that their delight in the temporary defeat of Mr. Bryan was shared only by the Federal officials. Some of these little fellows, in their blind vanity, could not see that Bryan really represented the overwhelming sentiment of the Nebraska Democracy. Others, however, very soon discovered their error. They soon learned that it is a very difficult task to destroy a man whose only sin had been that he struggled for a principle. The scene at the Nebraska convention of 1893 very much resembled that wherein a gang of jay-birds peck upon an eagle. In this instance at least no injury came to the eagle, for he soared above the petty persecutors and left them to the oblivion for which nature had so admirably fitted them.

Mr. Bryan returned to his Congressional duties while the administration put in much of its time branding for the slaughter men who were applicants for office and who had been known to sympathize with Mr. Bryan. The young Congressman began a determined advocacy of an income tax plan. He was so vigorous in his championship of this measure that he drew upon himself considerable criticism of eastern newspapers, but he was rewarded by the adoption of the income tax as suggested by him, by the Committee on Ways and Means.

On January 13, 1894, Mr. Bryan addressed the House on the tariff bill, in which address he maintained his high reputation.

On January 30, 1894, Mr. Bryan addressed the House on the subject of the proposed income tax. On that occasion he had pitted against him the eloquent Bourke Cockran, of New York. Mr. Cockran, although a Democrat, vigorously opposed the tax. From Mr. Bryan's speech in reply to Mr. Cockran the following extracts are taken:

"I need not give all the reasons which led the committee to recommend this tax, but will suggest two of the most important. The stockholder in a corporation limits his liability. When the statute creating the corporation is fully complied with, the individual stockholder is secure, except to the extent fixed by the statute, whereas the entire property of the individual is ordinarily liable for his debts. Another reason is that corporations enjoy certain privileges and franchises. Some are given the right of eminent domain, while others, such as street-car companies, are given the right to use the streets of the city—a franchise which increases in value with each passing year. Corporations occupy the time and attention of our Federal courts and enjoy the protection of the Federal Government, and as they do not ordinarily pay taxes, the committee felt justified in proposing a light tax upon them.

"Some gentlemen have accused the committee of showing hostility to corporations. But, Mr. Chairman, we are not hostile to corporations; we simply believe that these creatures of the law, these fictitious persons, have no higher or dearer rights than the persons of flesh and blood whom God created and placed upon His footstool. (Applause.) Their assessed valuation increased only a little more than $300,000,000. This bill is not in the line of class legislation, nor can it be regarded as legislation against a section, for the rate of taxation is the same on every income over $4,000, whether its possessor lives upon the Atlantic coast, in the Mississippi Valley or on the Pacific Slope. I only hope that we may in the future have more farmers in the agricultural districts whose incomes are large enough to tax. (Applause.)

"But the gentleman from New York (Mr. Cockran) has denounced as unjust the principle underlying this tax. It is hardly necessary to read authorities to the House. There is no more just tax upon the statute books than the income tax, nor can any tax be proposed which is more equitable; and the principle is sustained by the most distinguished writers on political economy.

"Adam Smith says:

"'The subjects of every State ought to contribute to the support of the Government, as nearly as possible in proportion to their respective abilities; that is, in proportion to the revenue which they respectively enjoy under the protection of the State. In the observation or neglect of this maxim consists what is called the equality or inequality of taxation.'

"The income tax is the only one which really fulfills this requirement. But it is said that we single out some person with a large income and make him pay more than his share. And let me call attention here to a fatal mistake made by the distinguished gentleman from New York (Mr. Cockran). You who listened to his speech would have thought that the income tax was the only Federal tax proposed; you would have supposed that it was the object of this bill to collect the entire revenue from an income tax. The gentleman forgets that the pending tariff bill will collect upon imports more than one hundred and twenty millions of dollars—nearly ten times as much as we propose to collect from the individual income tax. Everybody knows that a tax upon consumption is an unequal tax, and that the poor man by means of it pays far out of proportion to the income which he enjoys.

"I read the other day in the New York *World* —and I gladly join in ascribing praise to that great daily for its courageous fight upon this subject in behalf of the common people—a description of the home of the richest woman in the United States. She owns property estimated at $60,000,000, and enjoys an income which can scarcely be less than $3,000,000, yet she lives at a cheap boarding house, and only spends a few hundred dollars a year. That woman, under your indirect system of taxation does not pay as much toward the support of the Federal Government as a laboring man whose income of $500 is spent upon his family. (Applause.)

"Why, sir, the gentleman from New York (Mr. Cockran) said that the poor are opposed to this tax because they do not want to be deprived of participation in it, and that taxation instead of being a sign of servitude is a badge of freedom. If taxation is a badge of freedom, let me assure my friend that the poor people of this country are covered all over with the insignia of freemen. (Applause.)

"Notwithstanding the exemptions proposed by this bill, the people whose incomes are less than $4,000 will still contribute far more than their just share to the support of the Government. The gentleman says that he opposes this tax in the interest of the poor! Oh, sir, is it not enough to betray the cause of the poor—must it be done with a kiss? (Applause.)

"Would it not be fairer for the gentleman to fling his burnished lance full in the face of the toiler, and not plead for the great fortunes of this country under cover of the poor man's name? (Applause.) The gentleman also tells us that the rich will welcome this tax as a means of securing greater power. Let me call your attention to the resolutions passed by the New York Chamber of Commerce. I wonder how many poor men have membership in that body!

"They say that the income tax was 'only tolerated as a war measure, and was abrogated by universal consent as soon as the condition of the country permitted.' Abrogated by universal consent! What refreshing ignorance from such an intelligent source! If their knowledge of other facts recited in those resolutions is as accurate as that statement, how much weight their resolutions ought to have! Why, sir, there never has been a day since the war when a majority of the people of the United States opposed an income tax.

* * * * * *

"But they say that the income tax invites perjury; that the man who has a large income will swear falsely, and thus avoid the payment of the tax; and, indeed, the gentleman from Massachusetts (Mr. Walker) admitted that his district was full of such people, and he said that our districts were, too. I suppose these constituents whom he accuses of perjury are expected to pat him on the back when he goes home and brag about the compliment he paid them. (Laughter and applause.)

"If there is a man in my district whose veracity is not worth two cents on the dollar, who will perjure himself to avoid the payment of a just tax imposed by law, I am going to wait until he pleads guilty before I make that charge against him. (Laughter and applause.)

"They say that we must be careful and not invite perjury. Why, sirs, this Government has too much important business on hand to spend its time trying to bolster up the morality of men who can not be trusted to swear to their incomes. And let me suggest that gentlemen who come to this House and tell us that their districts are full of such persons are treading upon dangerous ground. If a man will hold up his hand to Heaven and perjure his soul to avoid a 2 per cent. tax due to his Government, how can you trust such a man when he goes into court and testifies in a case in which he has a personal interest?

"If your districts are full of perjurers, if your districts are full of men who violate with impunity not only the laws, but their oaths, do you not raise a question as to the honesty of the methods by which they have accumulated their fortunes?

(Applause on the Democratic side.) Instead of abandoning just measures for fear somebody will perjure himself, let them be enacted into law, and then if anyone perjures himself we can treat him like any other felon, and punish him for his perjury. (Applause.)

"But, gentlemen say that some people will avoid the tax, and that therefore it is unfair to the people who pay. What law is fully obeyed? Why are criminal courts established, except to punish people who violate the laws which society has made? The man who pays his tax need not concern himself about the man who avoids it, unless, perhaps, he is willing to help prosecute the delinquent. The man who makes an honest return and complies with the law pays no more than the rate prescribed, and if the possessors of large fortunes escape by fraud the payment of one-half their income tax, they will still contribute far more than they do now to support the Federal Government, and to that extent relieve from burdens those who now pay more than their share.

"The gentlemen who are so fearful of socialism when the poor are exempted from an income tax, view with indifference those methods of taxation which give the rich a substantial exemption. They weep more because fifteen millions are to be collected from the incomes of the rich than they do at the collection of three hundred millions upon the goods which the poor consume. And when an attempt is made to equalize these burdens, not fully, but partially only, the people of the South and West are called Anarchists.

"I deny the accusation, sirs. It is among the people of the South and West, on the prairies and in the mountains, that you find the staunchest supporters of government and the best friends of law and order.

"You may not find among these people the great fortunes which are accumulated in cities, nor will you find the dark shadows which these fortunes throw over the community, but you will find those willing to protect the rights of property, even while they demand that property shall bear its share of taxation. You may not find among them so much of wealth, but you will find men who are not only willing to pay their taxes to support the Government, but are willing whenever necessary to offer up their lives in its defense.

"These people, sir, whom you call Anarchists because they ask that the burdens of government shall be equally borne, these people have ever borne the cross on Calvary and saved their country with their blood.

"Let me refer again, in conclusion, to the statement made by the gentleman from New York (Mr. Cockran), that the rich people of his city favor the income tax. In a letter which appeared in the New York *World* on the 7th of this month, Ward McAllister, the leader of the 'Four Hundred,' enters a very emphatic protest against the income tax. (Derisive laughter.) Here is an extract:

"In New York City and Brooklyn the local taxation is ridiculously high, in spite of the virtuous protest to the contrary by the officials in authority. Add to this high local taxation an income tax of 2 per cent. on every income exceeding $4,000, and many of our best people will be driven out of the country. An impression seems to exist in the minds of our great Democratic Solons in Congress that a rich man would give up all his wealth for the privilege of living in this country. A very short period of income taxation would show these gentlemen their mistake. The custom is growing from year to year for rich men to go abroad and live, where expenses for the necessaries and luxuries of life are not nearly so high as they are in this country. The United States, in spite of their much boasted natural resources, could not maintain such a strain for any considerable length of time. (Laughter.)

"But whither will these people fly? If their tastes are English, 'quite English, you know,' and they stop in London, they will find a tax of more than 2 per cent. assessed upon incomes; if they look for a place of refuge in Prussia, they will find an income tax of 4 per cent.; if they search for seclusion among the mountains of Switzerland, they will find an income tax of 8 per cent.; if they seek repose under the sunny skies of Italy, they will find an income tax of more than 12 per cent.; if they take up their abode in Austria, they will find a tax of 20 per cent. I repeat, Whither will they fly?"

Mr. Weadock: "The gentleman will allow me to suggest that at Monte Carlo such a man would not have to pay any tax at all." (Laughter.)

Mr. Bryan: "Then, Mr. Chairman, I presume to Monte Carlo he would go, and that there he would give up to the wheel of fortune all the wealth of which he would not give a part to support the Government which enabled him to accumulate it. (Laughter and applause.)

"Are there really any such people in this country? Of all the mean men I have ever known, I have never known one so mean that I would be willing to say of him that his patriotism was less than 2 per cent. deep. (Laughter and applause.)

"There is not a man whom I would charge with being willing to expatriate himself rather than contribute from his abundance to the support of the Government that protects him.

"If 'some of our best people' prefer to leave the country rather than pay a tax of 2 per cent., God pity the worst. (Laughter.)

"If we have people who value free government so little that they prefer to live under monarchical institutions, even without an income tax, rather

than live under the stars and stripes and pay a 2
per cent. tax, we can better afford to lose them
and their fortunes than risk the contaminating influence of their presence. (Applause.)

"I will not attempt to characterize such persons.
If Mr. McAllister is a true prophet, if we are to
lose some of our 'best people' by the imposition
of an income tax, let them depart, and as they
leave without regret the land of their birth, let
them go with the poet's curse ringing in their
ears :

> "'Breathes there the man with soul so dead
> Who never to himself hath said,
>   This is my own, my NATIVE LAND!
> Whose heart hath ne'er within him burned,
> As home his footsteps he hath turned
>   From wandering on a foreign strand?
> If such there breathe, go mark him well;
> For him no minstrel raptures swell;
> High though his titles, proud his name,
> Boundless his wealth as wish can claim;
> Despite those titles, power and pelf,
> The wretch, concentered all in self,
> Living, shall forfeit fair renown,
> And, doubly dying, shall go down
> To the vile dust, from whence he sprung,
> Unwept, unhonored and unsung.'"

(Loud and long-continued applause.)
On February 23, 1894, the Union League Club
of Chicago gave a banquet of national interest.

Covers were laid for 500 guests. The speakers and their subjects were as follows:

Governor McKinley of Ohio, "'Washington is the Mightiest Name on Earth'—Lincoln;" John S. Wise of New York, "The Due Administration of Justice is the Firmest Pillar of Good Government;" Associate Justice David J. Brewer of Washington, D. C., "Lessons from Washington's Farewell Address;" Luther Laflin Mills of Illinois, "'Tis Essentially True That Virtue or Morality is a Necessary Spring of Popular Government;" Bishop Charles H. Fowler of Minnesota, "The Name of America Must Always Exalt the Just Pride of Patriotism;" William J. Bryan of Nebraska, "Patriotism."

Mr. Bryan's address on this occasion is of more than ordinary interest at this time. He spoke as follows:

" Patriotism is defined as love of country, and is everywhere recognized as the highest civic virtue. Some have regarded it as a sentimental attachment to their native or adopted land; some have called it devotion to the flag; and still others have seen in it that higher satisfaction which purchases natural advantages. But whatever may be its essence or the form of its expression, patriotism has ever been the inspiration of statesman, poet and orator. This was the theme of Pericles when he commemorated the death of those who fell at Salamis. This was the theme of Tennyson when he laid his graceful tribute of praise upon the tomb of England's greatest general. This was the theme of Patrick Henry when his eloquence aroused our revolutionary sires to armed resistance, and gave to them the immortal war-cry, 'Liberty or death.' This was the theme of those who, in memory of Washington, gave to their countrymen—not a poem nor an oration, but more than both combined—a monument, the most imposing shaft ever erected by human hands in gratitude to man.

"There is no more valuable literature than that which embalms the names and deeds of heroes; there is no money more worthily expended than that which expresses in granite, in marble or in bronze, a people's appreciation of their patriots; and, since we imitate that which we admire, there are no reasons more laudable in purpose and more ennobling in effect than those, like the present, which cultivate within us a love of country by the study of those who deserve their country's love. We render unto him due meed of praise whose sword leaps from its scabbard at his country's call; we bestow our heart's affection upon the volunteer whose time and means, and even life, are a nation's reliance in the hour of peril, but we are apt to overlook the labor of those whose devotion is as truly shown when the temple of Janus is closed and the implements of carnage give place to the tools of industry. Sad, indeed, would be the lot of this generation if loyalty could be proved only in the service of Mars. To those who are of the aftermath the lines of Milton bring sweet assurance:

> " ' Peace hath her victories
> No less renown'd than war.'

"Aye, peace hath her victories, and not her victories only, but her responsibilities as well. In this land of ours, where government derives its just powers from the consent of the governed and not from the divine right of kings, the call to duty is as imperative when it comes in the still, small voice, as when it issues from the cannon's mouth. Does it not require as much devotion to discharge with constant and conscientious care the daily tasks of the citizen as it does to carry a musket? Does it not require as much self-sacrifice to list all one's property for taxation as it does to enlist in the army? Does it not require as much patriotism to serve one's country well in the election booth as it does to march to the strains of martial music? Does it not require as much fortitude to place civil duty above private business and the common weal above party advantage as it does to command a company? Does it not require as much courage to resist the siege of a lobby as it does to capture a city?

"Time forbids more than a passing reference to a few of the principal duties which attach to

11

citizenship to-day. There is a growing disposition to avoid jury service and all manner of excuses are given by those who find it inconvenient to leave their work. But this sacrifice is not a matter of convenience, it is a matter of necessity. The jury system was never more correct than it is to-day, and to preserve it as a means of administering justice, men of 'ordinary intelligence and of approved integrity' must constitute the panel. If thieves are to be tried before thieves and criminals are to receive their acquittal at the hands of their associates, the system will become a hollow mockery. The rights of litigants cannot be safely submitted to the professional juror and the professional jury packer. If men plead pressure of business as a reason for shirking this duty, let them remember that large business interests are safe only under good government. How many, like Naaman, the leper, stand ready to do some great things for their country, but despise those humbler duties which make civil liberty possible.

"Another danger which we have to meet is corruption in official life. The boodler is abroad in the land, and the evidences of his handiwork are too often apparent. He is as dangerous to the welfare of the country as an army with banners, and as insidious as he is dangerous. Whether he enriches himself by his own malfeasance in office or finds a profit in using the legislative powers for private purposes, he is a public enemy and must be scourged from the temple. We cannot depend entirely upon criminal courts to remedy this evil, for guilt may exist in the absence of legal proofs sufficient to overcome all reasonable doubt. Public opinion, that ever potent force in popular government, must hold to strict accountability those who are trusted with authority. Mr. Jefferson has wisely said:

"'Confidence is everywhere the parent of despotism—free government is founded in jealousy and not in confidence,' and it may be added, the indifference of the citizen is the opportunity of the knave.

"If we were asked to name the greatest danger which threatens our political life as a nation, what danger would we point out? Not protection or free trade—a patriotic people will rid themselves of either if bad; not a gold nor a silver nor a paper standard—a patriotic people will settle the money question according to the best interests of all ; not extravagance nor stringency in appropriations—a patriotic people will support their Government with sufficient liberality, and will in time check unnecessary expenditures ; not State sovereignty nor the centralization of power—a patriotic people will wisely limit the authority of the general and local Governments. These are all great questions and may well occupy the best thought of the country and challenge the serious

consideration of both citizen and official, but
there is a question which is higher, deeper and
broader than any or all of these : Will the citizen
be as patriotic when he sits beneath the olive
branch of peace as when he follows the eagles of
war ?

"It has been said that the 'voice of the people
is the voice of God,' but that voice must be heard
to be effective. It must be expressed and obeyed
before it can assume supreme power. Some
boast that they take no part in politics and talk as
if participating in the business of the Government
were beneath them. Shame upon such ingrates.

"The man who is too good to take part in politics is not good enough to deserve the blessings
of a free Government. Suffrage is given to the
citizen not merely as a personal privilege, but as a
public trust, and should be exercised as such.
The man who tries to vote twice is scarcely more
to be feared than the man who is not interested
enough to vote once. The few who control primaries in the interest of the machine are scarcely
more to be blamed than the many who, by remaining away, not only permit, but invite, misrepresentation. The duty of the citizen does not end
when he contributes his just proportion of the
taxes collected by the Government; it does not
end when he goes to the polls and chooses between
the candidates nominated; his full duty requires
attendance upon conventions, mass meetings, cau-

cuses and primaries where public opinion finds expression and policies are initiated. Not only is there a prevalent disregard of political duties, but parents are often more solicitous about leaving a fortune to their children than they are about training them for the responsibilities of citizenship. If the political world is full of impurity, the son should be prepared to purify it, for in it he must live whether it be foul or clean. It was the boast of the Roman matron that she was able to rear strong and courageous sons for the battlefield; let it be the work of the American mothers that they are able to send forth to do battle for humanity brave and manly sons who can mingle in politics without contamination and serve their country without dishonor. No age has faced graver problems than those which now press us for solution. No generation ever enjoyed greater opportunities for intelligent, heroic devotion to the country's good. It is as important for us to preserve our liberties as it was for our forefathers to secure them, and as we meet about this board to do homage to him whose sword achieved our independence, and whose wisdom guided the footsteps of the infant Republic, I can propose no more appropriate sentiment than this:

"'The United States—secure in peace or war, when the people so act, at all times, in all places and under all circumstances, that each is worthy of that noblest of all names—an American citizen.'"

On March 2, 1894, Mr. Bryan introduced in the House of Representatives the following:

"Whereas, An act entitled 'An act directing the purchase of silver bullion and the issue of treasury notes thereon, and for other purposes,' approved July 14, 1890, provides 'that upon demand of the holder of any of the treasury notes herein provided for, the Secretary shall, under such regulations as he may prescribe, redeem such notes in gold or silver coin, at his discretion,' it being the established policy of the United States to maintain the two metals on a parity with each other upon the present legal ratio or such ratio as may be provided by law ; and

"Whereas, This provision and other similar provisions for redemption in coin have been construed to mean that the Secretary of the Treasury has no discretion, but must redeem in that coin which the holder of the obligation demands; and

"Whereas, such construction violates both the letter and the spirit of the law, destroys the principles of bimetallism and places the treasury at the mercy of any who may conspire to reduce the gold reserve for the purpose of forcing an issue of bonds, therefore

"Be it enacted by the Senate and House of

Representatives of the United States of America in Congress assembled:

"That all obligations heretofore or hereafter incurred by the Government of the United States, whether such obligations bear interest or not, which according to their terms call for payment in coin, shall be payable in gold or silver of present weight and fineness at the discretion of the Secretary of the Treasury, and the right of the holder of any such obligation to demand payment in a particular kind of coin, whether gold or silver, is hereby expressly denied; and that the Secretary of the Treasury is directed to maintain gold and silver coin on a parity with each other upon the present legal ratio, or such ratio as may be provided by law, by receiving the same without discrimination against either metal in payment of all public dues, customs and taxes."

Speaking of this in an interview, Mr. Bryan said:

"The object of the bill is to make certain a law now upon the statute books, and to prevent the misinterpretation and misconstruction of it. If it had been the object of the law to give to the note-holder the right to demand whichever coin he preferred, certainly the statutes would not have left it to the discretion of the Secretary of the Treasury to pay whichever one he preferred. The option cannot be given to the note-holder and the Government at the same time, and yet the department has construed a subsequent provision, in regard to maintaining the parity, in a way which absolutely destroys the discretion expressly given to the Secretary of the Treasury. If this bill can be brought before the House, it will enable those who believe in bimetallism and who believe that the Government owes as high duty to all the people as it does to those who attempt to injure its credit by raiding the gold reserve, to express themselves and to put the coin redemption provision in such a shape as to prevent further misunderstanding or misconstruction. We are brought face to face with the single standard and it is well to have the record made before the next election."

By this time the administration was using its utmost endeavors to rebuke Bryan for his defense of Democratic principles. In one district in the State a man was appointed to office who it was known had worked openly and avowedly against the regular Democratic nominee for Congress and in favor of the Republican candidate. On the day following that appointment, a number of Bryan's recommendations were turned down, and this policy of refusing every courtesy to the young Congressman was adhered to to the end by the Cleveland administration. The situation in this respect is well described in an editorial from the *World-Herald*, March 15, 1894.

"There are some strange influences at work in

the distribution of patronage in Nebraska. It
has been demonstrated that while George D.
Meiklejohn, the Republican Congressman, can
have some of his friends appointed to office,
friendship for William J. Bryan, the one Democratic Congressman from this State, is quite fatal
to an applicant's chances. There is little use of
the friends of Mr. Bryan keeping their eyes
closed to the real situation. The defeat of Mr.
Bryan's candidate at Nebraska City shows beyond
all doubt—if any doubt has existed—that the
anti-Bryan influences are the strongest with the
administration. It will be said that Nebraska City
being the home of Secretary Morton, he should
be permitted to name the postmaster, but everyone understands what Mr. Morton has so often
and so plainly stated, that he is not interfering
with Federal appointments. It might with equal
propriety be claimed that Mr. Bryan should be
permitted to name the postmaster at his home.
But this privilege was not granted him. A second choice was forced upon him, and his opponents now claim that they suggested this second
choice to the President.

"It may be true that the President was warranted
in refusing to appoint Calhoun at Lincoln because
of Calhoun's criticism of Presidential action. But
in the Nebraska City case there was no question
of Boydston's 'straight democracy.' He is a
young man of high character. He supported Mr.

Morton for Governor with the same zeal that he labored for Mr. Bryan for Congress. In Nebraska City's democracy Boydston has been the cheerful hewer of wood and drawer of water. Because of his ability and his enthusiasm he came to be known as Bryan's personal representative at Nebraska City. Against either Boydston's democracy or his character nothing could be said. He was, however, guilty of the unpardonable sin —he was a 'friend of Bryan.' The fact that he had also been a zealous friend to every other Democratic nominee could not make amends for the greatest 'crime' in Nebraska's political calender.

"He had not criticised Cleveland, but on the contrary was one of the President's enthusiastic admirers. Anticipating the punishment for his offense in being zealous in the election of Nebraska's one Democratic Congressman, Mr. Boydston recently accepted the Democratic nomination for City Clerk at Nebraska City. It will be seen that he anticipated correctly.

"The Third District Democratic patronage has been distributed to reward friends of a Republican Congressman.

"In the First District, Democratic patronage has been distributed to rebuke friends of the one Democratic Congressman from Nebraska.

"These are samples of 'Tobe Castor Democracy.'

"This may be the way to build up the Democratic party, but we doubt it. And it may also be said that it is the poorest method imaginable to tear down Bryan.

"It is just as well to understand right now that Bryan's recommendation to the administration is hardly worth the paper upon which it is written. But it is equally true that the young Congressman stands closer to the people of Nebraska to-day than ever before. And every move that bears the indication of an effort to rebuke him will only serve to increase the number of his admirers in Nebraska."

On March 15, 1894, Mr. Bryan stopped in Omaha on his way to his home in Lincoln, from Washington. He had made such an admirable record in Congress that the Democrats of Omaha, many of whom had helped the administration to rebuke the young Congressman at the State convention, turned out en masse to give him an ovation. It was noticeable that many of those who had been most conspicuous in the effort to rebuke him in 1893 made themselves conspicuous in the effort to do him honor on this occasion. There were many in that vast audience who differed radically from the young Congressman in opinion on the money question, but he preached to them the gospel of bimetallism eloquently and earnestly as he had at every opportunity presented in his career. He spoke strongly and eloquently of the necessity of making silver as well as gold a money metal, the foundation for the currency of the country and of the world, and predicted that his audience would yet see gold and silver go arm in arm to the United States mint. It was the great coming question he declared and no party was great enough to live unless it met every question as it came up. In closing Mr. Bryan completely captivated his great audience when he at once graciously acknowledged the reception accorded him and declared his adherence to the principle to which he is so thoroughly committed.

"My friends," said Mr. Bryan in conclusion, "you have been very kind to me here. Kind far beyond my deserts. For your personal consideration and the political honors you have helped to confer upon me I owe you more than I can ever repay, but I feel so strongly upon this subject that even should every friend I have turn from me, believing as I do that inconceivable misery would be wrought by a single gold standard, still would I preach the doctrine of bimetallism from every stump." The great audience rose as one man and cheered the young orator for fifteen minutes. Thousands of people crowded upon the platform and congratulated him personally and bid him God speed in his good work.

On the day following this reception, the *Omaha World-Herald* contained an editorial under the

head line, "The Grave Gives Up Its Dead," as
follows:

"THE GRAVE GIVES UP ITS DEAD.

"Congressman Bryan has reason to be proud of
the splendid reception accorded him by the people
of Omaha. The Democrats seemed to be a unit
in doing honor to the young man, whose public
career has been an honor to his State. Men who
have disagreed with him upon the financial question were as enthusiastic as their free silver
brethren in paying a tribute of respect to the
young Congressman.

"It is not too much to say that if Mr. Bryan had
been offered as a member of a resolutions committee at the Exposition hall Thursday night, instead of the Douglas delegation being solidly
against him, it would have been solid in his favor.

"Mr. Bryan has always manifested a tender feeling for the people of Douglas county, for it was
here that he received in his first election a vote
that swelled his majority to immensity. It was
here, in fact, that he made the first speech that
stamped him as a student of political economy,
and here he has always had a host of friends
whose devotion to him could not be questioned.

"It is hardly necessary to refer to the breezy
incidents at the last State Convention, when, in
the language of one enthusiast, 'We laid the
Young Man Eloquent to rest in the grave.' But
the scenes at the Exposition hall on Thursday

night impressed one with the thought that 'the grave' has given up its dead.

"This splendid reception to Bryan, coming immediately upon the announcement that he has 'once more been turned down by the administration,' is not without its significance. It demonstrates that while the young Congressman's influence with the administration has become weaker and weaker, his power with the people has grown stronger and stronger.

"While the reception Bryan received was a splendid tribute to himself, like the blessing of mercy it was creditable alike to them that gave and him that received. Many men who were earnest in the successful attempt to 'sit down on Bryan' at the State Convention were equally earnest and enthusiastic in doing him honor at the great gathering on Thursday night. Many of these may not have changed their views since that time, but it is fair to believe that if that State Convention were to be held to-day the 'sitting down' process would be carried out in an entirely different manner.

"There are many men in Omaha who do not entirely agree with Bryan, who are proud of his record and his fame.

"Bryan's strength is in his candor as well as his ability. Before him at the Exposition hall were the members of the two local Democratic organizations and representative Democrats in every walk of life. Upon every issue of the day he made himself understood. He took issue with the administration upon the issue of bonds, upon the repeal of the Sherman law, and he did not hesitate to refer to the well-known words of the Democratic Secretary of the Treasury in the halcyon days of that gentleman's championship of free silver. No other Democrat has ever lived in Nebraska who could receive the open recognition and the explicit tribute of organized Democracy in this city at the moment when he boldly assailed the attitude of the Democratic administration upon the great issues of the day; and when he said, 'You have been very kind to me here, but if every friend I have in the world should turn against me, as long as I believe as I do on this question I will preach it from every stump'—when he said this, there was no man present who could restrain himself from joining in the applause which was given as a tribute to the sincerity and the courage of a public man.

"The Omaha reception to Mr. Bryan must be accepted as formal recognition of the fact that he is to-day the leader of the Nebraska Democracy. The White House may send its messengers through the political Charnel House for 'leaders' in the distribution of patronage, but the Democracy of Nebraska, unawed and uninfluenced by the hope of reward to any individual, will prefer to doff its hat in the interesting presence of William J. Bryan—the pigmy in Presidential favor, the giant in popular esteem."

On May 8, 1894, an incident occurred in the House which illustrates the conscientious activity of the Democratic nominee for President. The Committee on Public Lands and Buildings brought up a bill to appropriate $300,000 to buy a site for a new printing office. The debate ran along all through the day. After adjournment Mr. Bryan visited the various sites suggested, examined the Government land suitable for the purpose and consulted real estate agents as to the price of property near the proposed sites.

The following morning he took charge of the fight against the bill and showed that the land recommended by the committee was being valued at $100,000 to $150,000 above its actual market value. He also showed that the Government owned suitable land for the building and did not need to buy. He succeeded in carrying by a vote of 149 to 35 a resolution to instruct the committee to select a site on land owned by the United States. His presentation of the facts was so clear and convincing that he carried the House in spite of the unanimous opposition of the Committee on Public Lands and Buildings.

CHAPTER VIII.

HOW NEBRASKA WAS REDEEMED.

In the spring of 1894 the silver sentiment in Nebraska had undergone a wonderful increase and the Democrats in all parts of the State became restless. The party in Nebraska was dominated by inferior men who had obtained their power simply because they were the only ones who were willing to do the bidding of the administration, without regard to what the orders might be. The dominant element in control of the State Committee had the aid and co-operation of the greater number of the Federal officials. It was evident too that they had plenty of money at their command, and it is certain that they had all the railroad passes that were necessary for the convenience of their fellows. On the other hand, the silver men were without money, but they were not without courage and determination. The administration men felt confident of their ability to hold power in Nebraska, unquestioned for time to come, and certainly they had good reason for this confidence.

But one evening in the month of May 1894, there assembled in a private room in the Paxton Hotel, in Omaha, a number of Silver Democrats

of Nebraska.   It is just and proper that the
names of these gentlemen should go into history,
for they laid the foundation for one of the greatest
triumphs ever accomplished in the record of a
State.   Their labor was entirely disinterested, for
there was not one man among the number who
was a candidate for public office either present or
prospective.   They were all property holders and
men of wide business experience, and they had
learned at great personal expense to appreciate
the evils of the single gold standard.   The names
of these men are as follows: Judge Joseph E.
Ong of Geneva, Nebraska; J. B. Kitchen of
of Omaha, Nebraska; C. J. Smythe of Omaha;
Nebraska; J. H. Broady of Lincoln, Nebraska,
William H. Thomsen of Grand Island, Nebraska; James C. Dahlman of Chadron, Nebraska; State Senator John Thompson of Free-
mont, Nebraska; G. A. Luikhart of Norfolk,
Nebraska; John C. Vanhousen of Schuyler,
Nebraska; W. H. Kelligar of Auburn, Nebraska;
Frank J. Morgan of Plattsmouth, Nebraska;
Edwin Falloon, of Falls City, Nebraska, and C.
D. Casper of David City, Nebraska.

These gentlemen determined to call a State conference of the Free Silver Democrats of Nebraska
and they fixed June 21 as the date on which that
conference should be held.   They determined to
have the call for this conference signed by 250
representative Democrats from all parts of

the State, and they determined that the matter should be an entire secret until all these signatures had been obtained and the call had been formally issued. It will be readily understood that it required a great deal of skillful effort to keep such an interesting plan a secret, particularly when such a large number of persons were required to sign the call. But the plan was well carried out and like a lightning flash from a clear sky the newspapers of the State on May 24, 1894, contained, under glaring head lines, this formal call:

"CALL TO FREE SILVER DEMOCRATS.

"Believing that the question of the restoration of the double standard of gold and silver as money of ultimate redemption and standard of values is now one of the foremost issues in the minds of the voters of Nebraska, and that the change from the double to the single standard is, has been, and will continue to be, until reversed, a grievous wrong to the people of the United States and particularly to the people of Nebraska; and believing that nine-tenths of the Democrats of Nebraska so feel, and that they have not always been fairly represented on the subject by the Democratic conventions of Nebraska; and believing that the time has come when the welfare of the party in this State imperatively demands a plain, unequivocal statement of the party on that subject;

"Therefore, we, the undersigned Democrats of Nebraska, for the purpose of propagating the double standard doctrine in the Democratic party and enabling the masses of the Democratic party in this State to obtain the fairest expression of their views on that subject in the conventions of the future, do hereby call a State conference of Free Silver Democrats, to be held at Omaha, commencing at 2 o'clock in the afternoon of Thursday, June 21, 1894, at which conference will be organized a 'Nebraska Democratic Free Coinage League.'"

This call was signed by 250 representative Democrats. On June 21 this great conference was called to order. One thousand delegates were in attendance. The Nebraska Bimetallic League was organized and the following resolutions were adopted:

"We send greeting to our fellow-Democrats of Nebraska and ask their earnest co-operation and aid in electing delegates from every county in the State to the Democratic State Convention of 1894, pledged to vote for the insertion in the Democratic State platform of the following plank:

"'We favor the immediate restoration of the free and unlimited coinage of gold and silver at the present ratio of 16 to 1, without waiting for the aid and consent of any other nation on earth.'

Hon. W. J. STONE,
Governor of Missouri.

CLARK HOWELL,
Editor of the *Constitution*, Atlanta, Ga.

"In the effort to obtain a fair expression of Democratic sentiment, we urge upon every Democrat who believes in the principles herein enunciated to participate actively and vigorously in the selection of delegates to the State Convention.

"We recommend that in every county of the State the Democrats who oppose this proposed plank be invited to a thorough discussion of its merits, to the end that the Democratic party may act intelligently and harmoniously upon this great question.

"We propose that this contest shall be fought out upon clean lines and with intelligent methods, but, confident in the correctness of our position, we also propose that the fight shall be vigorous, and that no effort shall be spared to place in the platform of the Democratic party the same emphasis, the same unmistakable utterance concerning the great question of finance, as has been lastingly imprinted upon our platforms concerning the great question of tariff reform."

Mr. Bryan addressed the Conference on the money question and concluded his splendid effort in the following language:

"I bid you go forth to battle; upon you rests a grave responsibility, and going forth in the name of the party that you love, you can redeem this country. The restoration of silver is only one of the reforms, but if the Democratic party cannot accomplish it, it cannot accomplish the others, for

the same power opposes all the reforms demanded
by the people to-day. Here before me are gray
haired, men who have toiled for victory for long
years without hope of reward—or fear of punishment. Their eyes may not behold complete
success, but they may know that their labors have
not been in vain, and when the time comes lie
down happy in the promise:

> "' Yea, though thou lie upon the dust,
>   When they who helped thee flee in fear,
>   Die full of hope and manly trust,
>   Like those who fell in battle here.

> " 'Another hand thy sword shall wield;
>   Another hand the standard wave;
>   Till from the trumpet's mouth is pealed
>   The blast of triumph o'er thy grave.'"

The mighty determination of the silver men
thoroughly alarmed the administration forces. At
the same time it gave hope to the silver Democrats of the State and from all parts of Nebraska
came encouraging words and promises of loyal assistance from men who had become disgusted with
the manipulation of their party to base purposes.
The Silver Democrats at their conference adopted
a courteous resolution, requesting the gold-bug
State Committee to call an early convention, in
order that the contest might be properly carried
on. But the committee refused to adhere to the

request and insisted on calling a late convention
in the hope that the gold men would be able to
repair their shattered forces. The silver men
prepared for the fight and organized in every
county of the State. In the spring of 1894 Mr.
Bryan had announced his determination not to be
a candidate for a third term in the House on July
28, 1894. The following letter was sent to Mr.
Bryan :

"HEADQUARTERS NEBRASKA DEMOCRATIC FREE
COINAGE LEAGUE, GENEVA, Neb., July 28, 1894.—
[To Hon. William J. Bryan, Washington, D. C.]—

Dear Sir: The growing sentiment that United
States Senators should be the choice of the people
make it essential that Nebraska should be in line
with other States with this progressive idea. Believing that the great majority of the people of
Nebraska desire that you should represent this
State in the United States Senate, the executive
committee of the Nebraska Democratic Free
Coinage League, respectfully request that you announce yourself as a candidate for this high office.

"We desire that you shall at the same time announce the principles which will guide you in the
event that you are elected, and also that you shall
make a thorough canvass of the State.

"In the event that you make this announcement,
the friends of bimetallism in the Democratic party
propose to urge your nomination by that party.

"We are confident that every element in the

State favorable to the principles you have so ably championed are favorable to your election as United States Senator, and we are certain that the political party which does not champion your candidacy will not reflect the sentiment of the masses of the people of Nebraska.

"Awaiting an early reply we are yours, truly,

J. E. ONG, President,
F. J. MORGAN, Secretary,
G. A. LUIKHART, Treasurer,
JAMES C. DAHLMAN,
H. M. BOYDSTON,
C. J. SMYTHE,
ROBERT CLOGG,
W. D. OLDHAM,
JOHN THOMPSON,
WILLIAM H. THOMSEN,
W. H. KELLIGAR,
GEORGE WELLS,

Executive Committee."

On August 5, 1894, Mr. Bryan replied to this letter consenting to become a candidate for the United States Senate. In this letter he said that if he should be elected he would do his part to repeal the unjust laws now existing and to secure such new legislation as might be necessary to protect each citizen in the enjoyment of life, liberty and the pursuit of happiness. He said he would labor for an income tax as a permanent

part of our financial system, preferring a graduated tax, but accept ng the tax provided for in the
Wilson Bill as a step toward the restoration of
equality in the distribution of the burdens of
government. He said that the most important
and far-reaching question which would confront
the Senator then to be elected from Nebraska was
the money question. On this question Mr. Bryan
said :

"In my judgment it lies at the bottom of the
great industrial disturbance now prevalent
throughout the world, and no permanent prosperity can be expected until silver is restored to its
rightful place by the side of gold, or metallic
money is abandoned entirely. For reasons which
I have stated on former occasions, I prefer the
remonetization of silver to the complete demonetization of both of the precious metals, and I
therefore 'favor the immediate restoration of the
free and unlimited coinage of gold and silver at
the present ratio of 16 to 1, without waiting for
the aid or consent of any other nation on earth.'

" Believing that the creation of money is an attribute of sovereignty, I am opposed to farming
out the right to any private individual or corporation whatever, and, in case the precious metals do
not furnish a sufficient supply, favor the issue of
full legal tender paper, redeemable in coin, by the
General Government, in such quantities that the
volume of the currency, gold, silver and paper to-

gether, will be so adjusted to the needs of commerce that the dollar will be stable in its purchasing power, and thus defraud neither debtor nor
creditor.

"I shall also favor such legislation as will hereafter prohibit the making of contracts for a particular kind of money. No person should be
permitted to demonetize by contract a nation's
money.

"The fact that the purchasers of the bonds recently issued (and issued, as I believe, without
reasonable excuse,) drew from the treasury more
than $18,000,000 in gold, to pay for the bonds
sold to obtain gold, shows the viciousness of the
policy followed by the present administration and
by the preceding Republican administration, of
allowing the holders of greenbacks and treasury
notes to demand gold only for redemption. The
Government has, and should exercise, the option
of paying either gold or silver on all coin obligations. If the Government will exercise this option in the interest of the people generally, it will
not be necessary to further burden the taxpayers
by issues of interest-bearing bonds in time of
peace. Until the Government does exercise its
right to pay in silver, when that is most convenient, it will be at the mercy of any band of con-
spirators who may find a pecuniary advantage in
depleting the gold reserve. No issue of bonds,
however great or frequent, can maintain a gold

reserve so long as the option is given to the note-holder, and the moneyed interests find a profit in the increase of our bonded indebtedness."

Mr. Bryan also declared in favor of election of Senators by the people. He declared in favor of a liberal pension policy toward the nation's disabled soldiers. He favored the foreclosure of Government liens on all Pacific Railways, and their sale, in order that the people of Nebraska and other Western States might not be burdened by the tolls collected to pay interest on an exorbitant valuation. He favored the application of the principle of arbitration as far as Federal authority extends.

Mr. Bryan's letter contained one plank which is very significant at this time, taken in connection with his declaration immediately following his nomination at Chicago.

This plank is as follows:

"I am in favor of an amendment to the Constitution making the President ineligible to re-election, in order that he may not be tempted by ambition to use the enormous patronage at his disposal to secure a continuance in office."

This is only one instance indicating that the principles advocated by William J. Bryan are not those hewn out for the occasion, but that they are the same principles to which he has devoted his life and his earnest and consistent effort.

The contest for control of the Democratic State

Convention that year was the most spirited in the history of the State. County after county elected silver delegates and instructed for Bryan for United States Senator. The "gold bugs" felt confident of carrying Douglas county, in which Omaha is located, but the Bryan men invaded that domain and made such a vigorous warfare that a solid free silver delegation was elected from that county. The silver men controlled the State Convention which met September 27, 1894, by two to one, and that convention adopted a platform of which the following is an extract:

"We endorse the language used by Hon. John G. Carlisle, in 1878, when he denounced the 'conspiracy' to destroy silver money as 'the most gigantic crime of this or any other age,' and we agree with him that 'the consummation of such a scheme would ultimately entail more misery upon the human race than all the wars, pestilences and famines that ever occurred in the history of the world.' (Cheers.) We are not willing to be parties to such a crime, and in order to undo the wrong already done, and to prevent the further appreciation of money, we favor the immediate restoration of the free and unlimited coinage of silver and gold at the present ratio of 16 to 1, without waiting for the aid or consent of any other nation upon earth.

"We regard the right to issue money as an attribute of sovereignty and believe that all money

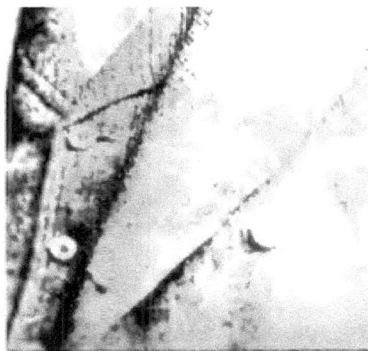

J. R. McLEAN, Esq.,
Editor of the *Enquirer*, Cincinnati, O.

Hon. G. G. VEST,
U. S. Senator from Missouri.

needed to supplement the gold and silver coinage of the Constitution, and to make the dollar so stable in its purchasing power that it will defraud neither debtor nor creditor, should be issued by the General Government as the greenbacks were issued; that such money should be redeemable in coin, the Government to exercise the option by redeeming them in gold or silver, whichever is most convenient for the Government. We believe that all money issued by the Government, whether gold, silver or paper, should be made a full legal tender for all debts, public and private (applause), and that no citizen should be permitted to demonetize by contract that which the Government makes money by law."

Mr. Bryan was nominated by that convention for United States Senator. There was considerable difference between this convention and the convention that assembled in Lincoln in 1893, when Bryan was rebuked. The convention of 1893 was dominated by the agents of the Cleveland administration, but the convention of 1894 was in the hands of the untramelled Democracy of Nebraska.

Mr. Bryan, in acknowledging his nomination to be United States Senator, said among other things:

"I look back over what I have tried to do with nothing of regret except that I have been able to do so little of what I have desired to do. I have realized, as each day passed, more and more the magnitude of the work, and more and more the exactitude of such a position. I want to say to you that I have striven as best I could to carry out your wishes as expressed at the convention and to protect your rights, as I understood them, and to do my duty as I saw it. I believe from your vote to-night that you will give me credit for having at least made an earnest attempt.

"I could not promise more fidelity in the future than I have tried to give in the past. The experience, which by your suffrages I have been able to earn, will be used, if by your suffrages again I am made a member of the upper part of Congress."

Although the State Convention was controlled two to one by the silver men and the "gold bugs" had been thoroughly whipped, thirty-nine of them, mostly Federal office-holders, or beneficiaries otherwise of the administration, bolted the convention and upon this slender pretext built up an organization which laid claim to be the regular Democratic organization of the State. The progeny of this organization was the delegation that went to Chicago and was seated by the votes of the "gold bug" members of the national committee and then ejected from the convention by the unanimous vote of the credentials committee, even the gold men of the credentials committee not being able to countenance such a shallow claim to recognition in a Democratic assemblage.

On the day following Mr. Bryan's nomination C. J. Smythe, chairman of the Democratic State Convention, issued a challenge to the Hon. John M. Thurston, who, although not formally nominated, was regarded as the Republican choice for Senator. It was very evident from the start that Mr. Thurston was not fond of punishment and it required considerable correspondence before he was induced, or perhaps forced, to meet Mr. Bryan in joint debate. Messrs. Bryan and Thurston opened their debate in Lincoln to a crowd of about 10,000 people. The second meeting was in Omaha where 15,000 people had gathered. It was a mighty contest in which Mr. Thurston, who is a man of great ability, acquitted himself with great credit. But his friends were not profuse in their compliments of his really worthy effort. They were content to congratulate their distinguished fellow-Republican that he had escaped from the contest with his life. Bryan overmatched the ablest Republican orator west of the Mississippi river exactly as he has overmatched every orator on either side of the Father of Waters.

Mr. Bryan was defeated for the Senate. Nebraska has a law whereby preference of the United States Senator may be expressed by the voter on his ballot. Of these expressions Mr. Bryan received 81,000 votes. Had the result been determined by the popular vote, no politician denies that Mr. Bryan would have been elected by a large majority. But the effect of many votes were lost for Mr. Bryan by the election of members for the Legislature by districts and thus the Republicans controlled that body. Mr. Bryan's defeat was a great disappointment to his many loyal friends in Nebraska, but if it was a serious disappointment to himself no one was ever able to discover it. He is not a man to "wear his heart on his sleeve for daws to peck at," and he accepted defeat gracefully. As soon as the result of the election was known, Mr. Bryan issued this splendid letter to his Nebraska friends.

"LINCOLN, NEB., November 8, 1894.

"The Legislature is Republican, and a Republican Senator will now be elected to represent Nebraska. This may be mortifying to the numerous chairmen who have introduced me to audiences as the 'next Senator from Nebraska,' but it illustrates the uncertainty of prophecies.

"I appreciate more than words can express the cordial good will and the loyal support of the friends to whom I am indebted for the political honors which I have received. I am especially grateful to those who bear without humiliation the name of the common people, for they have been my friends when others have deserted me. I appreciate also the kind words of many who have been restrained by party ties from giving me their votes. I have been a hired man for four years, and, now that the campaign is closed, I may be pardoned for saying that as a public servant I have performed my duty to the best of my ability, and am not ashamed of the record made.

"I stepped from private life into national politics at the bidding of my countrymen; at their bidding I again take my place in the ranks and resume without sorrow the work from which they called me. It is the glory of our institutions that public officials exercise authority by the consent of the governed rather than by divine or hereditary right. Paraphrasing the language of Job, each public servant can say of departing honors: 'The people gave and the people have taken away, blessed be the name of the people.'

"Speaking of my own experience in politics, I may again borrow an idea from the great sufferer and say: 'What, shall we receive good at the hands of the people, and shall we not receive evil?' I have received good even beyond my deserts, and I accepted defeat without complaint. I ask my friends not to cherish resentment against any who may have contributed to the result. If my election would have brought good to the State, those who have aided in the defeat will suffer as much as we; if my defeat has brought good to the State, we as citizens shall enjoy the advantage in common with those who secured it. If they were

13

conscientiously striving to carry out what they
believed to be right, we cannot criticise them, because each citizen has a right to contend in politics
for the measures and men desired by him, and he
is in duty bound to do so.   If our opponents were
actuated by unworthy motives, they will suffer
more than their victim.   Instead of finding fault
when it is too late to apply a remedy, let us rather
prepare for the work before us.   I have advocated
fusion because I believe it necessary to bring the
reform forces of society together in order to overcome a united and insolent opposition.   I still
advocate fusion as the only possible road to the
great reforms needed.

· "The enemies of good government, the beneficiaries of class legislation, act as one man, with
unlimited means at their disposal.   The common
people have only their votes, and they must cast
them together or suffer defeat.   In this State, fusion,
while only partial, has elected Judge Holcomb and
thus secured the defeat of as corrupt a ring as
ever cursed the State.   That is a great victory
for this year.   Where else have the Democrats
and Populists won such a triumph?   Let us rejoice that by our combined efforts we have elected
an honest man as Executive of this State.

"The friends of these reforms have fought a
good fight ; they have kept the faith, and they will
not have finished their course until the reforms
are accomplished.   Let us be grateful for the

progress made, and ' with malice toward none and charity for all ' begin the work of the next campaign.

"Those who fight for the right may be defeated, but they are never conquered. They may suffer reverses, but they never suffer disgrace.

"Yours truly,

"W. J. BRYAN."

CHAPTER IX.

BRYAN AT ARLINGTON.

On May 30, 1894, at Arlington, Washington, D. C., Mr. Bryan delivered the Memorial Day Address, which was listened to by the President and his cabinet, and many members of Congress. This address was admitted by Mr. Bryan's most bitter opponents, to be one of the best of memorial day productions. On this occasion Mr. Bryan said:

"With flowers in our hands and sadness in our hearts, we stand amid the tombs where the nation's dead are sleeping. It is appropriate that the chief executive is here, accompanied by his cabinet; it is appropriate that the soldier's widow is here, and the soldier's son; it is appropriate that here are assembled, in numbers growing less each year, the scarred survivors, federal and confederate, of our last great war; it is appropriate, also, that these exercises in honor of comrades dead, should be conducted by comrades still surviving. All too soon the day will come, when these graves must be decorated by hands unused to the implements of war, and when these speeches must be made by lips that never answered to a roll call.

"We, who are of the aftermath, cannot look upon the flag with the same emotions that thrill you, who have followed it as your pillar of cloud by day and your pillar of fire by night, nor can we appreciate it as you can who have seen it waving in front of reinforcements when succor meant escape from death ; neither can we, standing by these blossom-covered mounds, feel as you have often felt when far away from home, and on hostile soil you have laid your companions to rest ; but from a new generation we can bring you the welcome assurance that the commemoration of this day will not part with you. We may neglect the places where the nation's greatest victories have been won, but we cannot forget the Arlingtons which the nation has consecrated with its tears.

"To ourselves, as well as to the dead, we owe the duty which we discharge here, for monuments and memorial days declare the patriotism of the living no less than the virtues of those whom they commemorate.

"We would be blind indeed to our own interests and to the welfare of posterity, if we were deaf to the just demands of the soldiers and his dependents. We are grateful for the services rendered by our defenders, whether illustrious or nameless, and yet a nation's gratitude in not entirely unselfish, since by our regard for the dead, we add to the security of the living ; by our remembrance of those who have suffered, we give inspiration to those upon whose valor we must hereafter rely, and prove ourselves worthy of the sacrifices which have been made and which may be again required.

"The essence of patriotism lies in a willingness to sacrifice for one's country, just as true greatness finds expression, not in blessings enjoyed, but in good bestowed. Read the words inscribed on the monuments reared by loving hands to the heroes of the past; they do not speak of wealth inherited, or honors bought, or of hours in leisure spent, but of service done. Twenty years, forty years, a life or life's most precious blood he yielded up for the welfare of his fellows—this is the simple story which proves that it is now, and ever has been, more blessed to give than to receive.

"The officer was a patriot when he gave his ability to his country and risked his name and fame upon the fortunes of war; the private soldier was a patriot when he took his place in the ranks and offered his body as a bulwark to protect the flag; the wife was a patriot when she bade her husband farewell and gathered about her the little brood over which she must exercise both a mother's and a father's care; and if there can be degrees in patriotism, the mother stood first among the patriots when she gave to the nation her sons, the divinely-appointed support of her declining years, and as she brushed the tears away, thanked God that he had given her the strength to rear strong and courageous sons for the battlefield.

" To us who were born too late to prove upon the battlefield our courage and our loyalty, it is gratifying to know that opportunity will not be wanting to show our love of country. In a nation like ours, where the Government is founded upon the principle of equality and derives its just powers from the consent of the Government ; in a land like ours, I say, where every citizen is a sovereign and where no one cares to wear a crown, every year presents a battlefield and every day brings forth occasion for the display of patriotism.

"And on this memorial day we shall fall short of our duty if we content ourselves with praising the dead or complimenting the living and fail to make preparation for those responsibilities which present times and present conditions impose upon us. We can find instruction in that incomparable address delivered by Abraham Lincoln on the battlefield of Gettysburg. It should be read as a part of the exercises of this day on each returning year as the Declaration of Independence is read on the Fourth of July. Let me quote from it, for its truths, like all truths, are applicable in all times and climes :—

" 'We have come to dedicate a portion of that

field as a final resting place for those who here gave their lives that that nation might live. It is altogether fitting and proper that we should do this. But in a larger sense we cannot dedicate, we cannot consecrate, we cannot hallow this ground. The brave men, living and dead, who struggled here, have consecrated it far above our power to add or detract. The world will little note, nor long remember, what we say here, but it cannot forget what they did here. It is for us, the living, rather to be dedicated here to the unfinished work which they who fought here have thus far so nobly advanced.'

" 'The Unfinished Work.' Yes, every generation leaves to its successor an unfinished work. The work of society, the work of human progress, the work of civilization is never completed. We build upon the foundation which we find already laid, and those who follow us take up the work where we leave off. Those who fought and fell thirty years ago did nobly advance the work in their day, for they led the nation up to higher grounds. Theirs was the greatest triumph in all history. Other armies have been inspired by love of conquest, or have fought to repel a foreign enemy, but our armies held within the Union brethren, who now rejoice at their own defeat, and glory in the preservation of the nation which they once sought to dismember. No greater victory can be won by citizens or soldiers than to transform temporary foes into permanent friends. But let me quote again:

"'It is rather for us to be here dedicated to the great task remaining before us, that from these honored dead we take increased devotion to that cause for which they gave the last full measure of devotion ; that we here highly resolve that these dead shall not have died in vain ; that this nation, under God, shall have a new birth of freedom, and that government of the people, by the people and for the people shall not perish from the earth.'

"Aye, let us here dedicate ourselves anew to this unfinished work, which requires of each generation constant sacrifice and unceasing care. Pericles, in speaking of those who fell at Salamis, explained the loyalty of his countrymen when he said :

"'It was for such a country, then, that these men, nobly resolving not to have it taken from them, fell fighting, and every one of their survivors may well be willing to suffer in its behalf.'

"The strength of a nation does not lie in forts, nor in navies, nor yet in great standing armies, but in happy and contented citizens, who are ever ready to protect for themselves and to preserve for posterity the blessings which they enjoy. It is for us in this generation to prove ourselves worthy of our ancestors by making our Government so good, so just and so beneficent, that all who live beneath its flag will be willing if need be to die in its defense. It is for us of this generation to so perform the duties of citizenship that a 'government of the people, by the people and for the people shall not perish from the earth.'

"The man who gave expression to these thoughts is a safe man for any position where genuine patriotism and real ability are the essentials."

On September 1, 1894, Mr. Bryan became editor-in-chief of the Omaha *World-Herald*. His strongest and best editorial efforts were devoted to an education of the people on the money question. The following extracts are taken from some of Mr. Bryan's editorials, for which extracts this publication is indebted to the New York *World*:

"Editor Bryan attacked the secret bond deal arranged by Mr. Cleveland and Mr. Carlisle with J. Pierpont Morgan in an editorial on March 4, 1895. He said—

"'The enormous bonus that was given the Rothschild syndicate to take the last issue of bonds may prove, after all, to be one of the best investments the people have made in many a day. The deal reveals the cloven foot of a political syndicate, which undoubtedly has for its purpose the expenditure of foreign money to carry the next presidential and subsequent presidential elections in the interest of foreign and home capitalists, and the money the people have paid to get a glimpse of this enemy of our institutions will have been well and profitably invested if it causes them to rise in their might and send the American end of the conspiracy to its political grave.

" 'There is no doubt whatever that the Roths child syndicate will make its bond holdings an excuse to employ agents to influence nominating conventions that neither party shall designate a man for the Presidency who cannot be brought under the syndicate's influence. It is apparent that not a stone will be left unturned by Wall street and London to fasten upon the country at the next election an administration that is committed in advance to the gold standard. Every move of the monometallists in this country and Europe indicates as much, and when once mono-metallism is firmly fastened about the necks of the people, Eastern and foreign capital will be the people's taskmaster. Farmers, mechanics, laborers—the common people— think they already have greater burdens than they can bear, but if these bond syndicates get control of the Government the people will have to make bricks without straw. As an eye-opener, therefore, the bonus paid the Rothschild combine is not too great if the people will act, now that their eyes are open.' "

On April 28, 1894, Mr. Bryan editorially advocated the "initiative and referendum." Here are Mr. Bryan's words :—

"The principle of the initiative and referendum is Democratic. It will not be opposed by any Democrat who indorses the declaration of Jefferson that the people are capable of self-government, nor will it be opposed by any Republican who holds to Lincoln's idea that this should be a Government of the people, by the people and for the people. It is the duty of every good citizen to endeavor to make the machinery of government as perfect as possible.

"The anarchists in Chicago did not hold memorial services over the graves of those of their comrades who were executed for participating in the Haymarket riots. For seven years it has been their custom to hold exercises of this character in Waldheim Cemetery, where the remains of their misguided friends are buried, but the directors of the cemetery this year refused to permit it. It seems harsh to prohibit a tribute by the living to its beloved dead, but in this case the action of the directors was justifiable. These annual gatherings have not been those of genuine mourning, but the participants have used the place and occasion to teach their doctrines, and to stir up an animosity against the law and its officers.

"Anarchy has no place in this country, either in the busy walks of life or in the quiet city of the dead. Anarchy is an enemy to peace, to society and to happiness. It is not to be tolerated in any country. Much less has it any cause for existence or toleration in this country, and its friends and devotees cannot use the sacredness of the grave as a means for spreading their unwholesome doctrines and to stir up new strife against the law that accords to even the teachers of arson and assassination, a fair and impartial trial before a jury of their peers."

When the Senate Investigating Committee was probing the Sugar Trust, President Havemeyer acknowledged under oath that the principal object of the trust was to control the price on output of sugar. Mr. Bryan privately sent a copy of this evidence to Mr. Olney, then attorney-general, but he got no reply. On September 7th, Mr. Bryan published an editorial, rehearsing Mr. Havemeyer's testimony and quoting the statute forbidding trusts. This is Mr. Bryan's summary of the matter:

"A clear case would seem to be made out against the trust by the testimony of its President, which, be it said, is corroborated by the record of testimony in a suit brought in the United States Court by the North River Refining Company against the trust. Will Attorney-General Olney bring the officers of the trust to justice?"

Editor Bryan was strongly opposed to the marriage of rich American women to titled foreigners, and on November 3, 1895, said that the rearing of rich American girls in such a manner as to

make them desire titled husbands was "a reflection on the parents, who cultivated a love for aristocracy rather than a pride in American democracy." Mr. Bryan continued:

"Our forefathers decided that titles were
dangerous to liberty, and it is to be regretted
that the patriotism of Revolutionary days has
given place to a disgraceful scramble, among the
daughters of some of our multi-millionaires, for
lords and dukes and counts.

"When an Englishman or Frenchman or other
foreigner, with nothing to commend him but a
title, inherited from a remote ancestor (and possibly only retained because it could not be pawned),
reaches majority, he embarks for the United
States and enters into negotiations for some mar-
riageable heiress or heiress-apparent. Instead of
teaching their daughters to regard with favor the
suits of worthy sons of this country, too many
ambitious parents lead their daughters into the
market-place, and seek to barter a fortune for a
crown.

"Love may leap across the ocean and join in
holy wedlock 'two hearts that beat as one,' but
social ambition and hereditary avarice can never
weld two hearts into home-building material.

"When Cupid becomes a boodler, and court-
ship is carried on by brokers, marriage is a
mockery.

"It is significant that poor American girls, how-

ever accomplished, have no charms for impecu-
nious noblemen. It is also a source of congratulation that American sons do not seek foreign
alliances. It is a shame that some American
daughters do."

Now that Mr. Bryan expects to live in the
White House himself it is interesting to recall
what he wrote on March 31st, less than four months
ago, on the subject of former presidents and a
proposition to pension them. These are his
words:

"Ex-presidents ought to take care of themselves as ordinary citizens do. If it should ever
happen that one of our ex-presidents should be in
need of public or private aid, said aid would be
forthcoming. In recent years our presidents have
retired in comfortable circumstances. Gen. Harrison is earning fat fees at the bar, and his dignity
does not suffer one bit because he is eating his
bread in the perspiration of his gray matter.
When Mr. Cleveland retires he will not be in immediate want. The several millions which he is
credited with accumulating will help to keep the
wolf from the door for a while, and whenever his
reserve fund gets below one or two millions the
people will help him out cheerfully.

"This Government will attain more to the purpose of its founders when the notion that the
people owe their officials anything is entirely
eradicated. To be sure, we owe the faithful

official our appreciation and respect. We have
paid him for his time, and he loses nothing in
dignity if he steps from his official place to the ranks
of the laborers. If he is broken down in health
or should otherwise be unfortunate, the American
people would not permit an ex-president to
suffer."

After the nomination of McKinley and Hobart,
at St. Louis, Mr. Bryan editorially attacked Mr.
Hobart and reprinted *The World's* criticism. Of
Mr. McKinley he said :—

" In selecting William McKinley as its standard-
bearer, the Republican party chose the strongest
man within its ranks. He is a man of good character and personally no objection can be urged
against him.

" It is amazing that a man for whom the people
of this country entertain such a high regard as
they do for Mr. McKinley would consent to become the standard-bearer of a cause that has
brought upon us all of our woe, and the continuation of which will make prosperity impossible.
But the people will vote for the measures, not
men, this year, and Mr. McKinley, as the representative of an un-American measure, will go
down to defeat."

On January 14, 1895, the *World-Herald* contained an editorial from Mr. Bryan's pen on the
subject of "vast wealth." He said :—

" It is possible for one citizen to injure another

with a club or with a weapon, but that is not the only way. The gamblers on the Board of Trade may injure the farmer by decreasing the price of his grain, or they may injure the person who buys farm products by increasing the price. Whether their manipulations of the markets hurt the one class or the other they do an injury. Trusts crush out small competitors, and, then having a monopoly, extort higher prices from purchasers. There are many indirect methods by which one person can injure another, methods by which one person virtually takes the property of another person without his consent.

" If the Government properly restrains each citizen intent on wrong-doing and fully protects every citizen in the 'enjoyment of life, liberty and the pursuit of happiness,' many great fortunes will be prevented.

"People may well ask themselves whether our form of government will stand an indefinite aggravation of the tendency which has been observed for the last generation. Great inequality in wealth fosters social and political inequality and arouses class prejudices when great accumulations are found to arise from unjust legislation.

" The main contention of some of our financiers is, that we should so arrange our monetary system as to continually increase the investment of foreign capital among us. The *World-Herald* believes that it is better for the Government to

14

furnish a sufficient supply of money to do the business of the country, than to depend upon borrowing abroad and paying interest upon it.

"There is an economy in exchanging that which we can produce at a low cost, for something which we can only produce here at a high cost. That is the principle which lies at the foundation of all commerce between individuals and between nations. But there can be no justification for a financial system in this country, built upon the theory, that the more money we borrow abroad, the better we are off, and which permits the sale of a few American securities in London to create a panic in this country."

Mr. Bryan closed his editorial by declaring that the only remedy for our present financial ills, was independent and free coinage of silver, and the issue, by the Federal Government, of whatever paper money is needed to preserve stability in the purchasing power of the dollar.

In July, 1895, the Salvation Army was in trouble and Mr. Bryan wrote an editorial defending it. He said :

"The Salvation Army is not a nuisance. It is 'noisy,' but Satan is a rather noisy fellow himself, and no one can object if these people choose to 'fight the devil with fire.' * * * If it is 'a noisy crowd,' the noise will never induce any man or woman to do wrong, and there are thousands of instances where this 'noise' has induced many persons to quit their meanness. Such an organization is entitled not only to respect, but to the earnest co-operation of every good citizen."

On February 16, 1895, Mr. Bryan wrote this :—

"The cry that the Democratic party is dead is the cry of the enemy, of the coward and of the traitor. The Democratic party is not dead, nor is it asleep. When the Democratic party dies Democratic principles will die, and in the same grave will be buried the hope of humanity, the incentive to work for a broader and better plan of existence and the power to go from strength to strength in advancing and maintaining liberty and freedom. The principles of Jefferson, of Jackson and of Lincoln—the same—all are the heart and the soul of every government by and for the people that now is or ever will be ; and, moreover, they are the life-blood which courses through the arteries of liberty and makes the all-powerful agency in the mighty work of lifting mankind Godward.

"Man may be born and man may go hence, and nations may be established and nations may be overthrown, but the principles of Democracy are of God and they must return to him bearing in their arms a perfect humanity.

"The onward way of these principles has always been and always will be more or less impeded by the Judases of the world, but the right always prevails—the people triumph ultimately.

It is true that the Democratic party—the custo-
dian and proclaimer of these principles of human
progress—is for the moment wrenched and torn
by fierce onslaughts from daggers in the hands of
members of its own household, who, like Bene-
dict Arnold, were caught in the act of selling
their fellows for British gold, but they have made
their own graves deep and wide in the morasses
of their own treachery, and there is no inclination
anywhere to hinder the operations of the law of
retribution."

The last editorial written by Mr. Bryan appeared on July 1st, nine days before he was nominated. It was an answer to the charge made by
the Atchison *Globe* that he had advised the people to always oppose the bankers. The following extract contains the germ of Mr. Bryan's
argument :—

"The banker is a man, nothing more, nothing
less, and his opinions are entitled to all due consideration. But no man should permit another
man to do his thinking for him. There are many
bankers who are sincere and consistent bimetallists. There are others who are sincere gold
bugs. There are some who advocate the single
gold standard when they do not believe its preservation will be beneficial to the country, but for
reasons best known to themselves they adhere to
the advocacy of that standard.

"The opinions of all bankers are entitled to

SENATOR STEPHEN M. WHITE,
Permanent Chairman Democratic National Convention.

Hon. J. P. ALTGELD,
Ex-Governor of Illinois.

unusual consideration, because of their experience in financial matters; but the banker must be able to back up his opinion with logic.

" Because the banker has had wide experience in money matters, is no reason that another man should believe the banker's mere statement that black is white, particularly when the other man knows that black is not white."

CHAPTER X.

BRYAN AS A LAWYER.

William J. Bryan, the lawyer, has largely been obscured by the greater reputation which has been attained by the orator and as a student of governmental questions. His career as a lawyer is practically confined to the period prior to his election to Congress the first time. As this event occurred when he was just passed thirty years old, his achievements, and the demonstration of the possession of those qualities which go to make great lawyers, have been as conspicuous as his opportunities permitted.

Those lawyers who have had the best opportunity to judge of his abilities in this direction say, that had his destiny not directed him into another channel, he would have taken his place as high in the ranks of the legal profession, as he has attained in the political arena.

The influence, which his contact with Lyman Trumbull had upon the future professional career of Mr. Bryan, had been detected by some who were in a position to judge. With men possessing characters as strong as that of W. J. Bryan, it is doubtful if the influence of any association ever directs them into one path or another. Influences of other strong minds, when brought into contact with them during the receptive period of earlier years, may remain with them in after years, but their province is more that of lights which show the surroundings, than that of pilots who select the routes.

While pursuing his legal studies in Union College, W. J. Bryan occupied himself outside of recitation hours in the office of Lyman Trumbull, where such time as was not taken up with the minor duties imposed upon him was given to study.

After graduating from the law school at the age of twenty-three, he commenced to practice in Jacksonville, Ill., beginning at the bottom as young lawyers without influential connections must do. During the four years he lived in Jacksonville, he increased his professional income each year. After his removal to Lincoln, he was again a young lawyer, and one who had not made a reputation large enough to precede him to the new home in the West. Again, he had to commence over the work of building up a practice. Surrounded as he was by strangers, the first step was necessarily to make acquaintances and friends, out of whose ranks clients were afterwards to come. Again he saw his income from his law practice gradually increasing, until 1890, when he was elected to Congress. During his service of two terms in Congress, he did not practice, giving his whole time and attention to the questions which came up and to the business of the office to which he had been chosen. After his return from Congress at the close of his second term, it was his intention to at once take up the practice, but he found that this plan could not be carried out, on account of the demands made upon his time for speeches in different parts of the country, in behalf of the silver movement. In spite of the constant work and travel in the interests of the silver cause, several important cases involving questions of great interest were tried by him in the State Courts; the principal one of these was the Lincoln bond case, referred to in another place.

During the time since his retirement from Congress, and while at work in the interest of the silver cause, Mr. Bryan has sometimes lectured before Chautauquas and other societies for stated sums, and at others a liberal allowance was made by communities in which he spoke to meetings. Sometimes there was no compensation received but his income from this source, which, together with his salary as editor of the Omaha *World-Herald*, was sufficient to support himself and family.

His financial and professional success, when it is considered that he made two beginnings in seven years, each time as a young man among strangers, has been enough to demonstrate that he has the qualities which make successful lawyers.

The only case which he carried to the United States Supreme Court was won by him.

One of the cases of more than local importance which Mr. Bryan carried to a successful issue in the State courts was the Lincoln bond case. In this, the city council sought to authorize the issue of a series of refunding bonds, with a proviso inserted that the bonds should be payable in gold. The obnoxious clause had been inserted, or it was sought to be inserted, by the city council after the voters of the city had authorized a bond issue. The bond syndicate which had made a bid for the bonds demanded that the gold-payment clause be inserted. Mr. Bryan, as a citizen of Lincoln, in connection with others, joined in a petition to the State courts for an injunction restraining the city officials from issuing a gold bond as proposed. Mr. Bryan was the attorney for the petitioners and the court granted the injunction prayed for, making it perpetual. This case is regarded as of largely greater importance than the mere amount of half a million involved in the Lincoln city bonds would indicate. There were involved in it important and unsettled principles of constitutional law which were far reaching in their effects. Its determination against the city officials was one of the victories of the silver forces in the battle against the gold. This case was one in which there was no opportunity for the orator to win by swaying the jury, but, being an equity case, it was only on the application of cold logic, that would appeal to the judgment of the chancellor, that the attorney could depend for success.

Two other cases of lesser importance, but involving governmental principles, tried by Mr. Bryan as attorney, consisted of one wherein the right of officers to refuse to serve papers in criminal cases without their fees being paid in advance, was questioned and settled in the negative. Another was where the right of a township to vote bonds to beet sugar factories was combated and decided against any such issue. It is of interest to note that in these cases Bryan, the lawyer, appeared as the advocate of the rights of the many—of the people—as against the assumption of special rights, by the preferred class.

The same impulses which have made him among political leaders conspicuous for his advocacy of the cause of the masses of the people dominated him as a lawyer. His friends, who were solicitous for his pecuniary success, noted this, and some of them sought to give well-meant advice against what they considered faulty business policy. Bryan, in his practice, congratulated himself whenever he was able to bring about a settlement without going into court and entailing the extra expense and sometimes bitter feelings which litigation brings about between neighbors and friends. On one occasion, when an old friend thought to advise him that this was not the best policy, because his fees were smaller than if a fight in court had been carried on, he silenced the objector by saying that it would pay best in the long run, because these men would be happier and better citizens by reason of being friends instead of enemies, and then "they will be my friends, too."

As a lawyer, his practice was general, covering nearly the whole range. The line was drawn at one place. He had no corporation practice. The natural bent of his mind, and perhaps his inclinations, are such as are supposed to distinguish the jury practitioner from the equity lawyer. There are cases on the records in the State courts of Nebraska which show, that, although it was the opinion of W. J. Bryan's friends that he could make useful his powers of persuasive eloquence to more readily establish his standing at the bar, he did not lack those other qualities which make a successful equity lawyer, —the best paid and generally conceded to be the highest type of the lawyer. In the Lincoln bond case, Mr. Bryan exhibited the grasp of the broad principles, and the intimate knowledge of the history of previous cases having bearing on the subject which only comes to the delver in musty books. This case was won besides upon a presentation of the theories of the constitutional principle contended for with such clearness that the judges were convinced by the mastery of the case displayed by the lawyer. This case was even to some of Mr. Bryan's friends the means of revealing qualities of mind which they had not given him credit for possessing. It was shown that as a lawyer, he did not have to depend alone upon the powers of persuasion and appeals to the emotions which mark the jury lawyer. While possessing in an imminent degree the faculty of doing this, he showed that the ordinarily-considered incongruous branch of the profession, the equity practice, presented no closed doors against his entrance, but the gates flew open at his approach as if to welcome one who by right can claim a place of honor within. As a jury lawyer, older citizens of Southern Nebraska have many vivid recollections of his triumphs by means of the same qualities of persuasive eloquence which have gained him fame in Congress, on the lecture platform and before excited political gatherings. An old friend and intimate acquaintance of Mr. Bryan's ascribed the success which met his practice before juries to the fact that the lawyer was in close touch with the great body of the people; knew what they thought about and how they are affected by a given condition or occurrence. As the juries are drawn from this mass of the common people, he always found himself before men whose every-day thoughts and feelings were as an open book to him. No time had to be lost in lawyer and jurors getting into sympathy with each other.

A review of Mr. Bryan's legal life and analysis

Hon. CLAUDE MATTHEWS,
Governor of Indiana.

Hon. ALEX. M. DOCKERY,
Congressman from Missouri.

of his legal method and bent of mind has shown a curious likeness to that of Abraham Lincoln. While both coming from the people, depended largely upon their keeping in touch with the masses by constant association with those around them, while with both, this desire for social intercourse came from a cordial and real friendship for those around them it was the source of greatest strength in professional battles. It can be safely said that Mr. Bryan has demonstrated that he is as strong a lawyer as ever was selected by the people as president, with the exception of Lincoln and Benjamin H. Harrison. The achievements of Lincoln and Bryan as lawyers, up to the time Lincoln arrived at Mr. Bryan's age, are so nearly on a par that the two might fittingly be said to run side by side. Great legal reputations have not been regarded as prime essentials in the selections of presidents, and the history of the country shows that but one really strong lawyer—who had a strong record before his election—has ever been honored with the presidency. Men who might have been strong lawyers if their time and attention had not been taken up with governmental affairs and other questions, the mastery of which required as fine a quality of mind, have been presidents. Benjamin Harrison is the sole representative of the lawyer who was recognized by the profession, and had made a reputation as a great lawyer before election to the office of chief magistrate of the union.

CHAPTER XI.

BRYAN AS AN ORATOR.

Bryan is an orator of the people. Earnestness, simplicity and beauty are the chief characteristics of his style. The subject upon which he would speak is thoroughly studied in all its bearings. The best that has been written or said upon it is examined and re-examined, if necessary, until it is mastered. Nor is the investigation confined to the side of the question to which he is predisposed; every conceivable objection to the position he favors is looked for and thoroughly studied in the light of the strongest thought of its ablest advocates. Having digested with the utmost minuteness all that can be said for or against his position, he then selects from the mass the most forceful thoughts on both sides of the question. This done, he then looks for language suitable to express them. Long, involved sentences will not do; unusual words must not be employed; the thought which burns within the mind and would impress itself upon the hearts of others must not have any of its strength impaired or its beauty dimmed by the language selected to convey it. The simplest words are chosen and they are formed into short, pithy

(246)

sentences. No word is used solely for its sound; the mere jingle of words has no place in the mental workshop of our orator. To him words are the servants of thought, and take their real beauty from the thought that blazes through them. From this let it not be concluded that he undervalues the importance of the best literary style. His style is as pure and captivating as that of Irving, or Addison, and not dissimilar to either. But style, with him, as with those two great masters, is valued not for itself, but because it conveys in the most pleasing manner the thoughts which he would have others know. Here are some of his sentences culled from different speeches:

They call that man a statesman whose ear is tuned to catch the slightest pulsations of a pocketbook, and to denounce as a demagogue anyone who dares to listen to the heart-beat of humanity.   *   *   *   *   *

The poor man who takes property by force is called a thief, but the creditor who can by legislation make a debtor pay a dollar twice as large as he borrowed is lauded as the friend of a sound currency. The man who wants the people to destroy the government is an anarchist, but the man who wants the government to destroy the people is a patriot.   *   *   *

Some who are ready to use the power of the government to limit the supply of money, in order to prevent injustice to the creditor, are slow to admit the right of the government to increase the currency when necessary to prevent injustice to the debtor. I denounce the cruel interpretation of governmental power which would grant the authority to starve, but would withhold the authority to feed our people—which would permit a contraction of our currency, even to the destruction of all prosperity, but would prohibit the expansion of our currency to keep pace with the growing needs of a growing nation !   *   *   *   *   *

The gentlemen who are so fearful of socialism when the poor are exempted from an income tax, view with indifference those methods of taxation which give the rich a substantial exemption. They weep more because $15,000,000 is to be collected from the incomes of the rich than they do at the collection of $300,000,000 upon the goods which the poor consume. And when an attempt is made to equalize these burdens, not fully, but partially only, the people of the south and west are called anarchists. I deny the assertion, sir. It is among the people of the south and west, on the prairies and in the mountains, that you find the staunchest supporters of government and the best friends of law and order. You may not find among these people the great fortunes which are accumulated in cities, nor will you find the dark shadows which these fortunes throw over the community, but you will find those willing to protect the rights of property, even while they demand the property shall bear its share of taxation. You may not find among them as much of wealth, but you will find men who are not only willing to pay their taxes to support the government, but are willing whenever necessary to offer up their lives in its defense. These people, sir, whom you call anarchists because they ask that the burdens of government shall be equally borne, these people have ever borne the cross on Calvary and saved their country with their blood.   *   *   *   *   *

I may be in error, but in my humble judgment he who would rob man of his necessary food or pollute the springs at which he quenches his thirst, or steal away from him his accustomed rest, or condemn his mind to the gloomy night of ignorance, is no more an enemy of his race than the man who, deaf to the entreaties of the poor and blind and the suffering he would cause, seeks to destroy one of the money metals given by the Almighty to supply the needs of commerce.　·　　*　　　*　　　*　　　*　　　*

The line of battle is laid down.　The President's letter to Governor Northern expresses his oppostion to the free and unlimited coinage of silver by this country alone.　Upon that issue the next congressional contest will be fought.　Are we dependent or independent as a nation?　Shall we legislate for ourselves or shall we beg some foreign nation to help us provide for the financial wants of our own people?　　*　　*　　*

You may think that you have buried the cause of bimetallism; you may congratulate yourselves that you have laid the free coinage of silver away in a sepulchre, newly made since the election, and before the door rolled the veto stone.　But, sirs, if our cause is just, as I believe it is, your labor has been in vain; no tomb was ever made so strong that it could imprison a righteous cause.　Silver will yet lay aside its grave clothes and its shroud.　It will yet rise, and in its rising and its reign will bless mankind.　　　*　　　*　　　*

Alexander "wept for other worlds to conquer" after he had carried his victorious banner throughout the then known world.　Napoleon "re-arranged the map of Europe with his sword" amid the lamentations of those by whose blood he was exalted; but when these and other military heroes are forgotten and their achievements disappear in the cycle's sweep of years, children will still lisp the name of Jefferson, and freemen will ascribe due praise to him who filled the kneeling subject's hearts with hope and bade him stand erect a sovereign among his peers.　　*　　　*　　　*　　　*

The State of Indiana has declared that no police power shall be conferred on the Pinkerton detectives; and if the people of the State of New York do not desire such powers to be conferred upon them, it is the business of the State of New York, or any other State which entertains that view, to regulate it by its own legislative enactment.　It is not within the purview of Congress, it is not the business of Congress to interfere with the police powers of the several States of the

15

union. I believe that the time has come when we ought to squarely draw the line between the powers conferred upon the federal government and those reserved to the States, and that we ought to stop this indiscriminate investigation where we clearly have no power to legislate. * * *

I have been opposed to the issuing of money by national banks, for the reason that this function of government should not be surrendered to any corporation or any private concern whatever. On the same ground I am opposed to the States authorizing private corporations to issue money, or so-called money.

Mr. Bryan is not averse to the employment of the thoughts of others wherever they add force and attractiveness to the argument in hand. Accordingly, we find his speeches interspersed with quotations from some of the best writers in prose and poetry, but in each instance the quotation has a natural fitness for the place in which it is found. No straining of the lines of the argument is permitted that the quotation may find a place. There are some productions which pass for oratory that are mere mechanisms—the offspring of minds cold and plodding without a ray of genius to illumine their path. In them, words have been dragged together in the vain hope of producing a flower worthy to be laid at the feet of oratory, but they are as painted leaves, they are without the odor of life. The work of genius springs spontaneously from the depths of a heart ruled by purity—"Genius sees by intuition, illustrates by pictures, and speaks in music. The phraseology in which its sentiments are clothed is not a kind of patch-work laboriously tagged together, but is part and parcel of the thought, and is born mature and splendid, like Minerva glittering from the brow of Jove."

Briefly we have sketched the mere outlines of the work employed by Mr. Bryan in the preparation of his great deliverances in behalf of human rights. First, he masters the whole field of argument, and thus he prepares himself not only to prove the correctness of his own position, but to meet every objection that may be offered against it. He is enabled, too, by this means to state correctly the position of his opponent. Not a little of his force in debate is due to the fact that he states with absolute fairness the argument of his adversary, and then, with crushing effect, hurls against it the clean-cut, well-considered, overwhelming reply. His care in arranging the matter which he has gathered is no less than that employed in the gathering. By this means he has everything in its place, subject to his instant command, and when sent forth on its mission of truth, goes with a force that carries conviction. The most acceptable language is chosen, and so clear and simple do the most profound thoughts appear when they come fresh-coined from his brain, that men have no difficulty in comprehending them in all their force. This power was noted by a critical observer of one of the debates in which Mr. Bryan engaged when a candidate for Congress. The observer was asked what kind of an argument Mr. Bryan's opponent made. He replied that the argument was very good, but its strength was obscured by involved and awkward sentences, and most listeners could not comprehend it when delivered. On the other hand, Mr. Bryan's argument, he continued, came forth in language so simple and pleasing that the listener had not to hesitate for a moment to grasp its full force, and thus the orator carried along with him a convinced as well as an enthusiastic audience. Superficial observers have spoken of this feature of Mr. Bryan's style as "catchy," and frequently have they said that while he might charm a "common country audience" by what they termed "catch words," he would fail utterly when he came to address "men of culture." But these critics did not recognize in the simplicity of his work the hand of genius, and they have lived to see their anticipations dashed to atoms. Twice the lower house of Congress was enraptured by Mr. Bryan's luminous powers of eloquence. The morning after his great tariff speech the nation awoke to hail him as the peer of Webster or Prentice. A few years later he discussed the financial question before the same body only to win a repetition of the plaudits which greeted the close of his tariff speech. The next day, and for weeks thereafter, the press of the nation gave him unstinted praise and crowned him one of America's greatest orators.

But all his work would accomplish but little if not presided over by "a mind stamped with the patent of Divinity" and acting in the glow of a heart throbbing with the noblest and purest impulses. Nor does the great care employed by Mr. Bryan in the preparation of his speeches make him an orator. Preparation does not enable him to sway the minds of others and place in them impressions that live. It is something else. It is a power equalled by few and excelled by none. It comes from an unseen hand—the hand of God—and is entrusted to him for noble ends.

"There's a charm in deliv'ry, a magical art,
That thrills like a kiss, from the lip to the heart;
'Tis the glance—the expression—the well-chosen word—
By whose magic the depths of the spirit are stirr'd—
The smile—the mute gesture—the soul-stirring pause—
The eye's sweet expression, that melts while it awes—
The lip's soft persuasion—its musical tone;
Oh! such were the charms of that eloquent one!"

In personal appearance as well as in mental gifts, Mr. Bryan is highly favored. Before he utters a word, his presence wins for him the favor of his audience. Simplicity itself rules his delivery and bearing, but it is a simplicity in which the highest art wears all the graces of nature. As he stands before his audience, he presents a striking picture; every feature of his strong face is instinct with intelligence; his eyes dance with the light of a soul on fire as he marches through the depths of his discourse, pleading for the rights of the poor and of the masses. He "illustrates in his own person the ancient apologue of the youthful Hercules, in the pride and strength of beauty, surrendering his own soul to the worship of human rights and exalted virtue in public places."

He commences in a soft, pleasant, conversational tone; instantly your attention is riveted upon him; or rather upon what he has to say. You have little disposition to study either the man or his manner—his thought is what holds you. Nothing occurs either in tone, posture, or gesture to divert your attention, or break the spell that is upon you, Every movement of arm, head and body, every modulation comes as an inseparable part of the thought he is expressing. Your eyes are fastened upon the orator: as he moves, you in spirit move with him; as he advances to his climax the listener advances with him; not a step is missed, not a break occurs; in perfect harmony orator and audience travel over the path of thought until the climax is reached and then, as the last tone of the deep, rich, melodious voice of the orator is uttered with a dramatic force which thrills every fiber, there breaks forth the full, earnest, uproarious applause that marks the approval and admiration of those who listen.

The hand of the orator is raised, instantly perfect silence follows. The sweet tones of that marvelous voice are again heard by every one within the enclosure, no matter how vast. Under the influence of that voice and the magic of words that convey the thought of a master mind, men sit enraptured and applaud sentiments which but a moment before they ridiculed; they came to scoff, but remain to worship.

It has been said in describing the auditor under the influence of the orator's power, " He is thrilled in every nerve, he is agitated with rapture. He blends all his emotions with the speaker, and is subdued or inspired under his power. He soon becomes stripped of all defence, and willingly exposed to every blow, so that the greatest effects are produced by the slightest words adroitly directed and skillfully expressed." That this exactly portrays the auditor sitting under the influence of Mr. Bryan's orations will not be denied by those who have listened to his greatest efforts. Mr. Bryan never delivers a poor speech; he always pleases, but to reach those heights of impassioned eloquence which none but a master dares to tread, he must have the occasion and the subject. " It is only when God's creative breath fans the fires of patriotism in the soul sublimely endowed, that a true orator is fashioned for sovereignty over the hearts of mankind." If the highest oratory consists in the power to persuade and the force to chain in the blazing fires of the purest enthusiasm the intellects of men, then Mr. Bryan is an orator with few peers in ancient or modern times. Well we may say of him what the great Fenelon says of Demosthenes: "He moves, warms and captivates the heart. He was sensibly touched with the interests of his country. His discourses gradually increase in force, by greater light and new reasons, which are always illustrated by bold figures and lively images. One cannot but see that he has the good of the Republic entirely at heart, and that nature itself speaks in all his transports."

There is much in Mr. Bryan's oratory that recalls Demosthenes, Fox, O'Connell and Fisher Ames, but unlike any of them he never indulges in invective. Search his speeches through, whether in Congress, before the Convention, or on the stump, and you will find them absolutely free from personalities. Methods and classes he may denounce; individuals never. No audience ever sat within the sound of his most fervid utterances and caught a word that would appeal to the lower passions of anger, hate or revenge. The intellect, and the purer, higher affections of the human heart present the only field in which he loves to labor. He is always a master of himself. The noblest passions may surge and fiercely burn within his breast, but they are like the fires of the volcano, confined within the snow-capped mountain.

Many have constructed arguments as logical as
Mr. Bryan. Nor would it be difficult, perhaps, to
find speeches of equal depth and bold imagery to
those delivered by him, but this is true of all the
great tribunes of the people. Quintilius says,
"Logicians can be found everywhere, an able argument is not rare, but seldom has that orator appeared whose eloquence could carry the judge
out of his depth, who could throw him into what
disposition of mind he pleased, fire him into resentment, or soften him into tears. Many have
constructed arguments as logical as those of
Demosthenes, or Cicero, but none ever arrayed
them before their audiences with such magic
power."

One of Bryan's best speeches was that on the
subject " Money," in which he gave his famous
apostrophe to Jefferson. It is as follows :

" There are wrongs to be righted; there are
evils to be eradicated ; there is injustice to be removed ; there is good to be secured for those who
toil and wait. In this fight for equal laws we cannot fail, for right is mighty and will in time triumph
over all obstacles. Even if our eyes do not behold success, we know that our labor is not in
vain, and we can lay down our weapons, happy in
the promise given by Bryant to the soldier :

    " ' Yea, though thou lie upon the dust,
       When they who helped thee flee in fear

Die full of hope and manly trust,
Like those who fell in battle here.

" 'Another hand thy sword shall wield;
Another hand the standard wave;
Till from the trumpet's mouth is pealed
The blast of triumph o'er thy grave.'

"Let us then with the courage of Andrew Jackson, apply to present conditions the principles taught by Thomas Jefferson—Thomas Jefferson, the greatest constructive statesman whom the world has ever known ; the grandest warrior who ever battled for human liberty! He quarried from the mountain of eternal truth the four pillars, upon whose strength all popular government must rest. In the Declaration of American Independence he proclaimed the principles with which there is, without which there cannot be 'a government of the people, by the people, and for the people.' When he declared that 'all men are created equal; that they are endowed by their Creator with certain unalienable rights ; that among these are life, liberty, and the pursuit of happiness ; that to secure these rights governments are instituted among men, deriving their just powers from the consent of the governed,' he declared all that lies between the Alpha and Omega of Democracy.

"Alexander 'wept for other worlds to conquer' after he had carried his victorious banner throughout the then known world. Napoleon 'rearranged the map of Europe with his sword' amid the lamentations of those by whose blood he was exalted ; but when these and other military heroes are forgotten and their achievements disappear in the cycle's sweep of years, children will still lisp the name of Jefferson, and freemen will ascribe due praise to him who filled the kneeling subject's heart with hope and bade him stand erect—a sovereign among his peers."

CHAPTER XII.

BRYAN AT HOME.

In a country where no man is born to authority, but where each must acquire place through his own achievements, it is inevitable that the private life of public men should be closely scrutinized. This country has never ceased to be a democracy in spite of the efforts of some of its worst enemies, and in a democracy the good citizen is the bulwark. The American people still believe that a man who does not fulfill his obligations to the community as a good husband and father, and an honorable man of business, can not be fit to administer the highest office in the gift of the people. Moreover, this is a country where the sentiment of women counts for much, and the influence of women is frankly acknowledged. The home-life of a man, and those who make his home-life, have much to do, it is maintained, with his success.

Mr. Bryan has been very fortunate. Twelve years ago he married a sensible and lovely woman, who has made it easy for him to remain the domestic man that he is. What has been the duty of many men, has been his pleasure. Home is and always has been, the fairest spot on earth to him, and he is to be congratulated as much as praised for his unswerving fidelity to it.

Concerning Mr. Bryan's devotion to his home, the eulogistic language he himself used in speaking of the happy home of a colleague is entirely appropriate:

"He found his inspiration at his fireside, and approached the ideal in his domestic life. He and his faithful wife, who was both his helpmeet and companion, inhabited as tenants in common that sacred spot called home, and needed no court to define their relative rights and duties. The invisible walls which shut in that home and shut out all else had their foundations upon the earth and their battlements in the skies. No force could break them down, no poisoned arrows could cross their top, and at the gates thereof love and confidence stood ever upon guard."

Mrs. Wm. J. Bryan was Mary Elizabeth Baird. Her father, John Baird, was born in Northampton county, Pennsylvania. Mr. Baird is of Scotch-Irish descent. There is a record of his ancestry running back at least thirteen generations, which reveals many men and women of more than ordinary ability, all of whom have taken, as even those of the last generation may take, pride in the fact that not a taint has ever rested upon that good family name. Mr. Baird moved west in 1838 and in 1852 was married to the daughter of Col. Darius Dexter of Dexterville, New York.

Mr. Baird located at Perry, Illinois; and here on the 17th day of June, 1861, Mary was born.

In those days Perry was a trading-post of quite a large territory. Mr. Baird engaged with a partner in an extensive business which comprised, in the earlier days, a general store—a shoe-shop, harness-shop, pork-packing house and a general grain and shipping business. This firm did quite an extensive business in shipments to the city of St. Louis, using the river steamboats for transportation. Mr. Baird was a gentleman of scholarly instincts and a great reader. Although a very busy man, he became the companion of his daughter who was his only child, and he related to her the stories of the Iliad and Odyssey and of Greek mythology at the time when the little girl could not read them for herself. Mr. Baird was himself a self-educated man, and he appreciated the great value of a thorough education; consequently, he devoted his best energies to making a perfect woman, intellectually, of his beloved child.

Mrs. Bryan's mother was an invalid and upon the daughter rested a great deal of the care of her mother. Mrs. Bryan attended the High School at Perry, and at the age of sixteen went to Monticello Seminary at Godfrey, Illinois, remaining there for one year, but on account of the serious condition of her mother's health she found it necessary to be nearer home and in the following year entered the Presbyterian Academy at

Jacksonville, from which institution she was graduated in 1881 with the first honors of her class.

While Miss Baird was attending the Presbyterian Academy at Jacksonville, Mr. Bryan was a student at the Illinois College in the same city. The two young people first met at a reception in the Academy parlors. A very pretty story has been going the rounds to the effect that Miss Baird heard Mr. Bryan recite "A Soldier of the Legion," and was captivated with him. The story, however, is without foundation. The fact is that the young people met at this college reception and they fell in love with one another just as two good-looking and sensible people would be expected to do, and at the time Miss Baird had never detected the fire of oratory in her young lover and did not know that he could even deliver "Casabianca" with more than ordinary effect until long after their first meeting. The young people were engaged for a period covering a little more than four years. During the year preceding their marriage, Mr. Bryan practised law in Jacksonville. The young man had already built up a paying practice and the young lovers planned and built their first home before they were married, and on October 1, 1884, the marriage ceremony took place and they began housekeeping in their own home. This house stands to-day on College Hill in Jacksonville, near the Illinois College. Mr.

Bryan continued the practice of law in Jacksonville for three years after his marriage. On October 2, 1885, their first child, Ruth, was born.

In 1887 they removed to Nebraska, Mr. Bryan feeling that in the stirring West was more opportunity for success. Mrs. Bryan agreed with him. From the first she liked the West and made herself perfectly at home at Lincoln. She took up the study of the law, desiring to fit herself for the consideration of legal questions, not with any expectation of practising herself, but that she might be of assistance to her husband, and also that she might have the mental training resultant from such study.

The Bryans have now three children, Ruth, who is nearly eleven, William, who is seven, and Grace, who is five. All of the children are comely, well behaved, well taught, and very dearly beloved. In short, the home of the Bryans is the simple American home. Mrs. Bryan, who has never been a society woman, spends the early part of her evenings reading to her children. They have always received her direct personal care. Her responsibilities have not been light in any respect. Besides her young children, she has had her aged father and mother with her, and her affection for them has been such that she has been closely kept at home. Her mother is now dead, but her father remains, and he receives her solicitous care.

Mrs. Bryan has a singular activity of mind. She is logical, studious, industrious and aspiring. Above all, she is sensible. She has kept in touch with each detail of her husband's advancement in a political way. She knows the political situation and all the minutiæ of local political affairs accurately, giving them their due importance, and regarding them in a philosophic manner. She has been a faithful critic to her husband, assisting in the collection of material for his speeches, and giving him the benefit of her advice. She has been his closest confidante, and, probably, his most trusted adviser. Hers is not a mind to be swayed by prejudice. She is not given to undue enthusiasm. In short, she is possessed of that poise which makes her one of the safest of companions for a man of affairs, who is about to be plunged into a historic campaign.

Mrs. Bryan has maintained her democratic principles in her household, where intelligent liberty prevails. The children are directed, but not tyrannized over. She does not believe in doing anything likely to destroy their individuality. In religion her children are taught reverence, tolerance and devotion. She has tried to teach them that it is a sacred duty to do the best they can with their lives. To educate, not to coerce, is Mrs. Bryan's simple policy.

The home of the Bryans is substantial, hospitable and well-kept. Within, one is greeted by an

16

atmosphere of unpretentious comfort, simple cordiality and unaffected refinement. The rooms are quietly and comfortably furnished. Pictures, books, statuettes, souvenirs of certain historic occasions in their lives, mementoes of distinguished persons, and gifts from admirers compose what is precious in the house. In the library there is a double desk, one side of which belongs to Mr. Bryan and one to his wife. Here they work together in their quiet hours. At times this happy intimacy has filled them with a sort of dread.

"I am not so sure I like this desk," she once said. "What should I do with it if you were to leave this life before I do? I sometimes wonder if it is not dangerous for two lives to be so bound together. How could one bear parting after such association as this?"

Mrs. Bryan is an honest student of good literature. She is one of the organizers of "Sorosis," one of the women's study clubs, and she holds its highest office. She is a prominent worker in the Nebraska State Federation of Women's Clubs, and one of a committee which has in charge the traveling library of that association. Among club women she has won no little reputation for her work. She can speak extemporaneously on any subject in which she is interested, in a calm, concise, telling manner. She will never speak for the sake of speaking, or upon a subject with which she is unacquainted.

Mrs. Bryan's attire is always very simple. She wears only quiet colors, usually browns or greys. But her costumes are becoming and effective. She always appears to be a well-dressed woman ; that is to say, no one ever thinks about her clothes at all. They are in such good taste that they are not observed. She has a sense of propriety in dress, and always wears what is suitable to the occasion. She would always dress with modest propriety, just as she always speaks with modest propriety. Even these few sentences have laid more stress upon her toilet than she ever did.

Mrs. Bryan is sociable to a degree, and heartily enjoys meeting people. She is far too wholesome to have any of the affectations of a recluse. But a purely fashionable society would never please her. She would feel the need, always, in her social relations, for intelligent conversation. Any society which did not give her this would be distasteful to her. She would be impatient with a society which stood for competition in luxury, or in which pretention was conspicuous. Moreover, her nature is too affectionate, and she is too fond of real friendship, to endure the shallow relations of fashionable society.

She has been present at all of her husband's greatest forensic triumphs. When Mr. Bryan, in the beginning of his Congressional career, made his famous tariff speech, she listened from the galleries. She was present at the Chicago Convention when he turned the tide and made an epoch in his party. She sat on the stand when he received his nomination, and showed her profound gratification only with a few quiet tears. Throughout all the tremendously exciting scenes of that day she was one of the calmest persons in the house. When she joined him at the Clifton House, where he received the news of his nomination, a silent kiss expressed her congratulations. She probably was not in the least surprised. From the first she had felt perfect confidence in his ability. It would not be in her to be surprised at having her judgment confirmed.

Mrs. Bryan is comely. Her face is pale, well modeled and placid. It resembles that of her husband in some respects. At least, it gives a similar suggestion of strength and purity. It is the face of a sensible and affectionate woman; and it is typically American.

Mr. Bryan has been very fortunate, and he has shown his appreciation of his blessings in the best way possible, by unfaltering devotion.

CHAPTER XIII.

PERILS OF THE GOLD STANDARD.

Mr. James Dobson is known to the merchants throughout the United States. He is of the great manufacturing firm of John & James Dobson, of Philadelphia. In an interview in the *New York Mail and Express* Mr. Dobson shows very clearly the evil effects of the single gold standard.

Mr. Dobson said: "In 1890 there were imported into the United States from Japan 300,000 rolls of so-called China mattings at an average cost of twelve and three-eighths cents per yard. In 1895 the importation of China mattings had increased to 800,000 rolls, at five and one-fifth cents per yard. That is equivalent to 32,000,000 yards at five and one-fifth cents, instead of at twelve and three-eighths cents five years ago, all on account of the difference in exchange caused by the separation in value of the gold and silver dollar. I repeat that the price at which these mattings are imported in such enormous quantities, supplanting our own ingrain carpets, is wholly due to the rate of exchange caused by the fact that Japan is upon a silver standard while we are upon a gold standard. Japanese silks are affecting the domestic silk trade precisely as mattings are ruining the carpet trade. Let me quote figures to prove that also. In 1890 the United States imported only 12,000 pieces of Japanese silk. In 1895 we imported 404,164 pieces, or over thirty times more. This has demoralized the silk industry of this country, and so long as the rate of exchange remains as it is no duty could be imposed high enough to check these importations. So with silk handkerchiefs. In 1890 we imported 354,000 dozen. In 1895 the importation increased to 1,100,000 dozen. That shows graphically, I think, the abnormal and alarming increase of importations. So with many other lesser articles. Why, the Japanese are supplying the world to-day with tooth brushes.

"But another great industry is threatened. The Japs have gone largely into cotton manufacturing. No nation in the world has made such rapid progress in this industry as has Japan. Their 300,000 spindles in 1894 jumped at a bound to 750,000 in 1895, and they have orders placed in England to-day for 750,000 more. That is an increase of spindles at the astonishing rate of 100 per cent. a year. So I have shown you that in the three great items of mattings, silks and cotton cloth the difference in exchange between the Japanese silver standard and our present single gold standard is ruining three great branches of American manufacturing. The South must, in time, feel this, as well as Pennsylvania,

New York and New England, for the South is destined, under normal conditions, to be the home of the cotton factory."

Mr. Dobson, who favors a protective tariff, was asked: "Cannot these increased importations be charged in part to the lower duties of the Wilson-Gorman tariff law?"

Mr. Dobson replied as follows: "Take silks alone. The rate of duty on silks is only 5 per cent. lower under the present tariff than it was under the McKinley law. That is not difference enough to multiply the silk importations of 1890 by thirty in 1895. Matting under the McKinley act paid 20 per cent. duty. Now it is admitted free. Add 20 per cent. on the first cost in Japan—four cents per yard—and it makes the cost $\frac{80}{100}$ cents per yard more, making the cost, if imported under the McKinley law, six cents per yard, and under the present law five and one-half cents per yard, the difference being in the rate of exchange from a silver to a gold standard. In other words, when gold and silver were of nearly equal value, the cost of matting was twelve and three-eighths cents, as against five and one-fifth cents to-day."

"Why does not this oriental competition affect other manufactures, such as iron and steel?"

"It will in time. When a nation like Japan first enters the markets of the world, it naturally offers for sale the cheapest and plainest fabrics, requiring the least skill to make. As soon as this field is covered, as it already is in part, the new competing nation will turn its attention to costlier fabrics, requiring more labor and skill. Most woolen goods, as well as most iron and steel products, are thus far made in countries which are like ourselves, on a gold basis; so that in these branches of industry we are not yet confronted with a bounty of 100 per cent. in favor of the manufacturer in a silver country. Gradually, eastern competition may drive the single gold standard countries into killing competition with one another, and the United States will become the dumping ground of all foreign products, unless we protect ourselves."

Mr. Dobson was asked to give some illustrations of how these importations had affected American labor.

"That is the saddest part of the tale," was the reply. Mr. Dobson led the way to a window, which he threw open. "Look down there," said he, pointing down the hill. "You see a few lights gleaming yonder in the valley. Two years ago all the surrounding blackness would have been twinkling with the lighted windows of happy and prosperous homes." The manufacturer sighed as he gazed down upon the dark Schuylkill valley, and returned to his library. He resumed: "Here are more figures, but they have human interest and carry a pathetic meaning. The present importation of China mattings would keep busy 2,500 ingrain carpet looms. That means work, directly, for 7,500 weavers, dyers and spinners. That means labor and wages for one-half the ingrain carpet workers of Philadelphia. That means that about 30,000 people are indirectly caused to suffer by the stoppage of those 2,500 looms. Not one-half of the ingrain looms in the country are running to-day. That means that thousands of trained employés are out of work. And this does not apply to the weaving of ingrain carpets alone. What affects ingrains must affect other branches of the trade. The making of tapestries and Brussels suffers as well."

Mr. Dobson was so absorbed in this branch of his subject that he closed his eyes, and talking as if to himself, plunged into a little mental arithmetic.

"Let me see, 404,000 pieces of silk would be 16,000,000 yards a year. One loom weaves sixteen yards a day. That would mean about 3,300 looms a year to make the silk we imported in 1895 from Japan alone, not to speak of China. That, I believe, is just about the number of silk looms now idle at Paterson. That throws directly out of work 10,000 people—dyers, throsters and spinners. Indirectly, that brings hardship to 50,000 people. Those disasters have not yet struck our cotton mills. But they are coming, and coming soon, and they will strike New England and check the growth of the New South."

"Mr. Dobson, will you say to what extent these

oriental importations have stopped the payment
of wages within your personal knowledge?"

"I do not like that part of my story," he replied, "but I'll tell you approximately. In 1893
our pay-roll reached $136,000 a month. Our.
mills were then running full and gave steady
work to 5,000 people. To-day our pay-roll is
$60,000 a month. By reductions of time and like
devices we managed to distribute these wages
among about 4,000 people. We take care of as
many as we can, but there is so much less for
them to do and so much less for them to earn,
and so much less for them to spend, and so much
less for I don't know how many thousand other
people to receive and to respend in their turn. I
think those figures are sadly eloquent, and they
apply only to our own local community, right
here at the falls of the Schuylkill. But think of
the other communities. Go to Kensington—
Kensington, you know, is a northern suburb of
Philadelphia, on the Delaware River. There are
Dolan & Co.'s woolen mills. I am sure that not
one-half of their people who were working on full
time at good wages in 1893 can get any work at
all now. That statement will apply to every
branch of the woolen business, excepting only the
mills that make women's fancy dress goods. Most
of those mills, I believe, are still running full.
And then think of the Paterson silk mills!"

Mr. Dobson explained that he preferred to

confine his statement to the shrinkage of pay-rolls in dollars to his own experience, but suggested that the figures he had already given carried their own inference. Then he went on:

"All this means distress to both employés and manufacturers. The employés are earning either little or nothing at all, and yet they must live, and their necessity is dire. The manufacturer suffers because his expenses are constant for insurance, maintenance of plant and other items. These expenses in the aggregate are an enormous tax upon the capital invested in these crippled industries. For example, in the neighborhood of Providence, R. I., there are seventy-five woolen mills. Of them fifty-four are standing still and the rest are running only four days a week. It is hard to put into words what distress that means to both capital and labor.

"Why, in all my experience of many years I have never seen business in such a condition as it is to-day. People won't buy goods, because they think that at another time they can buy them cheaper. There is no stability in prices. For example, only last week 10,000 cases of ginghams were sold in New York at from three and one-half to three and three-quarter cents a yard. Only a few weeks ago the price of these goods would have been to jobbers six to seven cents a yard. To-day cotton cloth for converting purposes and for export sells in the South at thirteen cents per pound. That is simply unprecedented in the annals of manufacturing."

It was suggested that it would be difficult to trace the effect of these disasters upon other classes of capital and labor in our social and industrial system.

"Yes, to their furthest extent," said Mr. Dobson, "but it is comparatively easy to see how they affect the great business of transportation. I believe that the railroads employ one per cent. of all the employés of the country. Now, when the factories of the country are not busy, they furnish less freight to the railroads, whose earnings fall off until they go into the hands of receivers. That is the condition of sixty-two per cent. of the railroads of the country to-day. Unless we manufacturers can give business to the railroads I don't see how they can pay their interest charges and prosper. This, of course, finally reaches the pockets of the stockholders, big and little, at home and abroad, and carries distress to those who had hoped to live on their invested earnings. We owe an enormous foreign indebtedness to our railroads. Many of our railroads have borrowed all they can, until almost all their rolling stock is pledged to car trusts, and they have nothing left to borrow on. Not a railroad security falls due but that is paid off by issuing a new security. In other words, they are not paying their debts, but are keeping their borrowing capacity up to its extreme limit."

CHAPTER XIV.

A VOICE FROM BOSTON.

The following is an editorial taken from the *Boot and Shoe Record*, a representative business publication at Boston :—

"It is not easy to decide whether the financial authorities (?) who control the daily press in this part of the country are stupidly ignorant or lamentably disingenuous in their statements about our alleged dependence on foreign capital or about the threatened withdrawals of foreign capital by reason of the silver scare. Now foreign capital either refuses to go to silver-using countries or it does not. It is a question of fact and not of opinion. If doing business on anything but the gold standard scares off investors, then we will certainly find the proof in a silver-using country like Mexico, where gold is counted at nearly 100 per cent. premium. In the financial columns of the Boston *Herald*, which editorially tells of the terrible things that will happen if we favor silver in the slightest degree, we find the following :—

"A city of Mexico special says : "The Bank of London and Mexico will increase its capital to $10,000,000, in order to provide funds for its growing business. It had just paid 14 per cent. dividend.

" The National Bank of Mexico has purchased Hotel De La Gran Sociedad, and is expected to build a magnificent edifice on its site.

" The Deutsche Bank of Berlin has decided to open a branch here, with ample capital, on the first day of June. There is a great interest aroused in financial circles by this attempt of the greatest bank of Central Europe to secure business in this country, and the fact that it will open a branch is taken to indicate confidence in the financial solvency and continued prosperity of this country. The new bank will be managed by Baron Bleichroeder's former agent here, Dr. Gloner, and Pablo Kosidowski, German consul.

"A new private bank will also be opened here July 1st. It is reported that when the new banking law goes into effect, permitting the establishment of banks of issue in the interior, several institutions of credit will be opened.

" The Government has a heavy balance in cash, and is meeting all its obligations with punctuality. The national revenue is exceeding all expectations.

"There is a remarkable amount of residential buildings here, and every indication of solid and permanent prosperity. Bankers report everybody well supplied with funds, and business generally very satisfactory."

Does this look like a scare or not? Are any banks in this country paying 14 per cent. dividends? Can banks here or in any gold-standard country report "everybody well supplied with funds and business generally very satisfactory," or not? Isn't it about time that the hard-headed business men of the country used their common sense and stopped cowering like frightened children at the bug-a-boo threats of the great editors? Could we not stand a good deal of that kind of ruin and disaster?

Referring again to the evidence from Japan, we have the statements of Hon. Robert P. Porter, who has just returned from that country, where he has been investigating the industrial conditions. He says that he deems the question of Japanese competition one of the momentous problems that the American nation will have to solve, and that the danger lies not so much in the present competition in the undeveloped state of Japanese resources as in the enormous rapidity of the growth of the Japanese output in all lines of manufacture which they enter. Ten years ago, according to Mr. Porter, the whole Japanese trade amounted to $78,000,000, while last year it had increased to $300,000,000. The export of textiles alone increased from $511,000 to $23,-000,000 in the ten years.

The really important point to be noted in regard to this mass of evidence from Mexico,

Japan, and in fact from all the silver-using countries, is that the remarkable development has
been made during the last ten years, or since the
marked decline in the gold value of silver. In
the case of Japan, that country, by reason of the
commercial treaties forced upon it by England,
was prevented from levying protective duties on
imports. The native industries were able to
make but little headway against the imports from
Europe, and for fifty years there was no progress
to speak of. When England succeeded in forcing the gold standard on other countries and silver was displaced, the premium on gold in Japan
operated as a protective duty of about 100 per
cent. This gave the stimulus needed, and, as the
evidence proves, the development has been
something wonderful. Of course, great industries cannot be built up in a year, and we do not
feel much of the force of Japanese competition
as yet, but given another ten years, at the same
rate of progress, and how will our industries bear
up against it?

An editorial in the Boston *Herald*, on the subject of "Competition with Asia," admits the facts
as to the stimulating effect of the silver currency,
and also the fact that "to purchase the ordinary
country supplies an ounce of silver in the form of
coin will go nearly as far in the form of compensation as it would when the same ounce was
worth, as bullion, nearly twice as much as it is at

the present time, and this under conditions in one form or another of nearly free coinage." The editor attempts to explain this by the lack of intelligence and scant means of communication in those countries, so that the mass of the people do not realize the depreciation of silver. This would be plausible if it could be shown on the other hand that prices of ordinary country supplies in the gold-using countries had not fallen and the silver alone of all commodities had declined in value when measured in gold. As this is not true, and as the fact of the ruinous decline in all prices measured in gold is beyond dispute, the proof is absolute that the change in value is in the gold rather than in the silver.

Of course, the *Herald* yearns for the wage-earner. It continues that if we brought our currency to the Chinese basis, employers would pay wages in silver the equivalent of fifty cents in gold for what they are now paying 100 cents in gold. This, it claims, would be robbing the wage-earner. This is another form of the old stock free trade argument, which assumes that employers carry on business for the sole and only purpose of paying wages, and that the amount of wages paid is entirely optional with the employer, having no reference to profit or the selling prices of the products. Wages are considered as fixed and arbitrary, and political economy is, in effect, the science of giving the cheap-

17

est prices or the most goods for the wages. The employers are always despots, who can be forced to sell at low prices while paying the highest wages. It is hardly necessary to point out the absurdity of such assumptions. A few weeks since, for example, it was announced that the Baldwin Straw Plating Works, at Milford, Conn., had arranged to ship their entire machinery to Japan, as they were unable to continue the competition here. Will this concern maintain an office in Milford and continue paying wages to the old employés in gold or not? If not, how much do the wage-earners benefit by the gold standard? When manufacturers of silk, cotton, woolen, iron, leather, boots and shoes and other lines, find it profitable to follow the Baldwin example, who will continue to pay wages at 100 cents in gold to the idle workman? Where will the gain for the wage-earners come in?

What is the use of trying to keep up such humbug arguments? The people must come to their senses sooner or later. They must learn that employer cannot be separated from wage-earner, and that the latter depends absolutely on the prosperity of the former. Why not admit the fact that the gold standard and disuse of silver is forcing an unequal and ruinous competition in all industries? Every gold-using country feels it, and the people cannot always submit to be made slaves of the money-lenders, who exact their "pound of flesh nearest the heart." Let us have some fair discussion, instead of special pleading by the interested organ ; and for the good of common humanity, let us honestly seek an honest remedy.

CHAPTER XV.

CERNUSCHI ON THE ISSUE.

Henri Cernuschi was the famous French writer who won fame as a champion of international bimetallism and an opponent of independent bimetallism by any single nation. He has been frequently quoted by advocates of the gold standard in this country in their endeavor to combat the arguments of the advocates of " 16 to 1." The following is one of the last of Cernuschi's contributions : From the Paris *Economiste*.

"I have always combated the uncompromising silver men of America, who at bottom are really silver monometallists, because from the scientific point of view, their doctrine is as fallacious as that of the gold monometallists.

" The adoption of the free coinage of silver by the United States alone would, it is true, increase to a formidable extent the contingent of silver monometallic countries, but would not immediately bring about a true solution of the problem that international bimetallism has in view—namely, the instantaneous fusion of the two monetary standards in a single international money by the establishment of a fixed parity of value between gold and silver.

284

"With silver monometallism in the United States, the war to the knife between gold and silver will agitate yet for many years the civilized world, and you know as well as I do that the results of this struggle will be disastrous to those European countries which are at present living under a single gold standard, and in particular to England and France.

"I have always been the adversary of the out-and-out silver men of America, that is to say, the party which demands the free coinage of the silver dollar in the United States without reference to the action of European nations, because their monetary conception is diametrically opposed to mine. They are monometallists, like the monometallists of the city of London, and the triumph of their cause, so far from putting an end to the monetary anarchy in which the world has been writhing since 1873, will merely accentuate it, in rendering more burdensome for Europe the economic consequences of the diverge.

"But if I were a citizen of the United States and were convinced that Europe, by reason of England's attitude, is fixedly hostile to the establishment of a stable monetary parity between gold and silver, obstinately rejecting all ideas of international bimetallic agreement, then I should cease to be an international bimetallist (which nearly all my friends in the United States are), and should go over unhesitatingly to the camp of the silver men.

"As a matter of fact, in its present economic situation, the United States of America, that great and youthful nation, suffers much more from the merciless conflict that has been in progress between gold and silver since 1873 than England—a very wealthy country, creditor of the rest of the world, possessing resources of every kind and enormous financial reserves, which enable her to endure with comparative ease the economic competition of those nations whose monetary standard is depreciated in regard to gold, like the countries of the far east, Mexico, the Argentine Republic, etc.

"The United States of America, on the contrary, are debtors to Europe for a portion of the sums which they have employed in the development of their industrial system, and must necessarily liquidate their debts abroad by realizing upon the products of their soil and of their manufactures.

"Now, as their foreign debts are, on the one hand, contracted in gold, and as, on the other, American products in Europe have to reckon with the depressing competition of similar products exported by other countries having a silver standard or paper money, it follows that the appreciation of gold, in regard to silver, that has taken place since 1873, has had a two-fold result for the United States—which have remained faithful to the single gold standard since that date—namely: First—it has diminished by half, on American territory, the value in gold of all the national products which are subject to the said competition; and, second, it has doubled the real burden of the debts contracted abroad in gold, since double the quantity of American products is now required to discharge the annual liabilities arising from those debts.

"The native products of England have evidently felt the depressing influence of the same competition with similar products from countries whose monetary standard has been depreciated in regard to gold, and in this respect English agriculturists and manufacturers are prejudicially affected in the same way as the agriculturists and manufacturers of the United States. For this reason, an understanding between the two countries looking to the re-establishment of the equilibrium between the two monetary standards, and the maintenance of a stable parity of exchange for the future, was logical, reasonable and desirable for the world at large.

" But, if the interests of English agriculturists and manufacturers are seriously affected by the competition of countries having a depreciated monetary standard, the exterior finances of the United Kingdom do not suffer thereby, since England has no debts contracted abroad, and, in this respect at least, the English escape that particular evil from which the finances of the United States of America suffer so cruelly.

"Furthermore, England being a large creditor of foreign countries, the London bankers can argue—as Sir William Harcourt did in so categorical a manner in his speech of March 17th last in the House of Commons—that the English capitalists recover, by the increasing purchasing power of the gold due them from abroad, the amount which, owing to the fall in the gold price of products imported into England by debtor countries, is lost by the agriculturists and manufacturers of the United Kingdom.

"Is that the case with the United States of America? No, most assuredly not! for they are debtors in gold to foreign countries, and it is with the proceeds of these same products, the gold prices of which have been depreciated by the competition of silver standard or paper money countries, that they are obliged to pay their foreign debt.

"Therefore, the present monetary situation in the United States is doubly unfavorable to the economic interests of that great nation, since, owing to the state of affairs now obtaining, the gold standard countries of Europe, and particularly the manufacturing countries like England, find it enormously advantageous to purchase their raw materials in those countries whose standard depreciated with regard to gold, like Asiatic countries, Russia or the Argentine Republic, and, on the other hand, to sell their manufactured products in the American market, where they are paid for in gold currency.

"The present monetary policy of the United States is consequently very advantageous to the interests of England, a gold monometallic country, but it is utterly ruinous as regards the foreign financial relations of the United States, and especially for its native producers.

"This is why, inasmuch as England's attitude prevents the realization of international bimetallism and condemns one-half of the world to gold monometallism and the other half to silver mono metallism, I would not hesitate, were I a citizen of the United States, to become—I, Cernuschi, the father of international bimetallism, as I am everywhere called—a silver monometallist.

"From a theoretical point of view, the free coinage of silver at 16 to 1, re-established by the United States without the concurrence of Europe, would be a vicious solution, but it would nevertheless be a step in the direction of international bimetallism; for, under the regime of the new standard, the productive power of the United States would receive so enormous an impulse, and this development would have such a disastrous effect upon the economic and financial interests of England and the other European nations now governed by the gold standard, that it may be confidently predicted in advance, that the course of events would force the adoption of international bimetallism as the only true solution even upon those who to-day deny the possibility and efficacy of it."   HENRI CERNUSCHI.

CHAPTER XVI.

JOHN M. THURSTON ON MONEY.

The Republican National Convention for 1896, held in the city of St. Louis, selected a distinguished citizen of Nebraska to preside over its deliberations. Senator John M. Thurston needs no introduction to the people of the United States, and as the permanent chairman of the Republican National Convention, his utterances on the money question will be of more than ordinary interest.

By way of preface, and in exact justice to Senator Thurston, it should be said that there is no record showing that he declared explicitly in favor of the free and unlimited coinage of silver at the ratio of 16 to 1 ; but he seems to have regarded the question of the ratio as of secondary importance, while at the same time he favored restricting the coinage to the American product. But Senator Thurston's utterances on the money question, up to and including the very day of his election to the United States Senate, were directly, emphatically and explicitly antagonistic to the single gold standard.

In a letter addressed to Hon. J. Burrows, of

Lincoln, Nebraska, under date of July, 1893, Mr. Thurston said :—

"I am a profound believer in the use of both gold and silver as money. I advocated the restoration of free coinage before any of those who are now the self-selected champions of silver in Nebraska had ever opened their lips on the subject. At the opening of the corn palace in Sioux City, four years ago, I said :—

"At the risk of being tedious, I ask your careful attention to the presentation of another grave question, which, in my judgment, is of such momentous importance to the entire West that all our people should join in vigorous efforts to secure its early and favorable solution.

"We of the West must have cheap money, not money intrinsically cheap, but cheap in interest charges for its use.

"We are money borrowers, and we need vast sums with which to hasten the development of our wonderful resources.

"We have good security to give, and neither repudiation nor bankruptcy is to be feared.

"But the amount of money in circulation is becoming inadequate for the daily commercial necessities of the country. It is almost impossible to-day for our local banks to accommodate their regular customers at 10 per cent. They have not a dollar to loan on the best paper to anyone else.

"In popular parlance, 'money is scarce.'

"The country grows so fast that the demand increases almost by multiplication.

"An inadequate circulating medium adds to the relative value of the dollar, and cheapens the relative value of everything else.

"Every debtor must work harder or sell more property to meet his obligations than he otherwise would.

*   *   *   *   *   *   *

"But our mountain ranges produce a metal which, until a few years ago, was money the wide world over.   Silver was one of the standard coins of the United States from the birth of independence until its demonetization crept into the statutes of Congress, either by mistake or fraud.

"I assert that the American people, and especially those of the West, demand the free and unlimited coinage of silver.   I do not mean that the financial affairs of the country should be carried on by the actual use of silver, for it has been demonstrated that the silver certificates answer better.   Nor am I certain that the present standard should be adhered to.   But let us restore the law which made silver a legal tender for all debts, public and private.   Let us give the right to any man to deposit the bullion in the Treasury and receive for it certificates redeemable in silver coin, and the great problem of an adequate, flexible and stable currency is solved.

"The assertion that a government can have too much money, is not reliable. Inflation by issuance of irredeemable paper is one thing; expansion by coinage is another. If we coin all the silver produced in America, over and above what is used in manufactures and the arts, we will not any more than keep pace with the increased demands of our business growth. Every dollar issued in exchange for silver bullion will find its way into circulation and a new era of prosperity begin.

"From time to time thereafter, before the various Republican clubs and organizations in the United States, I maintained substantially the same views. My present position is quite fully set forth in a letter addressed by me to George Gunton, editor of *Social Economist*, New York City, on July 7, 1893, a copy of which I hereto attach."

On July 7, 1893, Mr. Thurston addressed a letter to George Gunton, editor of *The Social Economist*, No. 34 Union Square, New York City, in which Mr. Thurston said :—

"I have no doubt the remonetization of silver in the United States would speedily and certainly appreciate the price of silver, not only in this country, but throughout the whole world. No matter what other governments do, this country ought not to eliminate silver from use as a coin metal. Any legislation in that direction will be looked upon by the common people as in the in-

terest of the money power for the express purpose of increasing the purchasing power of money
and decreasing the selling price of everything
produced by human toil. It is a fact, which should
not be overlooked by statesmen, that the price of
American silver and the price of American wheat
reached low water mark on the same day.

＊　　＊　　＊　　＊　　＊　　＊　　＊

"Economists insist that the volume of money
in a country has nothing to do with the intrinsic
value of the dollar, and this is true so far as the
intrinsic value of the coin is concerned, but the
amount of money in circulation in a country has
almost everything to do with the interest rate on
money, with the ability to borrow money for use
in manufactures, improvements and speculation.
Since the recent monetary scare many branches
of industry have been closed to American workmen because of the inability of the manufacturers
to borrow money from the banks as heretofore,
and this, because a large part of the actual money
in the country had been taken out of circulation
by the panic. Small depositors have withdrawn
their money from the banks, and the deposit
vaults of the country have in them to-day millions
of dollars which, three months ago, were on deposit in our banks. Therefore, the interest rate
has increased and it is difficult, in most communities, to borrow money on any reasonable terms.

The result is stagnation of business, stoppage of all kinds of enterprises, and in a very short time thousands of American workmen will be out of employment.

     *   *   *   *   *   *   *

"The recent events, instead of bringing me to believe in the single gold standard, have had quite the opposite result. For the world at large to abandon the use of silver as money would be to greatly enhance the power of gold; to greatly diminish the volume of money, and thereby the borrowing classes and the producing classes would be more at the mercy of the money holders than they ever have been heretofore. The United States is a silver-producing country, and I do not believe it can afford to let those nations not silver producing compel it to abandon silver as a money.

"It is better that we should, if necessary, buy gold at a premium to settle our foreign balances with than that the American people should be compelled to pay higher prices in human labor and in human endeavor for a dollar because of the adoption of the single gold standard. I am an advocate of the American theory. We are not dependent either for manufactures or money on the outside world."

In an interview printed in the Omaha *World-Herald* of Monday, June 11, 1894, Mr. Thurston said :—

"So far as I am concerned, I think I only disagree with such Republicans as ex-President Harrison upon the question as to what steps ought to be first instituted to bring the commercial world back to the use of both gold and silver. He believes that it must be done through a monetary conference with the great commercial powers. In my judgment the United States can safely take the initiative by providing for the coinage of its own silver, and I believe that such action on its part would, within a comparatively short time, drive the other great countries of the world to similar action, and speedily pave the way for a monetary conference, which would establish gold and silver as the money of the world and fix the ratio for generations to come."

On January 16, 1895, Mr. Thurston addressed the Legislature of the State of Nebraska in formal acknowledgment of his election to the United States Senate. On that occasion Mr. Thurston said :—

"I would put a stop to the outflow of gold from the treasury; first, by requiring that all import duties should be paid in gold at the option of the treasurer of the United States; and, second, by insisting upon the right of redemption in either gold or silver, of outstanding notes, whenever it becomes apparent that redemption is being demanded for speculative purposes. It is said that such a policy would drive gold to a premium. In my judgment, we can better afford to have gold at a premium than prosperity at a discount.   *   *   *   *   *   *

"More money on hand than is necessary to supply the business demands may reduce interest rates, but the people can easily stand that. The bankers and the capitalists should not have power to contract the volume of currency in circulation or corner the money market of the country. I do not agree with those who would retire our greenbacks and treasury notes. I am in favor of keeping every one of them in circulation, and there can be no danger in so doing if we will adopt the policy already stated of meeting all speculative demands for redemption by tender of either gold or silver, at the option of the government, in accordance with the specific terms of the contract.

"I am in favor of American bimetallism, and in this the United States should lead the world.

"My position upon the American silver question has been thoroughly understood by the people of the State, and I accept my election by the united vote of the great Republican majority in the Legislature as an indorsement of my ante-election declaration in favor of coining the American product of gold and silver into honest dollars. To those who fear the effect of the American silver coinage, I have this to say: We are not realizing financial prosperty under existing gold monometallism, and it is worth our while to try the experiment of a return to bimetallism."

18

CHAPTER XVII.

MORETON FREWEN ON THE ISSUE.

(From the London *Financial News* of May 29, 1896.)

"It may be well to notice an error into which many persons ignorant of the currency question have fallen. They accuse the committee of desiring to rob the present public creditors in order to make up for the injury done to the public debtors in 1819. To such parties the committee recommends an inquiry as to how far the present relations and obligations of society are in accordance with the present gold coinage; and they will find that what the committee desires is to prevent further appreciation, or further robbery of the debtors, and not to rob the public creditor. The average of prices and wages is still about 25 per cent. above the present gold standard. It is the attempt at a further reduction which causes the present universal embarrassment. * * * Will or can the agricultural and commercial classes submit to this reduction? And, if so, would it be possible to collect the amount of revenue required by the government?"—From the memorial of the Birmingham Chamber of Commerce, addressed to Sir Robert Peel, December 2, 1842.

"To the Editor of the *News*—Sir: Your interesting leader of the 21st, upon the currency situation in the United States, may be shortly summed up in the following theses: (1) That no legislation by the United States, single-handed, can establish a parity between gold and silver; (2) That the free coinage of silver in the United States involves silver monometallism; (3) That gold monometallism is to be preferred to silver monometallism. Now, in the opinion of the silver party in the United States, if (1) is sound, (2) an honest silver currency such as Germany had until 1873, and India until 1893, is infinitely preferable to (3) an appreciating gold currency, even if—which is more than doubtful—that gold currency can be maintained at all. As a general statement of the financial position of the United States it may be said that she owes annually these interest payments: $150,000,000 on loans, $75,000,000 remittances to travelers and absentees, $75,000,000 to foreign ship-owners: so that either her exports have to exceed her imports by £60,000,000 sterling or she loses gold, or, failing this, she has to borrow to pay the interest, thus piling higher the permanent interest charges.

"I venture to think that the debts of this nation of 70,000,000 people are even larger than I have stated them. The general condition of financial

strain, and consequent political unrest in the
United States seems to be not less than is now
the case in Australia, where the annual interest
paid abroad by 4,000,000 people is known to be
some £15,000,000 sterling. If we take, for
example, the state of California; this state is in
population, in resources and climate about the
peer of New South Wales. The annual indebtedness of New South Wales is officially stated at
£5,000,000 sterling. May not the debt of California to New York and to Europe be about the
same? and, if so, how can California any more
than New South Wales permanently sustain the
burden of a 50 per cent. fall of prices, which fall
must have exactly doubled the burden of her
external debt? Thus the one issue in the United
States—which includes the other issues, such as
the mere color of her money and the fiscal
methods by which her revenue shall be collected
—the one paramount issue is this : How can the
United States secure a sufficient balance of exports to continue solvent? Now, I contend that
if, as you admit to be the case the world over, a
depreciating currency stimulates exports and
contracts imports, then that portion of public
opinion in America which favors silver rather
than gold is intelligent. For scheme, and re-ad-
just, and tinker with the tariffs as you will, you
cannot make a silk purse out of a sow's ear ; you
cannot restore the balance of trade to the United

States unless her currency legislation is such that
it drags up the exchanges between Europe and
Asia ; whereas every further movement, in
America or elsewhere, toward gold monometallism drags those exchanges down. In short,
gold monometallism in the United States involves
an increased competition for the industries of
white men everywhere, at the hands of the yellow races of the orient ; and there is not a consu-
lar report which comes to us from the far east
but emphasizes this statement. What, then, is
the argument for single-handed free coinage in
the United States? It is this. Either free coinage will establish bimetallism for the whole world,
or, failing this, there will be such a gold premium
in New York as to-day assists exporters in Russia, in all Asia, and in nine-tenths of South
America.

"This gold premium, unlike a protective tariff,
will stimulate the exports of the United States,
while acting, just as a protective tariff does, to
reduce imports ; therefore, either free coinage will
give bimetallism to the whole world, or, failing
this, it will tend to secure that excess of American exports over imports, which is the only possible alternative to further gold loans, leading to
ultimate insolvency. These, then, are the arguments which favor a non-appreciating, or even a
depreciating, currency in the United States. On
the other hand, I do not see, *qua* its economic

aspects, what possible advantage can accrue from a gold standard and a gold currency. A gold currency in America cannot raise—it cannot, indeed, fail to further depress—the European exchanges with 800,000,000 of Asiatic exporters. It cannot, therefore, fail to still further throw the balance of trade against the United States, unless, indeed, by further contracting the American currency, it forces down prices there to such a point as to contract violently America's import trades. And a pretty look-out for England that! In short, the clamor of our press that America shall become gold monometallic, seems to involve either the insolvency of our greatest debtor or the decline of our export trades to America, or both.

"There is this further point which you emphasize—that if America copies our gold standard 'confidence will be restored,' and we will lend her more money ; thus aggravating in the future the very disease from which she suffers. On the other hand, if she goes to free coinage we shall, in a panic, return her securities, and thus sell her back her railways and industrials at half price, just at that very moment when, her legislation having sent the rupee, the tael, and the yen to nearly, or quite, par, the export trades of the orient will be cut into, and the exports of the American farm, mine and factory will take their place. In other words, because of the inane

injunctions of a portion of the London press, our
investors there will be so misled as to sell
American stocks to Americans at that very moment when in America prosperity is about to set
in.   You remark that I describe America as 'the
greatest debtor nation on earth,' and you add
'that one fact is conclusive against taking any
course tending to lower its national credit.'   But
would free silver lower its credit, even should it
involve a gold premium ?   It certainly would not,
if trade and agriculture there improved, and the
railways did a larger business at better rates.
The credit of a country is not determined by its
currency, but by its prosperity.   Thus India's
credit, the rate at which she borrows, has greatly
improved side by side with the depreciation of
her currency.   So also has Russia's.   Of the
Argentine and Brazil it is not too much to say
that incontrovertible paper issues, and the stimulus thus afforded their exports because of depreciation, has alone enabled these countries to
continue paying the interest on their foreign
loans.   And what is lacking in the United States
is not really the lenders' confidence in the currency ; it is rather the conviction of both bor-
rower and lender that money invested in a farm
or factory will earn no profit ; that the pains and
perils of a fresh 'resumption' period are just
ahead ; and that while prices over there are even
now depressed below the point of possible profit,

they must be depressed 25 per cent. further yet before imports, under any tariff, can be so checked as to permit gold to remain at home in the currency. And, further than this, let me ask how, if imports are to be checked by a high tariff, is the necessary revenue to be secured for the Federal Government? If then, as I believe, the critical position of the United States results from the present conditions of exchange between Europe and Asia, and can only be remedied by some action which will raise those exchanges, much may be said for the policy of free silver, even should that policy involve a gold premium in New York. It is not the exporter from America who will be hurt by that premium; it is the exporter to America—in other words, the English manufacturer. But let me go further and ask your reasons for believing that the United States is unable to maintain the parity of 1 to 16, assuming, as we may assume, that if the American mints open to the free coinage of dollars, we shall open mints to the free coinage of rupees. Are there any scientific grounds for the conviction, so generally held, that such a monetary union as this bimetallism in America and silver monometallism in India would fail to maintain the world's parity. I do not venture, of course, to dogmatize as to this; but the problem is so interesting and the experiment by the United States—whether next year or in 1901—is so extremely probable, that it is worth while for those who hold that the experiment would be attended with disaster, to offer something for our consideration more convincing than prophecies.

" In the first place, then, free coinage in America would bring the Asiatic exchanges promptly to par—for the moment, at least—and assuming that you are right, and that there would be panic sales of American securities held here, perhaps £40,000,000 sterling of American gold would flow into Europe. This great flood of gold would be likely to inflate prices here to some extent, to thus increase the exports from the United States, and also to reduce the gold premium at Buenos Ayres and elsewhere, thus checking exports of wheat, etc., which compete with similar exports from America. And, again, the prodigious rise in the exchange with Asia would expand European exports to Asia, and, until gold prices here had risen, would greatly contract exports from Asia to Europe. Thus a double influence favorable to the balance of trade in the United States would be exerted. The United States would export more to England because Asia would export less, and thus America's gold as well as her securities, would go back to her. Secondly, because England, selling more goods to Asia, the rupee, the dollar, and the yen being at par, England could then also buy more produce from the United States. Thus, while free coinage in the

United States might, in the first place, tend to displace gold, there would almost simultaneously be exerted an even more powerful tendency for gold to be shipped west from Europe in order to liquidate what it seems to me must be an immense trade balance in favor of the United States. As to the absurd idea one frequently encounters, that Asia will dump silver upon the American mints and carry off gold, it is hardly necessary to examine this fallacy. It is for the objectors to show why Asia should give the metal which to her alone is money in order to buy the other metal which is not money; and why also the white metal should be withdrawn from the hoards of the orient at that moment when it appreciates, in order that it may be exchanged for the yellow metal, which has just depreciated almost one-half in terms of rupees.

"The present Lord Aldenham (then Mr. Hucks Gibbs), in his evidence before the currency commission in 1886, declared that, in his judgment, America with open mints could maintain the parity without help. There is no one who has had a larger practical experience of exchange problems than Mr. Gibbs; there is no one whose opinion is more entitled to respect. And since that evidence was given what have we seen? On a certain Monday in June, 1893, we saw the two metals at a parity of 1 to 24; on the Friday of that week the parity had become 1 to 30½. And why? Because the Indian mints had been closed to free coinage. Now, it is not possible to argue seriously that, while the closing of the Indian mints had thus enormously reduced the gold price of silver, yet the reopening of those mints would have failed to bring about a rise; so that it is fair to assume, that if between Monday and Friday the ratio fell from 1 to 24 to 1 to 30½, then between Friday and Tuesday, had the Indian mints been reopened, the ratio would have risen from 1 to 30½ to 1 to 24. And supposing, further, that on the Tuesday the United States had accepted free coinage at 1 to 16, is it inherently improbable that such a vast country, with such a boundless exporting capacity, could have lifted silver to 58½d?

"Permit me to recapitulate. The difference between open mints and closed mints in India has been demonstrated by the experiment of 1893 to be silver at 30½d and silver at 38½d, and, this having been ascertained, is it the folly, is it the lunacy, is it the dishonesty that the New York press so glibly declares it, if we venture to hold that the difference between open mints in the United States and closed mints in the United States, is the entire difference between 38½d and 58½d? In other words, if India contributes a 25 per cent. life to silver by giving it free coinage, why cannot America contribute a further 50 per cent? Why cannot she lift the ratio from 1 to 24 to 1 to 16? What, permit me to ask, with much respect, is your view as to this? We are

aware that you favor bimetallism, and not merely
' by and by metallism.' Either a monetary union
over a strictly limited area will establish the
parity, or, if not, then the whole system is chi-
merical; because if bimetallism needs to be
universal, then, also, it follows that our opponents
are correct in declaring that the system is imprac-
ticable, because the defection of one of two war-
ring nations would serve to destroy it.

"The new French Prime Minister, M. Meline,
when pointing to the rapid spread and acceptance by experts of the bimetallic theorem,
declared that what alone is now needed is the
'electric spark.' Such an electric spark may
very well prove to be a free-coinage plank in
the national Democratic convention, which met
at Chicago, on July 7th. For even if the Republican party should elect its president, still that plank,
unless countered by a similar move in the Republican party, will certainly secure to the Democratic
party the control until 1900 of the all important
senate; whereas, on the other hand, the monometallist counsels of Mr. Cleveland and Secretary
Carlisle, should they dominate the party at
Chicago, will both leave in that party the record
of a disgraceful surrender and will leave of that
party for a generation to come not one stone
standing upon another.

"Such is the great exchange crisis which to-day
confronts the whole world of trade. Its effects

on international trade, still dimly perceived, are probably infinitely greater and more complicated than any of us at all appreciate. We have seen, with the great rise in the gold premium at Buenos Ayres since 1890, the wheat area in that country increase from 2,990,000 acres in 1891 to 7,141,-000 acres in 1895; while in the same period the wheat exports jumped up from less than 2,000,-000 quarters to nearly 8,000,000 quarters. Here is a competition which, while the press is shouting for 'honest money,' has made Kansas and Minnesota not less desolate than Essex and Lincolnshire. On the other hand, we saw, in 1893, an artificial, a manipulated, rise in the exchanges between India and the far east strike the milling industries in Bombay as by lightning; so that 30,000 operatives there were thrown out of work in a few weeks, while yarn exports from Bombay fell off one-third, and the government of India was obliged to come to England because of the exchange disturbance and the contraction of exports, exactly as America has to-day to come to England, because of the contraction of her exports, in order to borrow gold. We have seen these experiments in exchange; we have seen experts, such as Mr. Hermann Schmidt, exactly foretell, in evidence before royal commissions, the results which were to follow from these experiments; and yet silly people there are who still declare that steady exchanges with four-fifths of mankind are immaterial, because 'international trade is merely international barter.'

"Let me only add, in conclusion, that Europe and America are indeed to be congratulated if, because of the intuitions of the common people in the western republic, we are now very near the dawn of better days. At a time when political leaders the world over are, as never before in history, disappointed and disgraced, the western nations, unguided and unguarded, groping in the dark as to the magnitude of the issues involved, have come within an ace of being routed and their industries decimated by that exchange crisis which has given their silver money to our oriental competitors at half price. If, then, we succeed in evading the greatest race danger with which we have ever been confronted, we shall owe our escape, not to our statesmen, who have failed us, but to the detection of pseudo-liberalism, false economics, and half-truths (worse than any lies) by the great American nation. Not without reason did Lincoln declare of that nation : 'You may fool some of them all the time, but not all of them all the time.' 'Everyone,' said Lincoln, again, 'knows more than anyone !' an utterance which, no doubt, his successor, the present occupant of the White House, and his 'cuckoo' cabinet consider frankly blasphemous.

"Yours faithfully,

"MORETON FREWEN.

"White's Club, London, May 25, 1896."

CHAPTER XVIII.

THE CHICAGO CONVENTION.

The Democratic National Convention for 1896, which had been called to meet in Chicago, July 7th, was destined by political conditions to be the most important gathering of the kind in recent years. The interest in the financial question had grown so rapidly during Mr. Cleveland's second administration that it became the one topic of national consideration. The action of the Republican National Convention at St. Louis, in June, in declaring for a single gold standard gave an impetus to the movement for a declaration for free silver coinage by the Democratic Convention. The people had listened to arguments on the important issue, had read and studied the question, and had discussed it among themselves until there was a demand by them that the issue must be fairly and honestly met at the polls.

The silver sentiment had taken a more aggressive form in the Democratic party than in its formidable competitor, and as the latter had gone on record for a gold standard, the democracy was looked to to take up the cause of silver. In every state convention held to select delegates to the National Convention, this one question was uppermost. No surprise was shown by the opponents of free coinage when the friends of silver secured the delegations from the Western States, but when that sentiment gave evidence of sweeping the Middle and some of the Eastern States, there was much alarm among the advocates of gold.

The Democratic national administration was for the gold standard, and used its power to enable that sentiment to control the National Convention. The repeated issuance of bonds by the administration to uphold the gold standard, thereby increasing the national debt to a startling extent, aroused the people to a sense of the need of a change in the financial policy of the Government. The result showed that this sentiment did not exist alone in the States which mined silver, as had been so frequently urged by the enemies of free coinage. Bimetallism carried the silver States, the Western States, with but two exceptions, the Southern States, and passed on into the enemy's camp, and carried all the Middle States but two. So strong did the movement become that it was conceded weeks before the National Convention met that the free-coinage men would control by a large majority.

The body which met at Chicago was a deliberative one, realizing at the outset that it had an important issue to meet, and that whatever position the party took on the question, there would inevitably be a great deal of dissatisfaction, followed by a bolt on the part of many prominent Democrats. It was composed of cool and determined men, who went there with a purpose, and bent on carrying that purpose out. They were not to be swayed from what they considered their duty, by personal friendship, local pride or political precedent. They held that new conditions had come into existence, requiring new men, new ideas, and new methods of party procedure. They worked upon this line, and the Democratic national ticket and platform of 1896 are the result. The convention met at noon, Tuesday, and did not adjourn till late the following Saturday afternoon. There was a contest royal from the moment the convention was originally called to order, till the fall of the gavel announced the dissolution.

Mr. Bryan was one of the duly-elected delegates-at-large from Nebraska, but his seat, and those of his delegation, were contested by a faction of the Democratic party in that State which had bolted from the regular organization, and called themselves "Administration Democrats," favoring a gold standard. This contest was acted upon by the National Committee previous to the assembling of the convention, and that organization being controlled by gold standard men, the contesting delegation was seated, forcing the regular delegation to take seats among the spectators in the convention.

Hon. William F. Harrity, of Pennsylvania, Chairman of the National Committee, called the convention to order at noon on Tuesday, July 7th, and after the usual formalities attending the opening of such a meeting, announced that the National Committee had selected Senator David B. Hill, of New York, as temporary chairman.

The silver men, being in a majority in the convention, refused to accept a single-standard man as the temporary presiding officer, even when he was possessed of the eminent ability and character of the senior senator from the Empire State, and presented as their choice, Senator John W. Daniel, of Virginia.

This action was contrary to precedent in Democratic conventions, but this convention was not following precedent. It was establishing precedent and making history for future conventions. A discussion was precipitated upon the phases of the question which continued all afternoon. Upon roll call, the silver men triumphed in their first contest, Senator Daniel being chosen to preside temporarily over the convention by a vote of 556, to 349 for Senator Hill.

The customary committees were selected, after which the first day's session came to an end.

The convention was slow in getting to work on Wednesday, owing to delay by committees in making their reports. After a few hours the committee on credentials sent in a partial report recommending the seating of the regular delegation from Nebraska, of which Mr. Bryan was a member, and this report was adopted by the convention without division. The departing of the contesting delegation, and the coming of the regular delegation, was the occasion for the first demonstration for Mr. Bryan, who, however, was not present at the time, being engaged with the committee on resolutions in preparing a platform.

Later, the committee on credentials reported in favor of seating four contesting silver delegates from Michigan, and this report was discussed during the larger part of the afternoon, being eventually adopted. With that, the work of this particular committee ended.

Permanent organization was then perfected by the election of Senator Stephen M. White, of California, as permanent chairman, after which the convention adjourned till Thursday.

Thursday morning the committee on resolutions reported. Senator J. K. Jones, of Arkansas, presented the majority report, embracing the free-silver plank, and Senator D. B. Hill presented the minority report, which called for the maintenance of the present gold standard until an international agreement could be reached for the free coinage of silver.

The committee had agreed to set aside two hours and forty minutes for debate on the platform, one hour and twenty minutes on a side.

Senator B. R. Tillman, of South Carolina, opened
the discussion for the silver men, followed by
Senator Jones, of Arkansas. Senator D. B. Hill
opened for the gold standard side, followed by
Senator William F. Vilas, of Wisconsin, and Ex-
Gov. William E. Russell, of Massachusetts. Mr.
Bryan closed for the silver men and closed the
debate. The discussion proved to be a forensic
contest of surpassing interest and of wonderful
force. Mr. Bryan's address on that occasion, and
a description of the manner in which it was received, can be best given by republishing the
report which appeared in the Chicago *Times-
Herald* the morning after the discussion, which
was as follows:

"The Silver Knight of the West," William
Jennings Bryan, of Nebraska, set the convention
on fire with a speech, which was followed by a
demonstration which never will be forgotten by
the 16,000 persons who witnessed it and partici-
pated therein.

Up to this time the convention had not been
dull for want of effective oratory. The tearful
and pleading Colonel Fellows, of New York; the
fiery and impulsive Blackburn, of Kentucky; the
forceful and aggressive Altgeld, of Illinois; and
such famous orators as Hill, Russell, Waller and
White had scored their triumphs and added new
leaves to their laurel wreaths. But when compared to the impassioned oratory of the " Black

Eagle of Nebraska," newly named "The Silver Knight of the West," the efforts were tame.

A reputation as an orator may prove either an advantage or a handicap to its possessor. From such a man the listener expects much. Woe is in store for such an orator if his effort fail to meet the sanguine expectations of the auditor, and triumph is sure if he reaches the heralded heights which have been promised. Bryan established a reputation as an orator in the scattered hamlets on the Nebraska plains and it wafted him into Congress. In one term he set a new mark for congressional eloquence. Yesterday, he set another new mark.

Senator Hill was given a storm of applause before he spoke ; Bryan, a cyclone of enthusiasm when he had concluded. When quiet had been restored by the chairman, Mr. Bryan then addressed the convention.

CHAPTER XIX.

SPEECH DELIVERED BY

HON. WILLIAM J. BRYAN

OF NEBRASKA

BEFORE THE DEMOCRATIC NATIONAL CONVENTION

JULY 9, 1896

— — —.

Mr. Chairman and Gentlemen of the Convention:

"I would be presumptuous, indeed, to pre-sent myself against the distinguished gentlemen to whom you have listened if this was a mere measuring of abilities ; but this is not a contest between persons. The humblest citizen in all the land, when clad in the armor of a righteous cause, is stronger than all the hosts of error. I come to speak to you in defense of a cause as holy as the cause of liberty—the cause of humanity.

"When this debate is concluded a motion will be made to lay upon the table the resolution offered in commendation of the administration and also the resolution offered in condemnation of the administration. We object to bringing this question down to the level of persons. The individual is but an atom ; he is born, he acts, he dies ;

318

but principles are eternal; and this has been a contest over a principle.

"Never before in the history of this country has there been witnessed such a contest as that through which we have just passed. Never before in the history of American politics has a great issue been fought out, as this issue has been, by the voters of a great party. On the fourth of March, 1895, a few Democrats, most of them members of Congress, issued an address to the Democrats of the nation, asserting that the money question was the paramount issue of the hour; declaring that a majority of the Democratic party had the right to control the action of the party on this paramount issue; and concluding with the request that the believers in the free coinage of silver in the Democratic party should organize, take charge of, and control the policy of the Democratic party. Three months later, at Memphis, an organization was perfected, and the silver Democrats went forth openly, courageously proclaiming their belief, and declaring that, if successful, they would crystallize into a platform the declaration which they had made. Then began the conflict. With a zeal approaching the zeal which inspired the crusaders who followed Peter the Hermit, our silver Democrats went forth from victory unto victory until they are now assembled, not to discuss, not to debate, but to enter up the judgment already rendered by the plain people of this country. In this contest brother has been arrayed against brother, father against son. The warmest ties of love, acquaintance and association have been disregarded ; old leaders have been cast aside when they have refused to give expression to the sentiments of those whom they would lead, and new leaders have sprung up to give direction to this cause of truth. Thus has the contest been waged, and we have assembled here under as binding and solemn instructions as were ever imposed upon representatives of the people.

"We do not come as individuals. As individuals we might have been glad to compliment the gentleman from New York (Senator Hill), but we know that the people for whom we speak would never be willing to put him in a position where he could thwart the will of the Democratic party. I say it was not a question of persons ; it was a question of principle, and it is not with gladness, my friends, that we find ourselves brought into conflict with those that are now arrayed on the other side.

"The gentleman who preceded me (ex-Governor Russell) spoke of the State of Massachusetts ; let me assure him that not one present in all this convention entertains the least hostility to the people of the State of Massachusetts, but we stand here representing people who are the equals before the law of the greatest citizens of the

State of Massachusetts. When you (turning to the gold delegates) come before us and tell us that we are about to disturb your business interests, we reply that you have disturbed our business interests by your course.

"We say to you that you have made the definition of a business man too limited in its application. The man who is employed for wages is as much a business man as his employer ; the attorney in a country town is as much a business man as the corporation counsel in a great metropolis ; the merchant at the cross-roads store is as much a business man as the merchant of New York ; the farmer who goes forth in the morning and toils all day—who begins in the spring and toils all summer—and who by the application of brain and muscle to the natural resources of the country creates wealth, is as much a business man as the man who goes upon the board of trade and bets upon the price of grain ; the miners who go down a thousand feet into the earth, or climb two thousand feet upon the cliffs, and bring forth from their hiding places the precious metals to be poured into the channels of trade are as much business men as the few financial magnates who, in a back room, corner the money of the world. We come to speak for this broader class of business men.

"Ah, my friends, we say not one word against those who live upon the Atlantic Coast, but the hardy pioneers who have braved all the dangers of the wilderness, who have made the desert to blossom as the rose—the pioneers away out there (pointing to the West), who rear their children near to Nature's heart, where they can mingle their voices with the voices of the birds—out there where they have erected school-houses for the education of their young, churches where they praise their Creator, and cemeteries where rest the ashes of their dead—these people, we say, are as deserving of the consideration of our party, as any people in this country. It is for these that we speak. We do not come as aggres-sors. Our war is not a war of conquest; we are fighting in the defense of our homes, our families and posterity. We have petitioned, and our petitions have been scorned; we have entreated, and our entreaties have been disregarded; we have begged, and they have mocked when our calamity came. We beg no longer; we entreat no more; we petition no more. We defy them.

"The gentleman from Wisconsin has said that he fears a Robespierre. My friends, in this land of the free, you need not fear that a tyrant will spring up from among the people. What we need is an Andrew Jackson to stand, as Jackson stood, against the encroachments of organized wealth.

"They tell us that this platform was made to catch votes. We reply to them, that changing conditions make new issues ; that the principles upon which Democracy rests, are as everlasting as the hills, but that they must be applied to new conditions as they arise. Conditions have arisen, and we are here to meet those conditions. They tell us that the income tax ought not to be brought in here ; that it is a new idea. They criticise us for our criticism of the Supreme Court of the United States. My friends, we have not criticised ; we have simply called attention to what you already know. If you want criticisms, read the dissenting opinions of the court. There you will find criticisms. They say that we passed an unconstitutional law ; we deny it. The income tax law was not unconstitutional when it was passed ; it was not unconstitutional when it went before the Supreme Court for the first time ; it did not become unconstitutional, until one of the judges changed his mind, and we cannot be expected to know when a judge will change his mind. The income tax is just. It simply intends to put the burdens of government justly upon the backs of the people. I am in favor of an income tax. When I find a man who is not willing to bear his share of the burdens of the government which protects him, I find a man who is unworthy to enjoy the blessings of a government like ours.

"They say that we are opposing national bank currency; it is true. If you will read what

Thomas Benton said, you will find he said that, in searching history, he could find but one parallel to Andrew Jackson ; that was Cicero who destroyed the conspiracy of Cataline and saved Rome. Benton said that Cicero only did for Rome what Jackson did for us when he destroyed the bank conspiracy and saved America. We say in our platform that we believe that the right to coin and issue money is a function of government. We believe it. We believe that it is a part of sovereignty, and can no more with safety be delegated to private individuals than we could afford to delegate to private individuals the power to make penal statutes or levy taxes. Mr. Jefferson, who was once regarded as good Democratic authority, seems to have differed in opinion from the gentleman who has addressed us on the part of the minority. Those who are opposed to this proposition tell us that the issue of paper money is a function of the bank, and that the Government ought to go out of the banking business. I stand with Jefferson rather than with them, and tell them, as he did, that the issue of money is a function of government, and that the banks ought to go out of the governing business.

"They complain about the plank which declares against life tenure in office. They have tried to strain it to mean that which it does not mean. What we oppose by that plank is the life tenure which is being built up in Washington, and which excludes from participation in official benefits the humbler members of society.

"Let me call your attention to two or three important things. The gentleman from New York says that he will propose an amendment to the platform, providing that the proposed change in our monetary system shall not effect contracts already made. Let me remind you that there is no intention of affecting those contracts which according to present laws are made payable in gold but if he means to say that we cannot change our monetary system without protecting those who have loaned money before the change was made, I desire to ask him where, in law or in morals, he can find justification for not protecting the debtors when the act of 1873 was passed, if he now insists that we must protect the creditors.

"He says he will also propose an amendment which will provide for the suspension of free coinage if we fail to maintain the parity within a year. We reply that when we advocate a policy which we believe will be successful, we are not compelled to raise a doubt as to our own sincerity by suggesting what we shall do if we fail. I ask him, if he would apply his logic to us, why he does not apply it to himself. He says he wants this country to try to secure an international agreement. Why does he not tell us what he is going to do if he fails to secure an international agreement? There is more reason for him to do that than there is for us to provide against the failure to maintain the parity. Our opponents have tried for twenty years to secure an international agreement, and those are waiting for it most patiently who do not want it at all.

"And now, my friends, let me come to the paramount issue. If they ask us why it is that we say more on the money question than we say upon the tariff question, I reply that, if protection has slain its thousands, the gold standard has slain its tens of thousands. If they ask us why we do not embody in our platform all the things that we believe in, we reply, that when we have restored the money of the constitution, all other necessary reforms will be possible ; but, that until this is done, there is no other reform that can be accomplished.

"Why is it, that within three months, such a change has come over the country? Three months ago, when it was confidently asserted that those who believe in the gold standard would frame our platform and nominate our candidates, even the advocates of the gold standard did not think that we could elect a president. And they had good reason for their doubt, because there is scarcely a State here to-day, asking for the gold standard, which is not in the absolute control of the Republican party. But note the change. Mr. McKinley was nominated at St. Louis, upon a platform which declared for the maintenance of the gold standard, until it can be changed into bi-

metallism by international agreement. Mr. Mc-
Kinley was the most popular man among the
Republicans, and three months ago, everybody
in the Republican party prophesied his election.
How is it to-day? Why, the man who was once
pleased to think that he looked like Napoleon—
that man shudders to-day, when he remembers
that he was nominated on the anniversary of
the battle of Waterloo. Not only that, but as he
listens, he can hear with ever-increasing distinct-
ness, the sound of the waves as they beat upon
the lonely shores of St. Helena.

" Why this change? Ah, my friends, is not the
reason for the change evident to any one who
will look at the matter? No private character,
however pure, no personal popularity, however
great, can protect from the avenging wrath of an
indignant people, a man who will declare that he
is in favor of fastening the gold standard upon
this country, or who is willing to surrender the
right of self-government, and place the legislative
control of our affairs in the hands of foreign
potentates and powers.

" We go forth confident that we shall win.
Why? Because upon the paramount issue of
this campaign there is not a spot of ground upon
which the enemy will dare to challenge battle. If
they tell us that the gold standard is a good thing,
we shall point to their platform and tell them that
their platform pledges the party to get rid of the

gold standard and substitute bimetallism. If the
gold standard is a good thing, why try to get rid
of it? I call your attention to the fact that some
of the very people who are in this convention to-
day, and who tell us that we ought to declare in
favor of international bimetallism—thereby declaring that the gold standard is wrong and that the
principle of bimetallism is better—these very
people, four months ago, were open and avowed
advocates of the gold standard, and were then
telling us that we could not legislate two metals
together, even with the aid of all the world. If
the gold standard is a good thing, we ought to
declare in favor of its retention, and not in favor
of abandoning it; and if the gold standard is a
bad thing, why should we wait until other nations
are willing to help us to let go? Here is the line
of battle, and we care not upon which issue they
force the fight; we are prepared to meet them,
on either issue or on both. If they tell us that
the gold standard is the standard of civilization,
we reply to them that this, the most enlightened
of all the nations of the earth, has never declared
for a gold standard, and that both the great parties this year are declaring against it. If the gold
standard is the standard of civilization, why, my
friends, should we not have it? If they come to
meet us on that issue, we can present the history
of our nation. More than that; we can tell them
that they will search the pages of history in vain

to find a single instance where the common people of any land have ever declared themselves in favor of the gold standard. They can find where the holders of fixed investments have declared for a gold standard, but not where the masses have.

"Mr. Carlisle said, in 1878, that this was a struggle between 'the idle holders of idle capital' and 'the struggling masses, who produce the wealth and pay the taxes of the country,' and, my friends, the question we are to decide is: Upon which side will the Democratic party fight: upon the side of the 'idle holders of idle capital,' or upon the side of 'the struggling masses?' That is the question which the party must answer first, and then it must be answered by each individual hereafter. The sympathies of the Democratic party, as shown by the platform, are on the side of the struggling masses who have ever been the foundation of the Democratic party. There are two ideas of government. There are those who believe that, if you will only legislate to make the well-to-do prosperous, their prosperity will leak through on those below. The Democratic idea, however, has been that if you legislate to make the masses prosperous, their prosperity will find its way up through every class which rests upon them.

"You come to us and tell us that the great cities are in favor of the gold standard; we reply
20

that the great cities rest upon our broad and fertile prairies. Burn down your cities and leave our farms and your cities will spring up again as if by magic; but destroy our farms and the grass will grow in the streets of every city in the country.

"My friends, we declare that this nation is able to legislate for its own people on every question, without waiting for the aid or consent of any other nation on earth ; and upon that issue we expect to carry every State in the Union. I shall not slander the inhabitants of the fair State of Massachusetts nor the inhabitants of the State of New York by saying that, when they are confronted with the proposition, they will declare that this nation is not able to attend to its own business. It is the issue of 1776 over again. Our ancestors, when but three millions in number, had the courage to declare their political independence of every other nation; shall we, their descendants, when we have grown to seventy millions, declare that we are less independent than our forefathers ? No, my friends, that will never be the verdict of our people. Therefore, we care not upon what lines the battle is fought. If they say bimetallism is good, but that we cannot have it until other nations help us, we reply that, instead of having a gold standard because England has, we will restore bimetallism and then let England have bimetallism because the United States has it. If they dare to come out in the open field and defend the gold standard as a good thing, we will fight them to the uttermost. Having behind us the producing masses of this nation and the world, supported by the commercial interests, the laboring interests and the toilers everywhere, we will answer their demand for a gold standard by saying to them: 'You shall not press down upon the brow of labor this crown of thorns; you shall not crucify mankind upon a cross of gold.'"

CHAPTER XX.

CONVENTION—Continued.

At the conclusion of this speech there was a demonstration, the like of which had never been seen in a convention, and which is also best described by again calling upon the Chicago *Times-Herald*, that paper reporting the scene in this language:

"Nebraska was the central star around which all other silver delegations clustered, in the midst of the popular demonstration to the orator from the Platte Country. Chairman Smyth, of the Nebraska delegation, grasped the hand of Bryan when he returned from the stage, pale with victory and excitement. In another instant Smyth was on his chair waving the blue Nebraska standard with an energy born of ecstasy. The members of the Nebraska delegation pulled red bandannas from their pockets and waved them enthusiastically. The sight of the emblem of 'the old Roman' used in former campaigns, awakened the Ohio delegation across the aisle.

"Bush, of Georgia, bewhiskered and strong of lung, ran down the aisle with the Georgia standard toward the Nebraska chairs. A wild yell from the rear of the hall disclosed Joe Lacy, the dark-skinned Cherokee delegate from the Indian Territory corner, causing a panic in the New York delegation, through whose ranks this Indian plunged at breakneck speed with the territory standard, in an attempt to beat the Georgian to Bryan's side. Like a Tammany brave, this child of the southwest, walked all over dignity and feet of the passive New Yorkers, and reached the Nebraska section second.

"Then came the colors of Illinois, South Dakota, Missouri, Virginia, Alabama, Kentucky, Ohio, Iowa, Tennessee, Mississippi, Michigan, Utah, Nevada, Colorado and others in quick sequence.

"Standing on chairs and yelling at the full capacity of lung power, the men who held the delegation standards reached as high as possible in their effort to reach the roof of the building. Bo Sweeney, of Colorado, six feet three inches from head to heel, shoved his long arm up near the rafters, while Hugh Brady pushed the colors of Missouri against those of Nebraska, to kiss the emblem of the new conqueror. Then Alabama led a grand march of glory around the delegates' pit. It was a parade of silver States fencing in the Bryan boom, and framing the hopes of the young Nebraskan with the shadows of coming events.

"Bryan was carried off his feet in the rush. The air in his vicinity was a kaleidoscope of big hands, all eager to congratulate him. Some felt

honored to touch the hem of his alpaca coat.
They surged and jostled him into the North
Dakota delegation, three rows from his seat.
Eight brawny men, including Buck Hinrichsen, of
Illinois; Oldham, of Nebraska, and McLaurin, of
Mississippi, grasped him and lifted him upon their
shoulders. Bryan was physically a heavy load.
It was like lifting an ice wagon, or a Graceo-
Roman wrestling match with an upright piano in
a moving van.

"On the shoulders of his admirers Bryan en-
deavored to fold his arms and look pleasant, but
his bulk caused the support beneath him to
shake, and he grabbed the shoulders of his supporters in much the same manner as a passenger
seizes the last strap on an 'L' train at the
Sixty-third street curve.

"At his own request they lowered him to the
floor. In an instant the Nebraskan was the center of a stampede. The delegates swarmed
around him and blockaded every inch of space.
They sat on his lap, hugged him until his collar
wilted, shook his hand, shouted into his ears,
danced all over his feet and hemmed him in until he could scarcely get his breath.

"Virginia came to him and announced that the
old dominion delegation would vote for him and
desert Bland. Then came Georgia, Mississippi,
and other States. News came from the Ohio
boys that McLean had released them to vote for

whom they pleased. Before adjournment, twenty Bryan votes had materialized in Ohio.

"With face flushed with excitement into a deeper, darker red, the giant of the Georgia delegation returned to his seat, after planting the standard of the Southern States in its old place. His chest was extended with pride and his eyes shone with pleased delight. He had reason to be proud. It was he, Dr. E. B. Bush, who had led the demonstration of States. It was he who had carried the Georgia standard to the Nebraska fold and planted it among the Bryan delegates as a token of the enthusiasm and admiration of the Southern men for the silver orator. It was his example that brought the standards of the other silver States around Mr. Bryan in a wild wave of delight, such as had not often before been witnessed at a National Convention.

"Carried away by his own delirious enthusiasm for the orator and the excitement of the moment, his giant form leaped into the arena of victorious applause, and he brought with him a rushing, shouting, cheering mob of standard-bearers. As the leader of the standard-bearers, Dr. Bush leaped into fame in the few bounds needed to carry him to the Nebraska delegation. A moment before he had been simply the distinct delegate from Miller County, Georgia.

" 'When I am not here,' he said, 'I am in the Georgia penitentiary.'

"This did not mean that he had laid aside the stripes and hard labor and donned the badge of a delegate to the Democratic National Convention. Dr. Bush is the chief physician of the Georgia penitentiary, and only leaves his duties when the National Convention opens. He little thought he would become the leader this year of an extraordinary demonstration over the oratorical effort of William J. Bryan.

"Then the Georgia delegates began to send telegrams to their friends in the South, which read: 'Bryan will be nominated. He is the best man.' And this was the sentiment of the Georgia delegation after hearing the Nebraska man's speech. The Georgians said they were ready to throw the mantle of charity over New York, and to entreat it to return to the fold.

"The feeling that Bryan would be nominated on the second or third ballot was general among the delegates of those States, the standards of which had been planted in front of the Nebraska orator, with the exception of those who were pledged to favorite sons. The latter considered the demonstration only one of appreciation and pleasure at the eloquent speech of Mr. Bryan.

"Maine did not pluck its standard from its rest, but a feeling grew among the delegates that Mr. Bryan was the only silver man they would care to vote for. And then some of them said they would cast their ballots for him any way.

"Ollie M. James, chairman of the Kentucky delegation, was another man who shared somewhat in the honors that fell to the lot of Dr. Bush. After shouting himself hoarse in the waving of the standards in the Nebraska fold he led the march down the aisles and round the floor of the convention hall. It was meant only as a compliment to Mr. Bryan on his eloquent and masterly argument for free silver, he said, but he also thought the Nebraska man would be a dangerous rival for the other presidential candidates.

"Mississippi was not far from the Nebraska fold, but it was not until the giant of Georgia had leaped to the front that R. H. Henry clambered over his fellow-delegates and seized the standard. 'The demonstration was simply one of earnest admiration for the eloquence of Mr. Bryan,' said Governor McLaurin, 'and I do not think it means his nomination as President.'

" But some of the other Mississippi delegates were looking favorably on the Nebraska man as the solution of the difficulty caused by the multitude of favorite sons.

" Michigan delegates—the silver men, not the four gold delegates-at-large—were to the front in the demonstration. George P. Hummer, the silver man from Michigan who led the fight before the national committee in favor of seating the silver men, carried the standard to Nebraska. And he was ready to vote for Bryan if the latter's

name came up for nomination. And so all the
Michigan delegates talked, with the exception of
the gold men.

"Missouri was not backward in applauding
Bryan, and it sent J. D. Gibson to join the procession of the standards.

"The Boies men from Iowa were caught in the
swirl of enthusiasm and joined the procession.

"J. C. Rich was the man who carried the Idaho
standard. He said it was the feeling of the State
that Bryan would be nominated. So did Bo
Sweeney, who got in the procession of the standards for California.

"Alabama was so enthusiastic that two men—
A. H. Keller and J. A. Roundtree—carried the
standard to Nebraska. Alabama was delirious
for Bryan, and talked about having the nominating speech made by a member of the delegation.

"Louisiana sent Joseph St. Amant to the front
with the standard, and he thought Bryan would
be nominated. Sam Taylor seized the standard
for Arkansas and almost carried pledges for
Bryan as the nominee of the party. W. S. Hope-
well, of New Mexico, felt the same way, as well
as his fellow-delegates. J. G. Johnson, of Kansas,
the standard-bearer in the demonstration, was too
enthusiastic about Bryan to think of any other
possible nominee. Colonel R. W. Davis, of
Florida, carried off the standard because he wanted to be in the hurrah. And so it seemed with
other silver States."

A roll of the states was called on the resolutions, and the minority report was rejected,
the majority report being immediately afterward
adopted, and the money question was then and
there made the issue of the campaign. The
Platform is as follows :

We, the Democrats of the United States, in
national convention assemble to reaffirm our allegiance to those great essential princip'es of justice
and liberty upon which our institutions are founded, and which the great Democratic party has
advocated from Jefferson's time to our own—freedom of speech, freedom of the press, freedom of
conscience, the preservation of personal rights,
the equality of all citizens before the law, and
the faithful observance of constitutional limitations.

During all these years the Democratic party
has resisted the tendency of selfish interests to
the centralization of governmental power and
steadfastly maintained the integrity of the dual
scheme of government established by the founders of this republic of republics. Under its guidance and teachings the great principle of local
self-government has found its best expression in
the maintenance of the rights of the States and
in its assertion of the necessity of confining the
General Government to the exercise of the powers granted by the Constitution of the United
States.

The Constitution of the United States guarantees to every citizen the rights of civil and religious liberty. The Democratic party has always been the exponent of political liberty and religious freedom, and it renews its obligations and reaffirms its devotion to these fundamental principles of the Constitution.

Recognizing that the money system is paramount to all others at this time, we invite attention to the fact that the Federal Constitution names. silver and gold together as the money metals of the United States, and that the first coinage law passed by Congress under the Constitution, made the silver dollar the monetary unit, and admitted gold to free coinage at a ratio based upon the silver dollar unit.

We declare that the act of 1873 demonetizing silver without the knowledge or approval of the American people has resulted in the appreciation of gold, and a corresponding fall in the price of commodities produced by the people; a heavy increase in the burden of taxation, and of all debts, public and private; the enrichment of the money-lending class at home and abroad; prostration of industry and impoverishment of the people.

We are unalterably opposed to monometallism, which has locked fast the prosperity of an industrial people in the paralysis of hard times. Gold monometallism is a British policy, and its adoption has brought other nations into financial servitude to London. It is not only un-American, but anti-

American, and it can be fastened on the United States only by the stifling of that spirit and love of liberty which proclaimed our political independence in 1776 and won it in the War of the Revolution.

We demand the free and unlimited coinage of both silver and gold at the present legal ratio of 16 to 1, without waiting for the aid or consent of any other nation. We demand that the standard silver dollar shall be a full legal tender equally with gold for all debts, public and private, and we favor such legislation as will prevent for the future the demonetization of any kind of legal tender money by private contract.

We are opposed to the policy and practice of surrendering to the holders of obligations of the United States the option reserved by law to the Government of redeeming such obligations in either silver coin or gold coin.

We are opposed to the issuing of interest-bearing bonds of the United States in time of peace, and condemn the trafficking with banking syndicates, which in exchange for bonds and at an enormous profit to themselves, supply the Federal Treasury with gold to maintain the policy of gold monometallism.

Congress alone has the power to coin and issue money, and President Jackson declared that this power could not be delegated to corporations or individuals.

We, therefore, denounce the issuance of notes intended to circulate as money by national banks as in derogation of the Constitution, and we demand that all paper which is made a legal tender for public and private debts, or which is receivable for dues to the United States, shall be issued by the Government of the United States and shall be redeemable in coin.

We hold that tariff duties should be levied for purposes of revenue, such duties to be so adjusted as to operate equally throughout the country. and not discriminate between class or section, and that taxation should be limited by the needs of the Government honestly and economically administered. We denounce as disturbing to business the Republican threat to restore the McKinley law, which has been twice condemned by the people in national elections, and which, enacted under the false plea of protection to home industry, proved a prolific breeder of trusts and monopolies, enriched the few at the expense of the many, restricted trade, and deprived the producers of the great American staples of access to their natural markets. Until the money question is settled we are opposed to any agitation for further changes in our tariff laws, except such as are necessary to make up the deficit in revenue caused by the adverse decision of the Supreme Court on the income tax.

There would be no deficit in the revenue but

for the annulment by the Supreme Court of a law passed by a Democratic Congress in strict pursuance of the uniform decisions of that court for nearly one hundred years, that court having under that decision sustained constitutional objections to its enactment which have been overruled by the ablest Judges who had ever sat on that bench.

We declare that it is the duty of Congress to use all the constitutional power which remains after that decision, or which may come from its reversal by the court as it may hereafter be constituted, so that the burdens of taxation may be equally and impartially laid to the end that wealth may bear its proportion of the expenses of the Government.

We hold that the most efficient way of protecting American labor is to prevent the importation of foreign pauper labor to compete with it in the home market, and that the value of the home market to our American farmers and artisans is greatly reduced by a vicious monetary system which depresses the prices of their products below the cost of production and thus deprives them of the means of purchasing the products of our home manufactures, and as labor creates the wealth of the country we demand the passage of such laws as may be necessary to protect it in all its rights.

The absorption of wealth by the few, the con-

solidation of our leading railroad systems, and
the formation of trusts and pools require a stricter
control by the Federal Government of those arteries of commerce. We demand the enlarge-
ment of the powers of the Interstate Commerce
Commission and such restrictions and guarantees
in the control of railroads as will protect the
people from robbery and oppression.

We are in favor of the arbitration of differences between employers engaged in interstate
commerce and their employés, and recommend
such legislation as is necessary to carry out this
principle.

We denounce the profligate waste of the money
wrung from the people by oppressive taxation and
the lavish appropriations of recent Republican
Congresses, which have kept taxes high, while
the labor that pays them is unemployed and the
products of the people's toil are depressed in
prices till they no longer repay the cost of production. We demand a return to that simplicity
and economy which befit a democratic government and a reduction in the number of useless
offices, the salaries of which drain the substance
of the people.

We denounce the arbitrary interference by
Federal authorities in local affairs as a violation of
the Constitution of the United States and a crime
against free institutions, and we especially object
to government by injunction as a new and highly

dangerous form of oppression, by which Federal
Judges, in contempt of the laws of the States and
rights of citizens, become at once legislators,
Judges and executioners, and we approve the bill
passed at the last session of the United States
Senate, and now pending in the House, relative
to contempts in Federal courts and providing for
trials by jury in certain cases of contempt.

No discrimination should be indulged in by the
Government of the United States in favor of any
of its debtors. We approve of the refusal of the
Fifty-third Congress to pass the Pacific railroads
funding bill, and denounce the effort of the present Republican Congress to enact a similar
measure.

Recognizing the just claims of deserving Union
soldiers, we heartily indorse the rule of the present Commissioner of Pensions, that no names shall
be arbitrarily dropped from the pension roll, and
the fact of enlistment and service should be
deemed conclusive evidence against disease and
disability before the enlistment.

We favor the admission of the Territories of
New Mexico, Arizona and Oklahoma into the
Union as States, and we favor the early admission
of all the Territories having the necessary population and resources to entitle them to Statehood,
and while they remain Territories we hold that the ·
officials appointed to administer the government
of any Territory, together with the District of

Columbia and Alaska, should be *bona-fide* residents of the Territory or District in which their duties are to be performed. The Democratic party believes in home rule, and that all public lands of the United States should be appropriated to the establishment of free homes for American citizens.

We recommend that the Territory of Alaska be granted a delegate in Congress, and that the general land and timber laws of the United States be extended to said Territory.

The Monroe doctrine, as originally declared, and as interpreted by succeeding Presidents, is a permanent part of the foreign policy of the United States, and must at all times be maintained.

We extend our sympathy to the people of Cuba in their heroic struggle for liberty and independence.

We are opposed to life tenure in the public service. We favor appointments based upon merit, fixed terms of office, and such an administration of the civil service laws as will afford equal opportunities to all citizens of ascertained fitness.

We declare it to be the unwritten law of this Republic, established by custom and usage of one hundred years, and sanctioned by the example of the greatest and wisest of those who founded and have maintained our Government, that no man should be eligible for a third term of the Presidential office.

The Federal Government should care for and improve the Mississippi River and other great waterways of the Republic, so as to secure for the interior States easy and cheap transportation to tide-water. When any waterway of the Republic is of sufficient importance to demand aid of the Government, such aid should be extended upon a definite plan of continuous work until permanent improvement is secured.

Confiding in the justice of our cause and the necessity of its success at the polls, we submit the foregoing declaration of principles and purposes to the considerate judgment of the American people. We invite the support of all citizens who approve them and who desire to have them made effective through legislation for the relief of the people and the restoration of the country's prosperity.

After the adoption of the platform, the convention took a recess till evening.

Previous to this time the convention had not considered Mr. Bryan as a presidential nominee, but conditions had changed. States volunteered their support if his name should be presented. His name seemed to be upon the lips of everybody in the convention city, and the prediction was freely made that evening that he would be the nominee. Many States, which had no favorite sons of their own, and had not been committed to one of the other avowed candidates, were anx

ious for the honor to present the name of Mr.
Bryan as a candidate. There was no plan, and
no organization, but a genuine spontaneous sentiment that he was the logical candidate, made so
by the developments in the convention, and supported by his years of zealous work on the lines
laid down in the platform adopted. The delegates
claimed that the only organization they needed
was an opportunity to vote for him, Mr. Bryan.
This feeling did not decrease during the recess,
but gained strength as the convention proceeded
with its deliberations.

Upon reassembling in the evening, it was
decided to devote the time to the presentation of
candidates for the presidential nomination. In
pursuance of this plan, these names were placed
before the convention :

Richard P. Bland, of Missouri ; Horace Boies,
of Iowa ; Governor Claude Matthews, of Indiana ; .
John R. McLean, of Ohio ; Senator J. S. Blackburn, of Kentucky ; Robert E. Pattison, of Pennsylvania ; Sylvester Pennoyer, of Oregon, and
W. J. Bryan, of Nebraska.

All the oratory which Iowa could boast of tried
to enthuse the convention for Gov. Boies, and
failed utterly. Then a young woman took the
matter up and succeeded gloriously.

She was Minnie Murray, of Nashua, Floyd Co.,
Ia., and after Boies' name had been duly put in
nomination and both delegates and gallery had

received it in an apathetic sort of way, she stood up in her seat at the extreme southern end of the convention and in two minutes had converted that crowd of 20,000 people from an orderly assembly into a howling mob.

Miss Murray is tall and strong. She has the beauty which always goes with good health, and the attractiveness which is a necessary part of enthusiasm. And last night she was enthusiastic. She was dressed all in white, and, after the cold reception which had greeted the nomination of Boies had become so pronounced as to be almost painful, she did the only thing which could have been done to rescue her favorite candidate from what seemed an unfortunate situation.

With her eyes ablaze with enthusiasm and every fibre in her frame trembling with excitement, she stretched out her hands so that the white muslin sleeves fell back from her arms and began shouting for Boies.

Her voice was clear and could be heard. How she did shout! Some one near by handed her a small American flag, and she waved it frantically over her head, waved it so strongly that the stick was broken in an instant. By this time there was a crowd around her and a dozen more flags were reached to her at once. Then she had two and she waved them both, but again the sticks broke and again she had to be supplied with more.

By this time she had aroused the convention.

She was the focus of 20,000 pairs of eyes, and 10,000 people seemed, each one, to be trying to excel her in cheering for the candidate from Iowa. Every delegate was on his feet, the galleries were in an uproar, and from all over that vast hall went up one mighty roar, of which this Iowa girl was both the inciter and the controlling spirit.

By this time the band had begun to play. The crowd shouted in chorus, and Miss Murray waved her flags in time with the air. The Iowa delegates were already parading the hall with a large banner, on it a picture of Gov. Boies, and they made straight for this enthusiastic girl, who was so loyally backing up their cause. The banner was handed to her, and, although it was heavy, and she had been using every nerve and muscle she possessed for fully fifteen minutes, yet she grasped the big standard and swung the silken folds back and forth in the air.

Then that crowd did yell. It seemed as if it would take off the roof, and from everywhere and every side went up the shout of, "Three cheers for the girl in the white dress."

But there was more work for Miss Murray to do yet. The Iowa delegates insisted she must come down on the floor, so they put her and her companion, Miss Margaret Gorman, also of Nashua, at their head, and with these two girls as their standard-bearers marched through the aisles of the delegates' seats. Then, when the shouting was done, they gave the two women seats in their delegation.

Miss Murray, with Miss Gorman, runs a weekly newspaper in Nashua called the *Reporter*. They are each about twenty-two years old, as bright as they make girls out in Iowa, which is saying a good deal, and they conduct a lively paper. They are editors, reporters, proprietors, and business managers, and it is devoted to home news and local gossip. In politics it is independent, but Miss Murray is a strong supporter of Governor Boies, having been a personal friend of his daughter, now dead, and a frequent visitor at the Governor's home in Waterloo. She was born and raised in Iowa, and, as she expressed it last night, went into the newspaper business three years ago for the purpose of making a living.

Speaking of the affair after it was all over she said :—

" Nobody is as much surprised as I am at what I did. We all love Horace Boies out in Iowa, and when his name was being cheered there was not enough noise to suit me in our part of the hall. In order to do all I could I got up on a chair and hurrahed just as loud as I could. There was a Missouri flag near by, but they refused to let me have it, so I got a smaller one. I didn't know I was attracting so much attention until they brought the banner up to where I sat."

The act was undoubtedly absolutely without

premeditation. It was that of a spirited, enthusiastic girl, whose whole soul was wrapped up in what was going on.

Georgia, the first of the States to pledge its solid vote for him, furnished the man to place Mr. Bryan's name before the convention in H. T. Lewis, one of the delegates from that State. The nomination was seconded by Theodore F. Klutz, of North Carolina; George Fred Williams, of Massachusetts, and Thomas J. Kernan, of Louisiana.

The nominations were not completed till after 12 o'clock that night, and the convention adjourned until the next morning.

Friday was the fourth day of the deliberations, and it was fraught with much that will make the convention noteworthy in the political history of the country. There had been little campaigning for the individual candidates previous to this day, as had been customary in conventions of this character. The almost universal feeling among the delegates had been that a platform of principles should be framed which would best meet the existing political conditions, and then find a candidate to fit the platform. The first and most important part of the work was completed. The next step was to be taken. The delegates had nothing else to do after a night for rest and reflection but calmly consider the many candidates before them, and select the one they thought best represented the spirit of the platform, and would best interpret it to the people. A roll call was ordered, and the work upon which so much depended, and upon which the eyes of a nation were turned, was begun.

The result of the first ballot was as follows: Bland 235, Boies 85, Matthews 37, McLean 54, Bryan 119, Blackburn 83, Pattison 95, Pennoyer 8, Teller 8, Hill 1, Russell 2, Campbell 1, Stevenson 7, Tillman 17, not voting 178.

All of the delegates from New York and New Jersey, and part of those from Connecticut, Delaware, Maine, Maryland, Massachusetts, Michigan, Minnesota, New Hampshire, Rhode Island, Vermont and Wisconsin, refused to vote for a candidate for president, giving as a reason that they could not endorse the platform adopted by the convention. With varying numbers they maintained that position throughout the balloting.

The second ballot resulted as follows: Bland 283, Boies 41, Matthews 33, McLean 53, Bryan 190, Blackburn 41, Pattison 100, scattering and not voting 189.

The third ballot: Bland 291, Boies 36, Matthews 36, McLean 54, Bryan 219, Blackburn 27, Pattison 97, scattering and not voting 172.

The fourth ballot: Bland 241, Boies 33, Matthews 36, McLean 46, Bryan 280, Blackburn 27, Pattison 97, scattering and not voting 170.

Bryan was now in the lead and confusion

reigned in the convention hall. It became apparent he was destined to be the winner and
Blackburn and McLean both withdrew and threw
their strength to the Nebraska man. It was some
time before sufficient order could be secured in
the convention to permit another roll call. When
it was ordered it resulted as follows :

Bland 106, Boies 26, Matthews 31, Bryan 500,
Pattison 95, scattering and not voting 170.

It required 512 votes to secure a nomination
and Mr. Bryan just lacked 12 at the completion of
the roll call, but there was a stampede at this
time by States which changed their votes to Mr.
Bryan, giving him the nomination without question, which was afterward made by acclamation
on the part of those participating in the convention.

The reader will pardon a further reproduction
from the report in the Chicago *Times-Herald* at
this time, reading as follows :

"Without any motion the chairman then declared an informal recess of an indefinite length,
and the convention readily fell into the scheme in
order to permit the Bryan men to give vent to
their enthusiasm, which had not all escaped in the
previous demonstration made by them in favor of
their candidate. Every person in the hall arose
to his or her feet, and, almost too tired to yell,
still sent up a shout for the Nebraska man. Once
more the procession of the standards paraded
about the hall, all taking part in the march but
those of Rhode Island, Pennsylvania, New York,

Hon. HORACE BOIES,
Ex-Governor of Iowa.

Hon. ADLAI E. STEVENSON,
Vice-President of the United States.

New Jersey, New Hampshire, Maine, Wisconsin, Massachusetts, Delaware and Connecticut, which remained solidly rooted in their places, while the crowd seethed and shrieked around them.

The Bland Marching Club and its band, which had been headed off many a time from parading through the hall, now got in their fine work and headed the procession. With 'Marching Through Georgia' and 'Dixie' by the band, and the tramp, tramp, tramp of thousands of feet, the crowd entertained itself through a period of ten minutes, with an occasional shriek of 'Bryan, Bryan.' Not much attempt was made by the officials of the convention to reduce the riotous elements to submission, but after twelve minutes of chaos the outburst died out through exhaustion."

After order had been restored, the Convention took a recess till evening, but, upon reassembling, then as promptly adjourned until Saturday morning.

The selection of a candidate for Vice-President was the only work before the convention on Saturday, and fifteen names were voted for on the first ballot. After that they dropped out one by one, until on the fifth ballot Arthur Sewall, of Maine, received the necessary number of votes, and his nomination was made by acclamation.

The purpose for which the convention had assembled was now accomplished, and it adjourned *sine die* to refer the result of its deliberations to the people for their approval.

CHAPTER XXI.

HON. W. J. BRYAN'S SPEECH AT NOTI-FICATION MEETING, MADISON SQUARE GARDEN, N. Y.

August 12, 1896.

Mr. Chairman, Gentlemen of the Committee and Fellow Citizens: I shall, at a future day and in a formal letter, accept the nomination which is now tendered by the Notification Committee, and I shall at that time touch upon the issues presented by the platform. It is fitting, however, that at this time, in the presence of those here assembled, I speak at some length in regard to the campaign upon which we are now entering. We do not underestimate the forces arrayed against us, nor are we unmindful of the importance of the struggle in which we are engaged; but, relying for success upon the righteousness of our cause, we shall defend with all possible vigor the positions taken by our party. We are not surprised that some of our opponents, in the absence of better argument, resort to abusive epithets, but they may rest assured that no language, however violent, no invectives, however vehement, will lead us to depart a single hair's breadth from the course marked out by the National Convention. The citizen, either public or private, who assails the character and questions the patriotism of the delegates assembled in the Chicago convention, assails the character and questions the patriotism of the millions who have arrayed themselves under the banner there raised.

It has been charged by men standing high in business and political circles that our platform is a menace to private security and public safety; and it has been asserted that those whom I have the honor for the time being, to represent, not only meditate an attack upon the rights of property, but are the foes both of social order and national honor.

Those who stand upon the Chicago platform are prepared to make known and to defend every motive which influences them, every purpose which animates them, and every hope which inspires them. They understand the genius of our institutions, they are staunch supporters of the form of government under which we live, and they build their faith upon foundations laid by the fathers. Andrew Jackson has stated, with admirable clearness and with an emphasis which cannot be surpassed, both the duty and the sphere of government. He said:

Distinctions in society will always exist under every just government Equality of talents, of education or of wealth, cannot be produced by human institutions. In the full enjoyment of the gifts of Heaven and the fruits of superior industry, economy and virtue, every man is equally entitled to protection by law.

We yield to none in our devotion to the doctrine just enunciated. Our campaign has not for its object the reconstruction of society. We cannot insure to the vicious the fruits of a virtuous life; we would not invade the home of the provident in order to supply the wants of the spendthrift; we do not propose to transfer the rewards of industry to the lap of indolence. Property is and will remain the stimulus to endeavor and the compensation for toil. We believe, as asserted in the Declaration of Independence, that all men are created equal; but that does not mean that all men are or can be equal in possessions, in ability or in merit; it simply means that all shall stand equal before the law, and that government officials shall not, in making, construing or enforcing the law, discriminate between citizens.

I assert that property rights, as well as the rights of persons, are safe in the hands of the common people. Abraham Lincoln, in his message sent to Congress in December, 1861, said: " No men living are more worthy to be trusted than those who toil up from poverty; none less inclined to take or touch ought which they have not honestly earned." I repeat this language with unqualified approval, and join with him in the warning which he added, namely: " Let them beware of surrendering a political power which they already possess, and which power, if surrendered, will surely be used to close the doors of advancement against such as they, and to fix new disabilities and burdens upon them, till all of liberty shall be lost." Those who daily follow the injunction, "In the sweat of thy face shalt thou eat bread," are now, as they ever have been, the bulwark of law and order—the source of our nation's greatness in time of peace, and its surest defenders in time of war.

But I have only read a part of Jackson's utterance—let me give you his conclusion : " But when the law undertakes to add to those natural and just advantages artificial distinctions—to grant titles, gratuities and exclusive privileges—to make the rich richer and the potent more powerful—the humble members of society, the farmers, mechanics and the day-laborers, who have neither the time nor the means of securing like favors for themselves, have a right to complain of the injustice of their government." Those who support the Chicago platform indorse all of the quotation from Jackson—the latter part as well as the former part.

We are not surprised to find arrayed against us those who are the beneficiaries of government favoritism—they have read our platform. Nor are we surprised to learn that we must in this campaign face the hostility of those who find a pecuniary advantage in advocating the doctrine of non-interference when great aggregations of wealth are trespassing upon the rights of individuals. We welcome such opposition—it is the highest indorsement which could be bestowed upon us. We are content to have the co-operation of those who desire to have the government administered without fear or favor. It is not the wish of the general public that trusts should spring into existence and override the weaker members of society; it is not the wish of the general public that these trusts should destroy competition and then collect such tax as they will from those who are at their mercy; nor is it the fault of the general public that the instrumentalities of government have been so often prostituted to purposes of private gain. Those who stand upon the Chicago platform believe that the government should not only avoid wrongdoing, but that it should also prevent wrongdoing, and they believe that the law should be enforced alike against all enemies of the public weal. They do not excuse petit larceny, but they declare that grand larceny is equally a crime. They do not defend the occupation of the highwayman who robs the unsuspecting traveller, but they include among the transgressors those who, through the more polite and less hazardous means of legislation, appropriate to their own use the proceeds of the toil of others. The commandment "Thou shalt not steal," thundered from Sinai and reiterated in the legislation of all nations, is no respecter of persons. It must be applied to the great as well as to the small; to the strong as well as **the weak;** to the corporate persons created by law as well as to the person of flesh and blood created by the Almighty. No government is worthy of the name which is not able to protect from every arm uplifted for his injury the humblest citizen who lives **beneath the flag.** It follows as a **necessary** conclusion **that vicious** legislation **must be** remedied by the people **who** suffer from the effects of such legislation, and not by those who enjoy its benefits.

The Chicago platform has been condemned by some because it dissents from an opinion rendered by the Supreme Court declaring the income tax law unconstitutional. Our critics even go so far as to apply the name Anarchist **to** those who stand upon that plank of the platform. It must be remembered that **we expressly recognize the** binding force of **that** decision so long as **it stands as a** part of **the law of the land.** There is in the platform no suggestion of an attempt to dispute **the** authority of the Supreme Court. The party **is** simply to use all the constitutional power which remains after that decision, or which may come **from its reversal** by **the** court as it may hereafter be constituted. Is there any disloyalty **in** that pledge? **For** a hundred years the Supreme **Court of** the **United States** has sustained the principle which underlies the income tax. Some twenty years ago this same court sustained without a dissenting voice an income tax law almost identical with the one recently overthrown; has not a future court as much right to return to the judicial precedents of a century as the present court had to depart from them? When courts allow rehearings, they admit that error is possible; the late decision against the income tax was rendered by a majority of one after a rehearing.

While the money question overshadows all other questions in importance, I desire it distinctly understood that I shall offer no apology for the income tax plank of the Chicago platform. The last income tax sought to apportion the burdens of government more equitably among those who enjoy the protection of the government. At present the expenses of the Federal government, collected through internal revenue taxes and import duties, are especially burdensome upon the poorer classes of society. A law which collects from some citizens more than their share of the taxes, and collects from other citizens less than their share, is simply an indirect means of transferring one man's property to another man's pocket, and while the process may be quite satisfactory to the men who escape just taxation, it will never be satisfactory those who are overburdened. The last income tax law, with its exemption provisions, when considered in connection

MISS MINNA F MURRAY.

The Girl in White—The Iowa "Joan of Arc."

ARTHUR SEWALL, Esq.,

with other methods of taxation in force, was not
unjust to the possessors of large incomes, because
they were not compelled to pay a total federal tax
greater than their share. The income tax is not
new, nor is it based upon hostility to the rich.
The system is employed in several of the most
important nations of Europe, and every income
tax law now upon the statute books in any land,
so far as I have been able to ascertain, contains
an exemption clause. While the collection of an
income tax in other countries does not make it
necessary for this nation to adopt the system, yet
it ought to moderate the language of those who
denounce the income tax as an assault upon the
well-to-do.

Not only shall I refuse to apologize for the
advocacy of an income tax law by the national
convention, but I shall also refuse to apologize for
the exercise by it of the right to dissent from a
decision of the Supreme Court. In a government like ours every public official is a public
servant, whether he holds office by election or by
appointment, whether he serves for a term of
years or during good behavior, and the people
have a right to criticise his official acts. "Confidence is everywhere the parent of despotism;
free government exists in jealousy and not in
confidence"—these are the words of Thomas
Jefferson, and I submit that they present a truer
conception of popular government than that

entertained by those who would prohibit an unfavorable comment upon a court decision. Truth
will vindicate itself; only error fears free speech.
No public official, who conscientiously discharges
his duty as he sees it, will desire to deny to those
whom he serves the right to discuss his official
conduct.

Now let me ask you to consider the paramount
question of this campaign—the money question.
It is scarcely necessary to defend the principle of
bimetallism. No national party during the entire
history of the United States has ever declared
against it, and no party in this campaign has had
the temerity to oppose it. Three parties—the
Democratic, Populist, and Silver Parties—have
not only declared for bimetallism, but have outlined the specific legislation necessary to restore
silver to its ancient position by the side of gold.
The Republican platform expressly declares that
bimetallism is desirable when it pledges the
Republican party to aid in securing it as soon as
the assistance of certain foreign nations can be
obtained. Those who represented the minority
sentiment in the Chicago Convention opposed
the free coinage of silver by the United States
by independent action on the ground that, in
their judgment, it "would retard or entirely
prevent the establishment of international bimetallism, to which the efforts of the government
should be steadily directed." When they asserted

that the efforts of the government should be steadily directed toward the establishment of international bimetallism, they condemned mono-metallism. The gold standard has been weighed in the balance and found wanting. Take from it the powerful support of the money-owning and money-changing classes and it cannot stand for one day in any nation in the world. It was fastened upon the United States without discussion before the people, and its friends have never yet been willing to risk a verdict before the voters upon that issue.

There can be no sympathy or co-operation between the advocates of a universal gold standard and the advocates of bimetallism. Between bimetallism, whether independent or international, and the gold standard there is an impassable gulf. Is this quadrennial agitation in favor of international bimetallism conducted in good faith, or do our opponents really desire to maintain the gold standard permanently? Are they willing to confess the superiority of a double standard when joined in by the leading nations of the world, or do they still insist that gold is the only metal suitable for standard money among civilized nations? If they are, in fact, desirous of securing bimetallism, we may expect them to point out the evils of a gold standard and defend bimetallism as a system.

If, on the other hand, they are bending their energies toward the permanent establishment of a gold standard under cover of a declaration in favor of international bimetallism, I am justified in suggesting that honest money cannot be expected at the hands of those who deal dishonestly with the American people.

What is the test of honesty in money? It must certainly be found in the purchasing power of the dollar. An absolutely honest dollar would not vary in its general purchasing power; it would be absolutely stable when measured by average prices. A dollar which increases in purchasing power is just as dishonest as a dollar which decreases in purchasing power. Professor Laughlin, now of the University of Chicago, and one of the highest gold standard authorities, in his work on bimetallism, not only admits that gold does not remain absolutely stable in value, but expressly asserts "that there is no such thing as a standard of value for future payments, either in gold or silver, which remains absolutely invariable." He even suggests that a multiple standard, wherein the unit is "based upon the selling prices of a number of articles of general consumption," would be a more just standard than either gold or silver, or both, because "a long time contract would thereby be paid at its maturity by the same purchasing power as was given in the beginning."

It cannot be successfully claimed that monometallism or bimetallism, or any other system, gives an absolutely just standard of value. Under both monometallism and bimetallism the government fixes the weight and fineness of the dollar, invests it with legal tender quantities, and then opens the mint to its unrestricted coinage, leaving the purchasing power of the dollar to be determined by the number of dollars. Bimetallism is better than monometallism, not because it gives us a perfect dollar—that is, a dollar absolutely unvarying in its general purchasing power—but because it makes a nearer approach to stability, to honesty, to justice, than a gold standard possibly can. Prior to 1873, when there were enough open mints to permit all the gold and silver available for coinage to find entrance into the world's volume of standard money, the United States might have maintained a gold standard with less injury to the people of this country; but now, when each step toward a universal gold standard enhances the purchasing power of gold, depresses prices, and transfers to the pockets of the creditor class an unearned increment, the influence of this great nation must be thrown upon the side of gold unless we are prepared to accept the natural and legitimate consequences of such an act. Any legislation which lessens the world's stock of standard money increases the exchangeable value of the dollar; therefore, the crusade against silver must inevitably raise the purchasing power of money, and lower the money value of all other forms of property.

Our opponents sometimes admit that it was a

mistake to demonetize silver, but insist that we should submit to present conditions rather than return to the bimetallic system. They err in supposing that we have reached the end of the evil results of a gold standard; we have not reached the end. The injury is a continuing one, and no person can say how long the world is to suffer from the attempt to make gold the only standard money. The same influences which are now operating to destroy silver in the United States will, if successful here, be turned against other silver-using countries, and each new convert to the gold standard will add to the general distress. So long as the scramble for gold continues, prices must fall, and a general fall in prices is but another definition of hard times.

Our opponents, while claiming entire disinterestedness for themselves, have appealed to the selfishness of nearly every class of society. Recognizing the disposition of the individual voter to consider the effect of any proposed legislation upon himself, we present to the American people the financial policy outlined in the Chicago platform, believing that it will result in the greatest good to the greatest number.

The farmers are opposed to the gold standard because they have felt its effects. Since they sell at wholesale and buy at retail, they have lost more than they have gained by falling prices, and, besides this, they have found that certain fixed charges have not fallen at all. Taxes have not been perceptibly decreased, although it requires more of farm products now than formerly to secure the money with which to pay taxes. Debts have not fallen. The farmer who owed $1000 is still compelled to pay $1000, although it may be twice as difficult as formerly to obtain the dollars with which to pay the debt. Railroad rates have not been reduced to keep pace with falling prices, and besides these items there are many more. The farmer has thus found it more and more difficult to live. Has he not a just complaint against the gold standard?

The wage-earners have been injured by a gold standard, and have expressed themselves upon the subject with great emphasis. In February, 1895, a petition asking for the immediate restoration of the free and unlimited coinage of gold and silver at 16 to 1 was signed by the representatives of all, or nearly all, the leading labor organizations and presented to Congress. Wage-earners know that while a gold standard raises the purchasing power of the dollar it also makes it more difficult to obtain possession of the dollar ; they know that employment is less permanent, loss of work more probable, and re-employment less certain. A gold standard encourages the hoarding of money because money is rising ; it also discourages enterprise and paralyzes industry. On the other hand, the restoration of bimetallism will discourage hoarding, because, when prices are steady or rising, money cannot afford to lie idle in the bank vaults. The farmers and wage-earners together constitute a considerable majority of the people of the country. Why should their interests be ignored in considering financial legislation? A monetary system which is peculiarly advantageous to a few syndicates has far less to commend it than a system that would give hope and encouragement to those who create the nation's wealth.

Our opponents have made a special appeal to those who hold fire and life insurance policies, but these policy holders know that, since the total premiums received exceed the total losses paid, a rising standard must be of more benefit to the companies than to the policy holders.

Much solicitude has been expressed by our opponents for the depositors in savings banks. They constantly parade before these depositors the advantages of a gold standard; but these appeals will be in vain, because savings bank depositors know that under a gold standard there is increasing danger that they will lose their deposits because of the inability of the banks to collect their assets; and they still further know that, if the gold standard is to continue indefinitely, they may be compelled to withdraw their deposits in order to pay living expenses.

It is only necessary to note the increasing number of failures, in order to know that a gold standard is ruinous to merchants and manufacturers. These business men do not make their profits from the people from whom they borrow money, but from the people to whom they sell their goods. If the people cannot buy, retailers cannot sell, and, if retailers cannot sell, wholesale merchants and manufacturers must go into bankruptcy.

Those who hold, as a permanent investment, the stock of railroads and of other enterprises—I do not include those who speculate in stocks or use stock holdings as a means of obtaining an inside advantage in construction contracts—are injured by a gold standard. The rising dollar destroys the earning power of these enterprises without reducing their liabilities, and, as dividends cannot be paid until salaries and fixed charges have been satisfied, the stockholders must bear the burden of hard times.

Salaries in business occupations depend upon business conditions, and the gold standard both lessens the amount and threatens the permanency of such salaries.

Official salaries, except the salaries of those who hold office for life. must, in the long run, be adjusted to t he conditions of those who pay the taxes; and if the present financial policy continues, we must expect the contest between the taxpayer and the taxeater to increase in bitterness.

The professional classes, in the main, derive their support from the producing classes, and can only enjoy prosperity when there is prosperity among those who create wealth.

I have not attempted to describe the effect of the gold standard upon all classes—in fact, I have only had time to mention a few—but each person will be able to apply the principles stated to his own occupation.

It must also be remembered that it is the desire of people generally to convert their earnings into real or personal property. This being true, in considering any temporary advantage which may come from a system under which the dollar rises in its purchasing power, it must not be forgotten that the dollar cannot buy more than formerly unless property sells for less than formerly. Hence, it will be seen that a large portion of those who may find some pecuniary advantage in a gold standard will discover their losses exceed their gains.

It is sometimes asserted by our opponents that a bank belongs to the debtor class; but this is not true of any solvent bank. Every statement published by a solvent bank shows that the assets exceed the liabilities. That is to say, while the bank owes a large amount of money to its depositors, it not only has enough on hand in money and notes to pay its depositors; but, in addition thereto, has enough to cover its capital and surplus. When the dollar is rising in value slowly, a bank may, by making short-time loans and taking good security, avoid loss ; but when prices are falling rapidly, the bank is apt to lose more because of bad debts than it can gain by the increase in the purchasing power of its capital and surplus.

It must be admitted, however, that some bankers combine the business of a bond broker with the ordinary banking business, and these may make enough in the negotiation of loans to offset the losses arising in legitimate banking business. As long as human nature remains as it is, there will always be danger that, unless restrained by public opinion or legal enactment, those who see a pecuniary profit for themselves in a certain condition may yield to the temptation to bring about that condition. Jefferson has stated that one of the main duties of government is to prevent men from injuring one another, and never was that duty more important than it is to-day. It is not strange that those who have made a profit by furnishing gold to the government in the hour of its extremity favor a financial policy which will keep the government dependent upon them. I believe, however, that I speak the sentiment of the vast majority of people of the United States when I say that a wise financial policy administered in behalf of all the people would make our government independent of any combination of financiers, foreign or domestic.

Let me say a word, now, in regard to certain persons who are pecuniarily benefited by a gold standard, and who favor it, not from a desire to trespass on the rights of others, but because the circumstances which surround them blind them to the effect of the gold standard upon others. I shall ask you to consider the language of two gentlemen whose long public service and high standing in the party to which they belong will protect them from adverse criticism by our opponents. In 1869 Senator Sherman said: "The contraction of the currency is a far more distressing operation than senators suppose. Our own and other nations have gone through that operation before. It is not possible to take that voyage without the sorest distress; it is a period of loss, danger, lassitude of trade, fall of wages, suspension of enterprise, bankruptcy and disaster. It means ruin to all dealers whose debts are twice their business capital, though one-third less than their actual property. It means the fall of all agricultural production without any reduction of taxes. What prudent man would dare to build a house, a railroad, a factory or a barn with this certain fact before him?" As I have said before, the salaried officer referred to must be the man whose salary is fixed for life, and not the man whose salary depends upon business conditions. When

Mr. Sherman describes contraction of the currency as disastrous to all the people except the capitalist out of debt and those who stand in a similar position to his, he is stating a truth which must be apparent to every person who will give the matter careful consideration. Mr. Sherman was at that time speaking of the contraction of the volume of paper currency; but the principle which he set forth applies if there is a contraction of the volume of the standard money of the world.

Mr. Blaine discussed the same principle in connection with the demonetization of silver. Speaking in the House of Representatives on the 7th of February, 1878, he said: "I believe the struggle now going on in this country and other countries for a single gold standard would, if successful, produce widespread disaster in and throughout the commercial world. The destruction of silver as money, and the establishment of gold as the sole unit of value must have a ruinous effect on all forms of property, except those invested which yield a fixed return in money. These would be enormously enhanced in value, and would gain a disproportionate and unfair advantage over every other species of property." It is strange that the "holders of investments which yield a fixed return in money" can regard the destruction of silver with complacency? May we not expect the holders of other forms of property to protest against giving to money a "disproportionate and

unfair advantage over every other species of property?" If the relatively few whose wealth consists largely in fixed investments have a right to
use the ballot to enhance the value of their investments, have not the rest of the people the right to
use the ballot to protect themselves from the disastrous consequences of a rising standard?

The people who must purchase money with the
products of toil stand in a position entirely different from the position of those who own money or
receive a fixed income. The well-being of the
nation—aye, of civilization itself—depends upon
the prosperity of the masses. What shall it
profit us to have a dollar which grows more valuable every day if such a dollar lowers the standard
of civilization and brings distress to the people?
What shall it profit us if, in trying to raise our
credit by increasing the purchasing power of
our dollar, we destroy our ability to pay the debts
already contracted by lowering the purchasing
power of the products with which those debts
must be paid? If it is asserted, as it constantly
is asserted, that the gold standard will enable us
to borrow more money from abroad, I reply that
the restoration of bimetallism will restore the
parity between money and property, and thus
permit an era of prosperity which will enable the
American people to become loaners of money instead of perpetual borrowers. Even if we desire
to borrow, how long can we continue borrowing

under a system which, by lowering the value of property, weakens the foundation upon which credit rests?

Even the holders of fixed investments, though they gain an advantage from the appreciation of the dollar, certainly see the injustice of the legislation which gives them this advantage over those whose incomes depend upon the value of property and products. If the holders of fixed investments will not listen to arguments based upon justice and equity, I appeal to them to consider the interests of posterity. We do not live for ourselves alone; our labor, our self-denial, and our anxious care—all these are for those who are to come after us as much as for ourselves; but we cannot protect our children beyond the period of our lives. Let those who are now reaping advantage from a vicious financial system remember that, in the years to come, their own children and children's children may, through the operation of this same system, be made to pay tribute to the descendants of those who are wronged to-day.

As against the maintenance of a gold standard, either permanently or until other nations can be united for its overthrow, the Chicago platform presents a clear and emphatic demand for the immediate restoration of the free and unlimited coinage of silver and gold at the present legal ratio of 16 to 1, without waiting for the aid or consent of any other nation. We are not asking that a new experiment be tried; we are insisting upon a return to a financial policy approved by the experience of history and supported by all the prominent statesmen of our nation from the days of our first President down to 1873. When we ask that our mints be opened to the free and unlimited coinage of silver into full legal tender money, we are simply asking that the same mint privileges be accorded to silver that are now accorded to gold. When we ask that this coinage be at the rate of 16 to 1, we simply ask that our gold coins and the standard silver dollar—which, be it remembered, contains the same amount of pure silver as the first silver dollar coined at our mints—retain their present weight and fineness.

The theoretical advantage of the bimetallic system is best stated by a European writer on political economy, who suggests the following illustration: A river fed from two sources is more uniform in volume than a river fed from one source—the reason being that when one of the feeders is swollen the other may be low; whereas, a river which has but one feeder must rise or fall with that feeder. So in the case of bimetallism; the volume of metallic money receives contributions from both the gold mines and the silver mines, and, therefore, varies less; and the dollar, resting upon two metals, is less changeable in its purchasing power than the dollar which rests on one metal only.

If there are two kinds of money, the option must rest either with the debtor or with the creditor. Assuming that their rights are equal, we must look at the interests of society in general in order to determine to which side the option should be given. Under the bimetallic system, gold and silver are linked together by law at a fixed ratio, and any person or persons owing any quantity of either metal can have the same converted into full legal-tender money. If the creditor has the right to choose the metal in which payment shall be made, it is reasonable to suppose that he will require the debtor to pay in the dearer metal if there is any perceptible difference between the bullion values of the metals. This new demand created for the dearer metal will make that metal dearer still, while the decreased demand for the cheaper metal will make that metal cheaper still. If, on the other hand, the debtor exercises the option, it is reasonable to suppose that he will pay in the cheaper metal if one metal is perceptibly cheaper than the other; but the demand thus created for the cheaper metal will raise its price, while the lessened demand for the dearer metal will lower its price. In other words, when the creditor has the option, the metals are drawn apart; whereas, when the debtor has the option, the metals are held together approximately at the ratio fixed by law; provided the demand created is sufficient to absorb all of both metals presented at the mint.

Society is, therefore, interested in having the option exercised by the debtor. Indeed, there can be no such thing as real bimetallism unless the option is exercised by the debtor. The exercise of the option by the debtor compels the creditor classes, whether domestic or foreign, to exert themselves to maintain the parity between gold and silver at the legal ratio, whereas they might find a profit in driving one of the metals to a premium if they could then demand the dearer metal. The right of the debtor to choose the coin in which payment shall be made extends to obligations due from the government as well as to contracts between individuals. A government obligation is simply a debt due from all the people to one of the people, and it is impossible to justify a policy which makes the interests of the one person who holds the obligation superior to the rights of the many who must be taxed to pay it. When, prior to 1873, silver was at a premium, it was never contended that national honor required the payment of government obligations in silver, and the Matthews resolution, adopted by Congress in 1878, expressly asserted the right of the United States to redeem coin obligations in standard silver dollars as well as in gold coin.

Upon this subject the Chicago platform reads: "We are opposed to the policy and practice of surrendering to the holders of the obligations of the United States the option reserved by law to the government of redeeming such obligations in either silver coin or gold coin."

It is constantly assumed by some that the United States notes, commonly called greenbacks, and the Treasury notes, issued under the act of 1890, are responsible for the recent drain upon the gold reserve, but this assumption is entirely without foundation. Secretary Carlisle appeared before the House Committee on Appropriations, on January 21, 1895, and I quote from the printed report of his testimony before the Committee :

" Mr. Sibley : I would like to ask you (perhaps not entirely connected with the matter under dis- cussion) what objection there could be to having the option of redeeming either in silver or gold lie with the Treasury instead of the note holder ?

" Secretary Carlisle : If that policy had been adopted at the beginning of resumption—and I am not saying this for the purpose of criticising the action of any of my predecessors, or anybody else—but if the policy of reserving to the govern- ment, at the beginning of resumption, the option of redeeming in gold or silver all its paper pre- sented, I believe it would have worked beneficially, and there would have been no trouble growing out of it, but the Secretaries of the Treasury from the beginning of resumption have pursued a pol- icy of redeeming in gold or silver, at the option of the holder of the paper, and if any Secretary had afterwards attempted to change that policy and force silver upon a man who wanted gold, or gold upon a man who wanted silver, and especially if he had made that attempt at such a critical period as we have had in the last two years, my judgment is it would have been very disastrous."

I do not agree with the Secretary that it was wise to follow a bad precedent, but from his answer it will be seen that the fault does not lie with the greenbacks and Treasury notes, but rather with the executive officers who have seen fit to surrender a right which should have been exercised for the protection of the interests of the people. This executive action has already been made the excuse for the issue of more than \$250,-000,000 in bonds, and it is impossible to estimate the amount of bonds which may hereafter be issued if this policy is continued. We are told that any attempt on the part of the government at this time to redeem its obligations in silver would put a premium upon gold, but why should it? The Bank of France exercises the right to redeem all bank paper in either gold or silver, and yet France maintains the parity between gold and silver at the ratio of $15\frac{1}{2}$ to 1, and retains in circulation more silver per capita than we do in the United States.

It may be further answered that our opponents have suggested no feasible plan for avoiding the

dangers which they fear. The retirement of the
greenbacks and Treasury notes would not protect
the Treasury, because the same policy which now
leads the Secretary of the Treasury to redeem all
Government paper in gold, when gold is demanded, will require the redemption of all silver
dollars and silver certificates in gold, if the greenbacks and Treasury notes are withdrawn from
circulation. More than this, if the Government
should retire its paper and throw upon the banks
the necessity of furnishing coin redemption, the
banks would exercise the right to furnish either
gold or silver. In other words, they would exercise the option, just as the Government ought to
exercise it now. The Government must either
exercise the right to redeem its obligations in silver when silver is more convenient, or it must retire all the silver and silver certificates from circulation and leave nothing but gold as legal tender
money. Are our opponents willing to outline a
financial system which will carry out their policy
to its legitimate conclusion, or will they continue
to cloak their designs in ambiguous phrases?

There is an actual necessity for bimetallism as
well as a theoretical defence of it. During the
last twenty-three years legislation has been creating an additional demand for gold, and this law-
created demand has resulted in increasing the
purchasing power of each ounce of gold. The
restoration of bimetallism in the United States

will take away from gold just so much of its purchasing power as was added to it by the demonetization of silver by the United States. The silver dollar is now held up to the gold dollar by legal tender laws and not by redemption in gold, because the standard silver dollars are not now redeemable in gold either in law or by administrative policy.

We contend that free and unlimited coinage by the United States alone will raise the bullion value of silver to its coinage value, and this make silver bullion worth $1.29 per ounce in gold throughout the world. This proposition is in keeping with natural laws, not in defiance of them. The best-known law of commerce is the law of supply and demand. We recognize this law and build our argument upon it. We apply this law to money when we say that a reduction in the volume of money will raise the purchasing power of the dollar; we also apply the law of supply and demand to silver when we say that a new demand for silver created by law will raise the price of silver bullion. Gold and silver are different from other commodities, in that they are limited in quantity. Corn, wheat, manufactured products, etc., can be produced almost without limit, provided they can be sold at a price sufficient to stimulate production, but gold and silver are called precious metals, because they are found, not produced. These metals have been the objects of anxious search as far back as history runs, yet, according to Mr. Harvey's calculation, all the gold coin of the world can be melted into a 22-foot cube, and all the silver in the world into a 66-foot cube. Because gold and silver are limited, both in the quantity now in hand and in annual production, it follows that legislation can fix the ratio between them.

Any purchaser who stands ready to take the entire supply of any given article at a certain price can prevent that article from falling below that price. So the government can fix a price for gold and silver by creating a demand greater than the supply. International bimetallists believe that several nations, by entering into an agreement to coin at a fixed ratio all the gold and silver presented, can maintain the bullion value of the metals at the mint ratio. When a mint price is thus established, it regulates the bullion price, because any person desiring coin may have the bullion converted into coin at that price, and any person desiring bullion can secure it by melting the coin. The only question upon which international bimetallists differ is: Can the United States by the free and unlimited coinage of silver at the present legal ratio create a demand for silver which, taken in connection with the demand already in existence, will be sufficient to utilize all the silver that will be presented at the mints? They agree in their defence of the bimetallic principle, and they agree in unalterable opposition to the gold standard. International bimetallists cannot complain that free coinage gives a benefit to the mine owner, because international bimetallism gives to the owner of silver all the advantages offered by independent bimetallism at the same ratio. International bimetallists cannot accuse the advocates of free silver of being "bullion owners who desire to raise the value of their bullion ;" or "debtors who desire to pay their debts in cheap dollars ;" or "demagogues who desire to curry favor with the people." They must rest their opposition upon one ground only, namely : That the supply of silver available for coinage is too large to be utilized by the United States.

In discussing the question we must consider the capacity of our people to use silver and the quantity of silver which can come to our mints. It must be remembered that we live in a country only partially developed, and that our people far surpass any equal number of people in the world in their power to consume and produce. Our extensive railroad development and enormous internal commerce must also be taken into consideration. Now, how much silver can come here? Not the coined silver of the world, because almost all of it is more valuable at this time in other lands than it will be at our mints under free coinage. If our mints are opened to free and unlimited coinage at the present ratio, merchandise silver cannot come here, because the labor applied to it has made it worth more in the form of merchandise than it will be worth at our mints. We cannot even expect all of the annual product of silver, because India, China, Japan, Mexico and all the other silver-using countries must satisfy their annual needs from the annual product; the arts will require a large amount, and the gold standard countries will need a considerable quantity of subsidiary coinage. We will be required to coin only that which is not needed elsewhere; but, if we stand ready to take and utilize all of it, other nations will be compelled to buy at the price which we fix. Many fear that the opening of our mints will be followed by an enormous increase in the annual production of silver. This is conjecture. Silver has been used as money for thousands of years, and during all that time the world has never suffered from overproduction. If, for any reason, the supply of gold or silver in the future ever exceeds the requirements of the arts and the needs of commerce, we confidently hope that the intelligence of the people will be sufficient to devise and enact any legislation necessary for the protection of the public. It is folly to refuse the people the money which they now need for fear they may hereafter have more than they need. I am firmly convinced that by opening our mints to free and unlimited coinage at the present ratio we can create a demand for silver which will keep the price of silver bullion at $1.29 per ounce, measured by gold.

Some of our opponents attribute the fall in the value of silver, when measured by gold, to the fact that during the last quarter of a century the world's supply of silver has increased more rapidly than the world's supply of gold. This argument is entirely answered by the fact that during the last five years, the annual production of gold has increased more rapidly than the annual production of silver. Since the gold price of silver has fallen more during the last five years than it ever fell in any previous five years in the history of the world, it is evident that the fall is not due to increased production. Prices can be lowered as effectually by decreasing the demand for an article as by increasing the supply of it, and it seems certain that the fall in the gold price of silver is due to hostile legislation and not to natural laws.

Our opponents cannot ignore the fact that gold is now going abroad in spite of all legislation intended to prevent it, and no silver is being coined to take its place. Not only is gold going abroad now, but it must continue to go abroad as long as the present financial policy is adhered to, unless we continue to borrow from across the ocean, and even then we simply postpone the evil, because the amount borrowed, together with interest upon it, must be repaid in appreciating dollars. The American people now owe a large sum to European creditors, and falling prices have left a larger and larger margin between our net national income and our annual interest charge. There is only one way to stop the increasing flow of gold from our shores, and that is to stop falling prices. The restoration of bimetallism will not only stop falling prices, but will—to some extent, restore prices by reducing the world's demand for gold. If it is argued that a rise in prices lessens the value of the dollars which we pay to our creditors, I reply that, in the balancing of equities the American people have as much right to favor a financial system which will maintain or restore prices as foreign creditors have to insist upon a financial system that will reduce prices. But the interests of society are far superior to the interests of either debtors or creditors, and the interests of society demand a financial system which will add to the volume of the standard money of the world, and thus restore stability to prices.

Perhaps the most persistent misrepresentation that we have to meet is the charge that we are advocating the payment of debts in fifty-cent dollars. At the present time and under present laws, a silver dollar, when melted, loses nearly half its value, but that will not be true when we again establish a mint price for silver and leave no surplus upon the market to drag down the price of bullion. Under bimetallism, silver bullion will be worth as much as silver coin, just as gold bullion is now worth as much as gold coin, and we believe that a silver dollar will be worth as much as a gold dollar.

The charge of repudiation comes with poor grace from those who are seeking to add to the weight of existing debts by legislation which makes money dearer, and who conceal their designs against the general welfare under the euphonious pretence that they are upholding public credit and national honor.

In answer to the charge that gold will go abroad, it must be remembered that no gold can leave this country until the owner of the gold receives something in return for it, which he would rather have. In other words, when gold leaves the country, those who formerly owned it will be benefitted. There is no process by which we can be compelled to part with our gold against our will, nor is there any process by which silver can be forced upon us without our consent. Exchanges are matters of agreement, and if silver comes to this country under free coinage it will be at the invitation of some one in this country who will give something in exchange for it.

Those who deny the ability of the United States to maintain the parity between gold and silver at the present legal ratio without foreign aid point to Mexico and assert that the opening of our mints will reduce us to a silver basis and

raise gold to a premium. It is no reflection upon
our sister Republic to remind our people that the
United States is much greater than Mexico in
area, in population and in commercial strength.
It is absurd to assert that the United States is not
able to do anything which Mexico has failed to
accomplish. The one thing necessary in order to
maintain the parity is to furnish a demand great
enough to utilize all the silver which will come to
the mints. That Mexico has failed to do this is
not proof that the United States would also fail.

It is also argued that, since a number of nations
have demonetized silver, nothing can be done
until all of those nations restore bimetallism.
This is also illogical. It is immaterial how many
or how few nations have open mints, provided
there are sufficient open mints to furnish a monetary demand for all the gold and silver available
for coinage.

In reply to the argument that improved machinery has lessened the cost of producing silver,
it is sufficient to say that the same is true of the
production of gold, and yet, notwithstanding that,
gold has risen in value. As a matter of fact, the
cost of production does not determine the value
of the precious metals, except as it may affect the
supply. If, for instance, the cost of producing
gold should be reduced to 90 per cent. without
any increase in the output, the purchasing power
of an ounce of gold would not fall. So long as

there is a monetary demand sufficient to take at a fixed mint price all of the gold and silver produced, the cost of production need not be considered.

It is often objected that the prices of gold and silver cannot be fixed in relation to each other, because of the variation in the relative production of the metals. This argument also overlooks the fact that, if the demand for both metals at a fixed price is greater than the supply of both, relative production becomes immaterial. In the early part of the present century the annual production of silver was worth at the coinage ratio, about three times as much as the annual production of gold; whereas, soon after 1849, the annual production of gold became worth about three times as much, at the coinage ratio, as the annual production of silver; and, yet, owing to the maintenance of the bimetallic standard, these enormous changes in relative production had but a slight effect upon the relative values of the metals.

If it is asserted by our opponents that the free coinage of silver is intended only for the benefit of the mine owners, it must be remembered that free coinage cannot restore to the mine owners any more than demonetization took away; and it must also be remembered that the loss which the demonetization of silver has brought to the mine owners is insignificant compared to the loss which this policy has brought to the rest of the people.

The restoration of silver will bring to the people generally many times as much advantage as the mine owners can obtain from it. While it is not the purpose of free coinage to specially aid any particular class, yet those who believe that the restoration of silver is needed by the whole people should not be flettered because an incidental benefit will come to the mine owners. The erection of forts, the deepening of harbors, the improvement of rivers, the erection of public buildings—all these confer incidental benefits upon individuals and communities, and yet these incidental benefits do not deter us from making appropriations for these purposes whenever such appropriations are necessary for the public good.

The argument that a silver dollar is heavier than a gold, and that, therefore, silver is less convenient to carry in large quantities, is completely answered by the silver certificate, which is as easily carried as the gold certificate or any other kind of paper money.

There are some, who, while admitting the benefits of bimetallism, object to coinage at the present ratio. If any are deceived by this objection, they ought to remember that there are no bimetallists who are earnestly endeavoring to secure it at any other ratio than 16 to 1. We are opposed to any change in the ratio for two reasons—first, because a change would produce great injustice; and, second, because a change in the ratio is not necessary. A change would produce injustice, because, if effected in the manner usually suggested, it would result in an enormous contraction in the volume of standard money.

If, for instance, it was decided by international agreement to raise the ratio throughout the world to 32 to 1, the change might be effected in any one of three ways:

The silver dollar could be doubled in size, so that the new silver dollar would weigh thirty-two times as much as the present gold dollar; or the present gold dollar could be reduced one-half in weight, so that the present silver dollar would weigh thirty-two times as much as the new gold dollar; or the change could be made by increasing the size of the silver dollar and decreasing the size of the gold dollar until the new silver dollar would weigh thirty-two times as much as the new gold dollar.

Those who have advised a change in the ratio have usually suggested that silver dollars be doubled. If this change were made it would necessitate the recoinage of four billions of silver into two billions of dollars. There would be an immediate loss of two billions of dollars either to individuals or to the government, but this would be the least of the injury. A shrinkage of one-half in the silver money of the world would mean a shrinkage of one-fourth in the total volume of metallic money. This contraction, by increasing the value of the dollar, would virtually increase the debts of the world billions of dollars, and decrease still more the value of the property of the world, as measured by dollars. Besides this immediate result, such a change in the ratio would permanently decrease the annual addition to the world's supply of money, because the annual silver product, when coined into dollars twice as large, would make only half as many dollars.

The people of the United States would be injured by a change in the ratio, not because they produce silver, but because they own property and owe debts, and they cannot afford to thus decrease the value of their property or increase the burden of their debts.

In 1878 Mr. Carlisle said: "Mankind will be fortunate, indeed, if the annual production of gold and silver coin will keep pace with the annual increase of population and industry." I repeat this assertion. All of the gold and silver annually available for coinage, when converted into coin at the present ratio, will not, in my judgment, more than supply our monetary needs.

In supporting the act of 1890, known as the Sherman Act, Senator Sherman on June 5th of that year, said:

"Under the law of February, 1878, the purchase of $2,000,000 worth of silver bullion a month has by coinage produced annually an average of nearly $3,000,000 per month for a period of twelve years, but this amount, in view of the retirement of the bank notes, will not increase our currency in proportion to our increasing population. If our present currency is estimated at $1,400,000,000 and our population is increasing at the ratio of 3 per cent. per annum, it would require $42,000,000 increased circulation, each year, to keep pace with the increase of population; but, as the increase of population is accompanied by a still greater ratio of increase of wealth and business, it was thought that an immediate increase of circulation might be obtained by larger purchases of silver bullion to an amount sufficient to make good the retirement of bank notes and keep pace with the growth of population. Assuming that $54,000,000 a year additional currency is needed upon this basis, that amount is provided for in this bill by the issue of Treasury notes in exchange for bullion at the market price."

If the United States then needed more than $42,000,000 annually to keep pace with population and business, it now, with a larger population, needs a still greater annual addition; and the United States is only one nation among many. Our opponents make no adequate provision for the increasing monetary needs of the world.

In the second place, a change in the ratio is not necessary. Hostile legislation has decreased the demand for silver and lowered its price when measured by gold, while this same hostile legislation, by increasing the demand for gold, has raised the value of gold when measured by other forms of property.

We are told that the restoration of bimetallism would be a hardship upon those who have entered into contracts payable in gold coin, but this is a mistake. It will be easier to obtain the gold with which to meet a gold contract, when most of the people use silver, than it is now, when every one is trying to secure gold.

The Chicago platform expressly declares in favor of such legislation as may be necessary to prevent, for the future, the demonetization of any kind of legal tender money by private contract. Such contracts are objected to on the ground that they are against public policy. No one questions the right of legislatures to fix the rate of interest which can be collected by law; there is far more reason for preventing private individuals from setting aside legal tender law. The money which is by law made a legal tender must, in the course of ordinary business, be accepted by ninety-nine out of every hundred persons. Why should the hundredth man be permitted to exempt himself from the general rule? Special contracts have a tendency to increase the demand for a particular kind of money, and thus force it to a premium. Have not the people a right to say that a comparatively few individuals shall not be permitted to derange the financial system of the nation in order to collect a premium in case they succeed in forcing one kind of money to a premium?

There is another argument to which I ask attention. Some of the more zealous opponents of free coinage point to the fact that thirteen months must elapse between the election and the first regular session of Congress, and assert that during that time, in case people declare themselves in favor of free coinage, all loans will be withdrawn and all mortgages foreclosed. If these are merely prophecies indulged in by those who have forgotten the provisions of the Constitution, it will be sufficient to remind them that the President is empowered to convene Congress in extraordinary session whenever the public good requires such action. If, in November, the people by their ballots declare themselves in favor of the immediate restoration of bimetallism, the system can be inaugurated within a few months.

If, however, the assertion that loans will be withdrawn and mortgages foreclosed is made to prevent such political action as the people may believe to be necessary for the preservation of their rights, then a new and vital issue is raised. Whenever it is necessary for the people as a whole to obtain consent from the owners of money and the changers of money before they can legislate upon financial questions, we shall have passed from a democracy to a plutocracy. But that time has not yet arrived. Threats and intimidation will be of no avail. The people who, in 1876, rejected the doctrine that kings rule by right divine, will not, in this generation, subscribe to a doctrine that money is omnipotent.

In conclusion permit me to say a word in regard to international bimetallism. We are not opposed to an international agreement looking to the restoration of bimetallism throughout the world. The advocates of free coinage have on all occasions shown their willingness to co-operate with other nations in the reinstatement of silver, but they are not willing to await the pleasure of other governments when immediate relief is needed by the people of the United States, and they further believe that independent action offers better assurance of international bimetallism than servile dependence upon foreign aid. For more than twenty years we have invited the assistance of European nations, but all progress in the direction of international bimetallism has been blocked by the opposition of those who derive a pecuniary benefit from the appreciation of gold. How long must we wait for bimetallism to be brought to us by those who profit by monometallism. If the double standard will bring benefits to our people, who will deny them the right to enjoy those benefits. If our opponents would admit the right, the ability and the duty of our people to act for themselves on all public questions without the assistance and regardless of the wishes of other nations, and then propose the remedial legislation which they consider sufficient we could meet them in the field of honorable debate; but, when they assert that this nation is helpless to protect the rights of its own citizens, we challenge them to submit the issue to a people whose patriotism has never been appealed to in vain.

We shall not offend other nations when we declare the right of the American people to govern themselves, and, without let or hindrance from without, decide upon every question presented for their consideration. In taking this position, we simply maintain the dignity of seventy million citizens who are second to none in their capacity for self-government.

The gold standard has compelled the American people to pay an ever-increasing tribute to the creditor nations of the world—a tribute which no one dares to defend. I assert that national honor requires the United States to secure justice for all its citizens as well as do justice to all its creditors. For a people like ours, blest with natural resources of surpassing richness, to proclaim themselves impotent to frame a financial system suited to their own needs, is humiliating beyond the power of language to describe. We cannot enforce respect for our foreign policy so long as we confess ourselves unable to frame our own financial policy.

Honest differences of opinion have always existed, and ever will exist, as to the legislation best calculated to promote the public weal; but, when it is seriously asserted that this nation must bow to the dictation of other nations and accept the policies which they insist upon, the right of self-government is assailed, and until that question is settled all other questions are insignificant.

Citizens of New York: I have travelled from the centre of the continent to the seaboard that I might, in the very beginning of the campaign, bring you greeting from the people of the West and South and assure you that their desire is not to destroy but to build up. They invite you to accept the principles of a living faith rather than listen to those who preach the gospel of despair and advise endurance of the ills you have. The advocates of free coinage believe that, in striving to secure the immediate restoration of bimetallism, they are laboring in your behalf as well as in their own behalf. A few of your people may prosper under present conditions, but the permanent welfare of New York rests upon the producers of wealth. This great city is built upon the commerce of the nation and must suffer if that commerce is impaired. You cannot sell unless the people have money with which to buy, and they cannot obtain the money with which to buy unless they are able to sell their products at remunerative prices. Production of wealth goes before the exchange of wealth; those who create must secure a profit before they have anything to share with others. You cannot afford to join the moneychangers in supporting a financial policy which, by destroying the purchasing power of the products of toil, must in the end discourage the creation of wealth.

I ask, I expect, your co-operation. It is true that a few of your financiers would fashion a new figure—a figure representing Columbia, her hands bound fast with fetters of gold and her face turned toward the East, appealing for assistance to those who live beyond the sea—but this figure can never express your idea of this nation. You will rather return for inspiration to the heroic statue which guards the entrance to your city—a statue as patriotic in conception as it is colossal in proportions. It was the gracious gift of a sister Republic and stands upon a pedestal which was built by the American people. That figure, Liberty enlightening the world, is emblematic of the mission of our nation among the nations of the earth. With a government which derives its powers from the consent of the governed, secures to all the people freedom of conscience, freedom of thought and freedom of speech, guarantees equal rights to all and promises special privileges to none, the United States should be an example in all that is good and the leading spirit in every movement which has for its object the uplifting of the human race.

CHAPTER XXII.

HON. W. J. BRYAN'S LETTER ACCEPTING POPULIST NOMINATION.

Lincoln, Neb., October 3, 1896.

Hon. William V. Allen, Chairman, and others, members of the Notification Committee of the People's Party—Gentlemen : The nomination of the People's party for the Presidency of the United States has been tendered me in such a generous spirit, and upon such honorable terms, that I am able to accept the same without departing from the platform adopted by the Democratic National Convention at Chicago.

I fully appreciate the breadth of patriotism which has actuated the members of the People's party who, in order to consolidate the sentiment in favor of bimetallism, have been willing to go outside of party lines and support as their candidate one already nominated by the Democratic party and also by the Silver party.

I also appreciate the fact that while, during all the years since 1873, a large majority of the Democratic party, and a considerable minority of the Republican party, have been consistent advocates

of the free coinage of silver, at the present ratio,
yet ever since the organization of the People's
party its members have unanimously supported
such coinage as the only means of restoring bimetallism. By persistently pointing out the disastrous effects of a gold standard and protesting
against each successive step towards financial
bondage, the Populists have exerted an important
influence in awakening the public to a realization
of the Nation's present peril.

In a time like this, when a great political party
is attempting to surrender the right to legislate
for ourselves upon the financial question, and is
seeking to bind the American people to a foreign
monetary system, it behooves us as lovers of our
country and friends of American institutions to
lay aside for the present such differences as may
exist among us on minor questions, in order that
our strength may be united in a supreme effort to
wrest the Government from the hands of those
who imagine that the Nation's finances are only
secured when controlled by a few financiers and
that national honor can only be maintained by
servile acquiescence in any policy, however destructive to the interests of the people of the
United States, which foreign creditors, present or
prospective, may desire to force upon us.

It is a cause of congratulation that we have in
this campaign not only the support of Democrats,
Populists and Republicans who have all along be-

lieved in independent bimetallism, but also the active co-operation of those Democrats and Republicans who, having heretofore waited for international bimetallism, now join with us rather than trust the destinies of the Nation in the hands of those who are holding out the delusive hope of foreign aid, while they labor secretly for the permanent establishment of the single gold standard.

While difficulties always arise in the settlement of the details of any plan of co-operation between distinct political organizations, I am sure that the advocates of bimetallism are so intensely in earnest that they will be able to devise some means by which the free silver vote may be concentrated upon one electoral ticket in each State. To secure this result, charity towards the opinions of others and liberality on the part of all is necessary, but honest and sincere friends who are working towards a common result always find it possible to agree upon just and equitable terms. The American people have proven equal to every emergency which has arisen in the past, and I am confident that in the present emergency there will be no antagonism between the various regiments of the one great army which is marching to repel an invasion more dangerous to our welfare than an army with banners. Acknowledging with gratitude your expressions of confidence and good will, I am, very truly yours,

W. J. Bryan.

CHAPTER XXIII.

SPEECH AT LINCOLN, NEB.

I.adies and Gentlemen: I am only going to talk to you a little while. There are others here who are prepared to discuss these issues of the campaign in your presence, and I am trying to do as little work as possible. I think I have been doing my share so far as time is concerned; but I want to avoid getting tired by resting before I get tired, and, therefore, I am going to ask you to listen to me but a short time.

It is now just about one month since I left Nebraska and turned eastward. It has been an interesting trip. I want to assure you that the sentiment in favor of the free coinage of silver is a growing sentiment. (Applause.)

It far surpassed my expectations in the East, and I found people, the producers of wealth, the farmers and the laborers, who are joining with you to free themselves from the domination of those financial influences which have controlled our legislation and our financial policies. You will find in the very shadow of Wall Street as bitter hatred to the influences from which you have suffered as you will find among the farmers of Nebraska. (Applause.)

(408)

All through the East I found farmers, who had been Republicans, who were openly supporting the free coinage of silver, and were asserting that they had as much right to attend to their business as the New York banker had to attend to his business. Another thing I noticed, and that is the intense earnestness that characterizes this campaign. I have not found a lukewarm person anywhere. Politics is a serious business when you confront such issues as confront the American people now. (Applause and cries of "That's right.")

I don't know whether all of you fully realize the intensity of the struggle in which you are engaged. Our opponents began the campaign by asserting that the American people were not able to establish bimetallism, and then, when they found there was a revolt among the people against such a policy, they commenced a system of coercion and terrorism, insisting that the masses of the people even have not the right to determine what kind of a policy they want. (Applause.) This terrorism and coercion is manifested in two ways.

In the first place, the heads of many great corporations are undertaking to compel their employes to support the gold standard. (Cries of "That is so; shame!") My friends, if the heads of these corporations assert the right to control the votes of those who work for them, then we have presented to the American people even a greater question than the silver question. If a corporation has the right to control the vote of an employe on one question, it has the right to control on every question. (Cries of " Right you are.")

These corporations were not constituted for any such purpose. They are creatures of law. Has the law given unto these corporations any such power? No, my friends, and no people who love their government will ever entrust those powers to any person or corporation. If a corporation is not invested with the legal right to vote those employes as it will, then the corporation that attempts it usurps its right, and becomes a a dangerous power in a free country. (Applause.)

If there are those here who are opposed to us on the money question, they dare not approve of the conduct of those corporations that are attempting to coerce their employes. We may be the ones to suffer now; but I warn you, fellow citizens, that the time may come when these very corporations will turn themselves against you and your families with all the accumulated power that your endorsement of their conduct now will give them. (Applause.)

Not only have some of these corporations attempted to coerce their employes, but the great money power centered in New York has been attempting to coerce the people who do business with it. A paper a few days ago said of a Montana bank, which had failed, that the reason given was that the managers of the bank were advocating free silver, and, therefore, the New York banks refused to extend credit any longer and enforced the collection of notes which they held, which suspended the bank.

My friends, do you think you are under a government of the people? I want to ask you what you think will be the result if we get to be a government by banks? (Applause.) If we could trust our affairs to a New York banker we might endure it for a time; but when you remember that the New York banker is under the control of the London banker, I ask you to reflect before you submit the destinies of a free people to a few financiers. (Applause.)

We had a failure in this city last winter, a failure which, in my judgment, was largely due to the sale of bonds, and to the fact that the Eastern banks were drawing in money from circulation, from business, from the channels of trade, to invest it in government bonds. If you have a financial policy which permits a few financiers to close your banks at will and swallow up your deposits and impoverish your people, I want to ask you if it is not time for you to consider whether this cannot be stopped? (Applause.)

We have been told that we cannot borrow money from abroad unless we have a financial system that is satisfactory to the people abroad. My friends, you let them control your financial system, and you will never see a time when you can get out of the clutches of those who are dominating your financial policy. (Great applause.)

I assert the right of the people of this country to have their own financial system and to regulate their own affairs; and if foreign people do not want to loan money to us under these conditions, we will have the consolation of knowing that the conditions will be so favorable that we soon will have money to loan them. (Applause.)

In my humble judgment, a proper financial policy for the last twenty years would have left the people of the United States independent of foreign money. Our opponents tell us they want good money. So do we. We want good money as much as they do, but we differ as to what good is. They want a dollar so good that those who have the dollar can buy a great deal from those who need dollars. We want dollars that are not so good that we can't get hold of them when we have wheat and corn to sell. (Applause and cries of " Good.")

The interest of the farmer is not the same as the interest of the money changer. They tell us not to array one class of society against another. We do not. They are the ones who are arraying classes. I call your attention to the fact that the Republican Committee of this town has sent letters to lady school teachers showing them what their interest in the question is. (Great applause.)

In calling the attention of the school teachers to the fact that a gold standard gives them a salary which will buy more and more all the time, they neglect to say that the more the salary rises the harder it is for the taxpayer to pay that salary. (Applause.) And, more than that, they forget to say that if these times go on it will be necessary to cut down the salaries of those who are enjoying high salaries while the people are sinking more and more into debt.

If you will show me a school teacher who, because of a salary involved, and for the hope of getting larger dollars instead of more dollars, will favor the gold standard while the people of this county and State are suffering, I will show you a school teacher who does not deserve a place teaching the children of this county. (Applause.)

Talk about arraying one class against another. I want to ask you why it is that every Democrat who is interested in a syndicate or trust or has a salary from a railroad corporation is arrayed against the Democratic party. Why is it? It is because the Democratic party has declared against the issue of bonds in time of peace and the trafficking with syndicates. (Cries of " That's right "). It is because the Democratic party is opposed to the trusts and the prices which the trusts have instituted. It is because the Democratic party believes in the control, the regulation and the restriction of all corporations, so that they will serve the purposes for which they were allowed to exist. (Great applause).

If those connected with trusts are flocking together in the Republican party, may we not appeal to all the smaller business men who have felt the iron heel of the trust and who have been driven out of business by its unlawful competition? (Applause). If we are to lose all the attorneys of the great trusts—(A voice, "Let them go ")—may we not appeal with confidence to the support of the people who have been plundered by these trusts while their attorneys have received part of the plunder? (Applause and cries of "Yes").

We are not responsible for the arraying of one class against another. These people—not the producers of wealth, but the exchangers of wealth—are those who try to array a class against the rest of the people.

The Republican platform in the State of New York said that we ought to have a business administration conducted by business men in behalf of the business interests of the country. What do they mean by that? Do they call the farmers business men? (Cries of "No"). He simply produces wealth, but if a man goes on the Board of Trade and makes more in an hour betting on the price of what you raise than you make in a year he becomes a business man. These people have attempted to array a few of the people against the rest of the people, and have insisted that the affairs of this Government should be put in the hands of a few.

When we have complained, what euphonious names they have given us. They have been calling us disturbers of the public peace and they have called us Anarchists. (Applause).

My friends, those terms simply express the contempt which they have for the great mass of the people of this country. (Cries of "They have been doing it for twenty-five years"). These names they call us simply prove that they are not willing to trust the destinies of this Republic in the hands of the people who have created its wealth in times of peace and who have fought its battles in times of war.

Show me those people who now call us Anarchists and I will show you a class of people who, if we had war, would never go to the front; but they are the ones who abuse those who would fight and save their own property. (Applause and cheers). I believe that the men upon whom the nation most relies when it wants to increase its martial strength are its security in hours of peril. I believe that these people can be trusted to cast their ballot in time of peace to devise the various policies for this nation. (Applause).

I am glad to see the number of people who

have assembled here this afternoon. (Cries, " This aint half of them. They're working for corporations, and have to wear McKinley badges ").

I am willing to defend the principles embodied in my platform in Nebraska or in New York, or anywhere else. But, my friends, when they attack me and call me a disturber of the public peace, and when they say that I could not be trusted with executive power because I am in sympathy with the lawless, it is gratifying to me to have the toilers of my own city meet me and indorse me as one whom they, at least, are willing to trust. (Long and continued applause and three cheers for Bryan).

I have come among you and I am glad to meet you all. I have made campaigns before you and you know how those campaigns have been conducted. You know that I have never appealed to a man in this district to vote for me unless his conscience and his judgment followed his vote. (Applause).

It is gratifying to me to know that in this county, with its 2,500 Republican majority, the majority in the past against my candidacy has been only 440 and 331 respectively. (Applause). If I can judge anything from what I see here, and if I can place any reliance upon the reports which have come to me from everywhere, then when the election day comes we cannot only expect a majority in Lancaster County, but a majority of not less than 25,000 in Nebraska. (Applause).

You say that that estimate is not large enough and I will say that I know it is not, but I always was a conservative person. I want to say to you in this campaign, as I have said to you in every campaign, if there is one Democrat who believes that the election of the Chicago ticket will be injurious to his country we have no claim on his vote. (Applause). I am one who has never believed that the citizen should put his party above his country. I have not, and do not, intend to appeal to any man to support the Chicago ticket if he thinks that any other ticket will be better for him to vote for or for the land in which we all live. (Applause).

We want them to apply their intelligence and patriotism to this question and we are willing to abide the result. Men in New York called attention to the fact that sentiment was all on our side in this campaign, and one man said that a man could not write a poem in favor of syndicates running the business of this country. (Applause).

Do you know what word rhymes with syndicate? It is "hate," and you cannot write a poem, and you cannot sing a song in favor of the syndicate, controlling the financial policies of this nation, because their policy is a sentiment that appeals to the pocketbook and overshadows the appeal to the best feeling of man. (Applause).

Now I must stop or I will make a speech. You know that I would hate awfully to have the New York papers say that I had driven an audience away in my own town. (Cries of "Go on").

I have never met an audience in this city or in this district but what I felt that I should express the gratitude I feel to the good people of this district for all that you have done for me. I came among you a stranger and you took me in, not in the sense that people are sometimes taken in, but in the Bible sense. (Applause). You gave me an opportunity to study national questions at the National Capitol, and the study of these questions has led me to the convictions which I have expressed in this campaign.

Nothing that you can do hereafter can rob me of the benefits which you have already conferred. You may turn against me if you will, but your confidence that I have received in former campaigns is mine, and you cannot take it back, and I thank you for it.

CHAPTER XXIV.

SPEECH IN THE HOUSE OF REPRE-
SENTATIVES.

February 27, 1894.

The House being in Committee of the Whole and having under consideration the bill (H. R. 4956) directing the coinage of silver bullion held in the Treasury, and for other purposes, Mr. Bryan said:

Mr. Chairman: The House has been so kind to me on previous occasions that I shall not trespass long upon its patience, having reserved for myself only twenty-two minutes; but I desire to submit a few remarks in connection with this bill. I do not feel as some of our friends have expressed themselves toward our Eastern Democrats who fail to vote with us upon this question, or to vote at all.

This is not so much a conflict between men as it is a conflict between ideas. It has presented itself in various forms at different times, and we may expect it to present itself again, and I have no words of censure for those of our brethren who, from the importance of the subject, in their judgment, feel justified in refusing to vote.

Nor do I agree with those who would invoke the rule which prevailed in the Fifty-first Congress of counting a quorum in order to reach a vote. I believe it is the duty of the Representative to protect his constituents and to represent their interests upon this floor; and if the crisis is such that in his judgment he can best protect his people by refusing to vote, I do not criticise him for exercising that right.

For one hundred years or more it was the unbroken rule in this House that when the minority thought it of sufficient importance they might, by refusing to vote, compel those in favor of the pending proposition to bring in a majority of all of the members elected in order to pass the bill. To my mind that is a safeguard. Any other rule is invoked not in the interest of a majority government, but in the interest of a minority government; and one of the reasons why I feel called upon to criticise that rule is that it was invoked in the Fifty-first Congress for partisan purposes, invoked by those who denied its application when they were in the minority, and who in my judgment made better arguments when they were opposing the rule than they were able to make when they adopted the rule afterward. If we bring the members into this House and have a majority in favor of the bill, we do not need to count a quorum. If we have not a majority in favor of the bill, then we have no assurance that the majority of the people of the country, represented by a majority of the members upon this floor, are in favor of that bill.

I believe we had better stand by the old rule; and if the minority believe that there is sufficient justification, let them compel a majority to concur in legislation. We do it in our States. Perhaps three-fourths of the States of the Union provide in their constitutions that no bill can become a law until a majority of all the members elected have expressed themselves in the affirmative by a yea-and-nay vote; and, according to my judgment, it would be better for Congress if we had the same constitutional provision, and it was impossible to pass a law unless a majority expressed assent upon a yea-and-nay vote. It would make men stay here and attend to their business; if we count a quorum, it allows persons to be absent while the business goes on all the same. Instead of having the intelligence and judgment of all the people represented here to do the legislative work, we simply have the intelligence and the judgment of a majority of them when we count a quorum, and important measures may be passed by a minority of the members elected. It is true a minority may enact laws if a quorum votes, but under our new rules now the minority have it in their power to compel the concurrence of a majority, and it is too valuable a right to relinquish.

But I do not wish to speak longer upon this phase of the question. As I said, it is a conflict of ideas. We have the Eastern idea of finances proposed here, and it is antagonized by the ideas of the West and South. You may make fun of the West and South if you like. You may say that their people are not financiers. You may, even in your private conversation, deny to them the right to express views. You may belittle their judgment if you like; but these people have just as much right to express their ideas and to guard their interests as you have to guard yours, and their ideas are as much entitled to consideration as yours. Most of those who are opposed to this bill favor the gold standard. They may call it bimetallism if they like. They may say, as the gentleman from New York (Mr. Hendrix) said the other day, that he believed in bimetallism, but that (in bimetallism) gold will be the standard.

If, sir, that is the idea of some of those who advocate bimetallism, if they want it on a gold basis, I desire to say that there are bimetallists here who do not understand the meaning of the term in that way. We must choose between bimetallism and gold monometallism, and we might as well meet the question now. We have had it illustrated on a recent occasion by the treasury department when we were told that gold is the only real money, and must be paid when demanded. In order to get gold, bonds were issued, and just see what a ridiculous and absurd thing occurred in the attempt to get that gold. During the time that those bonds were being sold and paid for, those who wanted to buy the bonds drew out gold on treasury notes. I have a letter from the treasurer showing that between the first of February and the twentieth of February they presented $18,641,855 United States notes and treasury notes, and drew gold out of the treasury. Nearly one-third of the gold brought in by the bonds was drawn out to pay for them or to replenish the vaults. That this enormous withdrawal of gold from the treasury was to obtain the gold with which to buy the bonds issued for the purpose of drawing gold into the treasury is evident from the fact that during the entire month of December, 1893, only $506,638 in gold were withdrawn by the presentation of such notes, and during the month of January, 1894, only $356,121, while less than half a million dollars in gold have been withdrawn during the eight days since February 19th.

This was perfectly proper under the construction given to the law by the department. If a man who takes the note there has the option to demand gold or silver, whichever he pleases, we are at the mercy at any time of those who desire to deplete our gold reserve; and I wonder at the moderation of those who are buying the bonds. Instead of only taking $18,000,000, I do not understand why they did not draw from the treasury all the gold needed to buy the bonds. Just as long as we maintain the policy of giving the option to any holder, neither $50,000,000 nor $100,-000,000 is a sufficient reserve if our financiers attack it. We have $346,000,000 in greenbacks outstanding. You can take any amount of these and go and demand gold if the holder has the option.

If the treasurer gives up the right to pay in either coin, then just as long as you have greenbacks outstanding you can compel the issue of the bonds daily, monthly or yearly, to make up your gold reserve. As it is, the law is construed to compel their redemption in gold. Now, the difference between me and my friend from New York (Mr. Warner) is this—and I admire the frankness with which he stated the other day what a great many of the advocates of the gold standard are not willing to state, that in his judgment we ought to draw in these greenbacks, pay them off, and fill the void with bank notes of some kind; now, the difference, I say, between the gentleman and myself is this, that while he wants to extinguish the greenbacks by paying them off, and thus protect the reserves, and then fill the void with something else, I want to adopt bimetallism in fact, and compel the treasurer to exercise the option of paying in whichever coin he wishes to pay in and has at hand. There is no bimetallism which gives the option to the note-holder. Bimetallism always gives the option to the debtor, and if the treasurer would follow the law which stands upon the statute book and was intended to be exercised, there would be no danger of our gold being drained out as it has been.

Why, sir, the gentleman from Tennessee (Mr. Patterson) told us yesterday of the small amount of gold that was coming into the Treasury, I was sorry to hear, because that meant, if it means anything, that there will be another demand for bonds, but it only illustrates how helpless we are in the hands of those whom a republic in time of war called pirates. It only shows us how defenseless we are when these men who call themselves financiers attack the credit of the government under a pretence of keeping up an honest currency. We are told that less than one per cent. of the custom dues are now paid in gold. What does it mean? In my judgment it means that there is a concerted plan to hold gold and gold certificates, and they can be withheld easily. The banks and clearing houses pay these checks, and they can pay them in any money they like. They have commenced now to pay the silver certificates to the Treasury and to withhold the gold. Does it not look like they were simply trying to deplete the gold reserve in order to secure another issue of bonds? We were told a while back that we should issue bonds to keep the gold from going to Europe, and now we find that since the panic bank reserves have become so great that the banks are seeking the bonds as a safe investment for those reserves; but whatever the excuse it is always "bonds." I am in favor of the second section of this bill, which would substitute silver certificates for the coin certificates when they come in.

Just so long as our Treasurer or the administration admits the right of the note holders to demand gold just so long we are at their mercy; and if we destroy half, two-thirds, three-fourths or nine-tenths of our paper money they can drain the gold reserve just as well with that which is left as they could with all of it; but I favor the second section of the pending bill, I say, because it will partly take away their argument; but when you take away one argument they will resort to another. They told us before the Sherman act was repealed that the coin certificates were being used to deplete the gold reserve. The Sheman law was repealed and they are drawing out gold still with the certificates, and when you wipe them all out and put in their place silver certificates they can and will do the same with the greenbacks. We have to meet this question, Mr. Chairman, and I hope our people will be brave enough to meet it now and say that the Government of the United States is in duty bound to protect its common people, and owes to them an obligation as strong and as sacred as its obligations to the "financiers" who are drawing the gold out of the Treasury whenever they desire.

I have not criticised our eastern brethren. I presume they are carrying out the wishes of their constituents, at least we must take that for granted. But I do beg our western Republicans to be as independent in their actions as the eastern Democrats are in theirs. For years we talked tariff reform in the West and had it in our platforms. It was the faith of the party; yet when we came down here and attempted to put it in execution we found opposed to it eastern Democrats enough to prevent the bringing of relief to the people. When we went back we had to tell our people that while a large majority of the Democratic party was in favor of tariff reform we could do nothing. Eastern protectionist Democrats retard the growth of the party in the West. These eastern representatives have had the courage to defy the discipline of party; they have had the courage to separate from their party associates in order to protect what they believed to be the interests of their districts. Will the Republicans of the West blindly follow their eastern leaders rather than stand up for the interests of their constituents?

We have been voting here to get a quorum, and there are just a few Republicans of all those who preach bimetallism—who

> "Keep the word of promise to our ear
> and break it to our hope."

There are just a few of them who will vote here, against the dictation of their leaders, to bring this question before the House. But the great mass of the western Republicans who tell you that they are for bimetallism, that they are in favor of the use of silver; who "point with pride" to the Republican platform which speaks of the venerable use of gold and silver; these people—unlike the eastern Democrats, who stand up against their party because, as they say, their constituents demand it of them, refuse to vote, and bow to party discipline. They sacrifice not the interests only, but in my humble judgment, the rights of the people who sent them here. If, sir, this is a conflict of ideas; if the eastern idea is to divide our party; if it is to take men out of the Democracy and make them stand aloof from their party associates in order, as they say, that they may protect their constituents, I ask if the Republicans of the West and South must stand by and allow a party name to prevent them from representing the interests of their people. We need money. There is not a dollar being issued by the Federal Treasury. Our population increases and with it the demand for money increases.

Mr. Sherman said, in advocating the Sherman law, that we needed every year the $54,000,000 which that law was expected to give. If we needed it then, do we not need it now? I ask you, western Republicans, who will go back to your homes and tell your people that you want to give them more money, I ask you, what provision you are making now for more money for the people? There is practically no gold being coined. There is no material increase of the circulation from that source. There is none from the coinage of silver. There is none from the issue of certificates. There is none from the issue of greenbacks. There is none from the issue of national bank notes. There is a letter on the first page of this morning's Record which indicates that the national banks are withdrawing their circulation instead of increasing it. In fact the total amount of the national bank notes is constantly decreasing. On the 1st of November, 1893, the amount of such notes in circulation was $209,311,-993; the amount in circulation December 1, 1893, $208,948,105; the amount in circulation January 1, 1894; $208,538,844; the amount in circulation February 1, 1894. $207,862,107, and the amount in circulation to-day, (February 27, 1894) $207,-420,440. Yet here is a great people demanding money and the great western country waiting for development. To be developed it must have money.

What provision are you going to make? I ask that this bill shall be passed in order that you may coin and put in circulation $55,000,000 of silver which will not more than supply the yearly need of this country according to Mr. Sherman's statement of three years ago.

Mr. Coombs.—Will it interrupt the gentleman to ask him to tell us how the issue of fifty-five millions of silver is to get into the hands of the people?

Mr. Bryan.—In this way, Mr. Chairman: We coin these fifty-five millions; that money is put into the Treasury, and then, instead of issuing bonds to get money to run the Government, let that silver be used to pay the expenses of the Government. In that way it goes into circulation without any difficulty. Why, sirs, we need it so badly that we were told a few days ago by the gentleman from New York (Mr. Hendrix) that, while the ostensible purpose of the bond issue was to get gold for the reserve, the real object was to get money to run the Government. Was there ever a better time to coin this money than now? If our eastern Democrats and all our eastern Republicans are willing to give the people fifty-five millions of this coinage, which they can give easily, which they can give right now, when we need the money, when we are borrowing money to pay our running expenses; if they are not willing to give this money now, I want to ask when will they be willing to give the people more money?

Mr. Walker.—Does the gentleman want an answer?

Mr. Bryan.—Will it be in that sweet by-and-by that you are looking forward to, when the Republican party, as you say, will pay expenses by collecting more taxes?

Mr. Walker.—I will answer the gentleman. Never, never any flat money.

Mr. Bryan.—Mr. Chairman, I believe the gentleman speaks what he believes. I do not do him any injustice, for I repeat his own words. I believe that that gentleman would never give the people enough money to do their business with.

Mr. Walker.—I said flat money.

Mr. Bryan.—Never as long as he represents a constituency more interested in appreciating the value of the currency than in giving a sufficient quantity of money for our public needs. This is not flat money. It is silver coin.

Now, I want our friends to think about this. If we cannot justify the coinage of this seigniorage at this time when we need the money to meet the public expenditures; if we cannot justify it now, then I want you, gentlemen, to settle in your own minds when you are going to give the people a law that will supply them with money to keep pace with our population. Do you mean to say that you are going to confine the 67,000,000 of people in this country to the present currency? Do you mean to say that you never intend to give them more money of any kind? If you do intend to give them more money, here is the chance to do it.

If you do not want to give them this money, let it go forth that this Congress or those who are opposing this bill are in favor of confining a growing country, a developing country, to the present volume of currency, which must mean an appreciating dollar and fall in prices an increasing debt, increasing suffering and the piling up of the wealth of this country in the hands of the few even more rapidly than it has been done heretofore. If you are ready to say that, let us go out and fight the battle before the people. Let us leave it to them to determine the question. But, sirs, you cannot excuse yourselves for not giving the people this money unless you are prepared to show them how you can furnish a better money with which to do their business.

CHAPTER XXV.

SPEECH ON THE ROTHSCHILD-MORGAN BOND CONTRACT, DELIVERED IN THE HOUSE OF REPRESENTATIVES.

February 14, 1895.

The House having under consideration the joint resolution (H. Res. 275) authorizing the issue of $65,116,275 of gold 3 per cent. bonds, Mr. Bryan spoke as follows:

Mr. Speaker: This resolution embodies two purposes. It proposes to ratify the contract made by the Executive by authorizing the substitution of gold bonds to the amount of $65,116,275, bearing interest at a rate not exceeding 3 per cent., and payable not more than thirty years after date, in accordance with the request made in the President's message, and it also provides that greenbacks and Treasury notes redeemed with the gold purchased with these bonds shall not be re-issued.

I desire to call the attention of the House to the fact that the latter provision is intended to lock up in the Treasury $65,000,000 of legal-tender paper without making any provision whatever to supply the place of that currency. If we vote for this proposition, we vote to retire that much money without filling the void.

433

Mr. Warner. Will the gentleman allow me to ask him a question?

Mr. Bryan. I hope I shall not be interrupted.

Mr. Warner. Does not the gold fill the void?

Mr. Bryan. Mr. Speaker, the House knows that when I have time I never object to questions, and it is only because of my limited time to-day that I ask gentlemen not to interrupt me. In answer to the question, however, I would say that unless the greenbacks and Treasury notes are re-issued they will accumulate and a few more bond issues will retire all of them and deprive the country of that much of its circulating medium. For all practical purposes it is equivalent to a cancellation of this money and will offer a constant temptation to those who oppose greenbacks to draw out the gold and force further issues of bonds for the purpose of getting this kind of money out of the way.

But the main question presented by this resolution is whether we shall ratify the contract made by the Executive and issue gold bonds in order to save about a half million a year in interest. The supporters of this resolution urge us to consider it as a business proposition, and I shall discuss it as a business proposition. One gentleman has suggested that Democrats ought not to criticise the Administration. I want it understood that, so far as I am concerned, when I took the oath of office as a member of Congress, there was no mental reservation that I would not speak out against an outrage committed against my constituents, even when committed by the President of the United States.

The President of the United States is only a man. We intrust the administration of government to men, and when we do so, we know that they are liable to err. When men are in public office we expect them to make mistakes—even so exalted an official as the President is liable to make mistakes. And if the President does make a mistake, what should Congress do? Ought it to blindly approve his mistake, or do we owe it to the people of the United States, and even to the President himself to correct the mistake, so that it will not be made again? But some gentlemen say that the Democratic party should stand by the President. What has he done for the party since the last election to earn its gratitude? I want to suggest to my Democratic friends that the party owes no great debt of gratitude to its President. What gratitude should we feel? The gratitude which a confiding ward feels toward his guardian without bond who has squandered a rich estate. What gratitude should we feel? The gratitude which a passenger feels toward the trainman who has opened a switch and precipitated a wreck. What has he done for the party? He has attempted to inoculate it with Republican virus, and blood poisoning has set in. What is the duty of the Democratic party? If it still loves its President, it is its duty, as I understand it, to prove that it has at least one attribute of divinity left by chastening him whom it loveth.

Mr. Speaker, I do not intend to question the motives of officials who are responsible for this contract. We might criticise the conduct of the President in excluding all other advices and consulting only with the magnates of Wall street; and we might even suggest that he could no more expect to escape from asphyxiation if he locked himself up in a room and turned on the gas—but without questioning the motives of the President, I say, we have the right to express our judgment as to whether the discretion vested in the President has been wisely exercised. We are told that this is not only a business proposition, but a very insignificant question—just a little matter of saving half a million a year, that is all.

Mr. Speaker, I desire to ask these gentlemen who are always coming here with these " business propositions" why it is that no advocate of the gold standard dares to stand before the American people and unfold the full plan of the gold conspiracy. Why is it that our opponents keep bringing up one proposition at a time and saying, "An emergency is upon us; let us adopt this proposition at once, and leave the final settlement of the money question until some other time?"

Why is it that we never reach a time when these gentlemen are willing to consider the greatest of all the questions which are demanding settlement at the hands of the American people? Save $16,000,000 in thirty years? Why, sirs, this is a bigger question than $16,000,000.

Will you set a price upon human life? Will you weigh in the balance the misery of the people? What is the value of civilization to the human race—because the settlement of "this little question" may enormously affect the welfare of mankind? And yet gentlemen talk about its being a matter of small consequence, a little question, the mere saving of half a million dollars a year. Save the people $16,000,000 in thirty years—twenty-five cents apiece—by this resolution, and $16,000,000 will not measure the damage that may result to them in a third of that time.

What is this contract? I am glad that it has been public. It is a contract made by the Executive of a great nation with the representatives of foreign money-loaners. It is a contract made with those who are desirous of changing the financial policy of this country. They recognize by their actions that the United States has the right to pay coin obligations in either gold or silver, and they come to us with the insolent proposition, "We will give you $16,000,000, paying a proportionate amount each year, if the United

States will change its financial policy to suit us."
Never before has such a bribe been offered to our
people by a foreign syndicate, and we ought to so
act that such a bribe will never be offered again.
By this contract we not only negotiate with foreigners for a change in our financial policy, but
give them an option on future loans. They are
to have the option on all bonds which may be
issued before the first of next October.

What would be the effect of such a condition?
Do you suppose that anybody else will care to
bid when it is known that these men have the refusal of all bonds at any price? It makes a popular loan impossible. If these men alone did so
bid for the next issue, they can insist upon a condition that they shall have an option on a still
further issue of bonds. Shall we bind ourselves
to these men perpetually? I shall not raise the
question, because I am not prepared to discuss it
from a legal standpoint, whether the President
has a right to sell an option on bonds which may
be hereafter issued; but, sirs, I will say that if he
has the right, I believe he has made an inexcusa-
ble use of the discretion invested in him. We
cannot afford to put ourselves in the hands of the
Rothschilds, who hold mortgages on most of the
thrones of Europe.

The press despatches stated that the French
steamer La Gascogne, when she came into port a
few days ago, had the three red lanterns on her

foremasts, signifying: "Get out of the way; I cannot control my course." The President may be persuaded that this country has reached the point where it cannot control its own course, and it must supplicate foreign financiers to protect our Treasury; but he mistakes the sentiment of the American people if he thinks that they share with him in this alarm. The United States is able to take care of itself. It can preserve its credit and protect its people without purchasing at a high price the "financial influence" or the legitimate efforts of banking corporations, foreign or domestic.

I call attention also to the fact that these bonds may be made payable in thirty years. The contract does not call for thirty year bonds; it says that "any bonds of the United States," payable in gold, and drawing three per cent. interest, may be substituted in the place of the coin bonds. But there seems to be a fear that the bond-buyers may insist that the spirit of the contract may compel the issue of thirty-year bonds. In describing this contract, Mr. Speaker, I find in the "Merchant of Venice" language more expressive than any I can command. That language fits the contract which we are asked to ratify, and is as follows:

> "*Shylock.* This kindness will I show:
> Go with me to a notary, seal me there
> Your single bond, and, in a merry sport
> If you repay me not on such a day,

In such a place, such sum or sums that as are
Expressed in the condition, let the forfeit
Be nominated for an equal pound
Of your fair flesh, to be cut off and taken
In what part of your body pleaseth me.

* * * * *

"*Antonio.* Yes, Shylock, I will seal unto this bond."

Mr. Bowen.—Who wrote that, Shakespeare or Bacon?

Mr. Bryan.—I shall leave Mr. Donnelly and Mr. Ingersoll to settle the question of authorship. But, Mr. Speaker, it was decided that Mr. Shylock's bond, while it called for a pound of flesh, did not include any blood. The difference between the construction placed upon that bond and the construction which this House is asked to place upon the contract before us is, that we are asked to make the construction so liberal as to include the blood with the flesh. We have a right, according to the terms of the contract, to substitute a short-time bond, and yet the resolution permits the Secretary to issue a thirty-year bond.

This House is not prepared to give its sanction to a policy which contemplates a permanent public debt; but the rule adopted allows no opportunity for an amendment limiting the bonds to five or ten years. If we give the Secretary of the Treasury authority to issue a thirty-year bond, he is powerless to resist the demands of bond purchasers, because the contract is made. Ten days only are given for the exercise of the option. He cannot negotiate with anybody else; he cannot offer bonds to anyone else; he is in their hands; he must make a thirty-year bond if they ask it— and who doubts that they will ask it?

There is another objection to this contract. It provides for the private sale of gold bonds, running thirty years, at $1.04½ which ought to be worth $1.19 in the open market, and which could have been sold at public auction for $1.15 without the least effort.

Why this sacrifice of the interest of the United States? The Government's credit was not in danger; the bonds of the United States were selling in the market at a regular premium. The same kind of bonds having only twelve years to run were selling at over $1.12. What excuse was there for selling a thirty year bond for $1.04½? What defence can be made of this gift of something like seven million and a half dollars to the bond syndicate. We are told that we can avoid the sale of coin bonds at $1.04½ by authorizing three and a half per cent. gold bonds. What a privilege! Why, it is less than three months since ten year coin bonds were sold by the President at a premium which reduced the rate of interest to less than three per cent.

Has the credit of the country fallen so much in three months that a thirty year three per cent. gold bond is worth less now than a ten year three per cent. coin bond was then? Nothing has occurred within three months, except the President's messages to injure the credit of the country. If the President is correct in assuming that the financial world places a higher estimate on gold bonds than the coin bonds, why did he not secure a higher price for gold bonds? Did not purchasers know three months ago that coin bonds could be paid in silver? They certainly did and yet they were willing to loan money on those bonds for a short time at a lower rate of interest than Messrs. Morgan and Rothschild now offer to loan on long time gold bonds.

But why are gold bonds demanded? Gentlemen say that all our bonds are in fact payable in gold now. They either are payable in gold or they are not. If they are, then this legislation is not needed. If they are not, then the proposed legislation is a radical and violent change of policy. We insist that outstanding bonds are payable in gold or silver and that the United States has the right to choose the coin. The men who contracted for coin bonds understood this, and insisted upon a higher rate of interest on the ground that they be paid in silver. By what authority, then, does the President declare in his message: "Of course there should never be a doubt in any quarter as to redemption in gold of the bonds of the Government which are made payable in coin." Is he not aware of the fact that the debtor always has the choice of the coin, where only coin is mentioned? Is he not aware of the adoption of the Matthews' resolution in 1878? That resolution expressly declared the right of the Government to pay its bonds in either gold or silver. The resolution reads as follow:

"That all the bonds of the United States issued or authorized to be issued under the said act of Congress herein before recited, are payable principal and interest at the option of the Government of the United States in silver dollars of the coinage of the United States containing 412 one-half grains each of standard silver, and that to restore its coinage such silver coin as a legal tender in payment of said bonds, principal and interest, is not in violation of the public faith nor in the derogation of the rights of the public creditors."

That policy has never been changed by law, but the resolution before us makes a departure from the settled policy of the Government and provides for a bond payable specifically in gold. Do members realize the influence which would be exerted upon the public generally by the adoption of this resolution? The gentleman from Florida (Mr. Cooper) told us that his city recently issued gold bonds and we know that pressure is being brought to bear on other cities and on individuals to induce them to enter into gold contracts. If the Government discredits silver by making these bonds payable in gold only it will set an example which will go far towards compelling all borrowers to compromise payment in gold. As gold contracts increase in number the demand for gold will increase.

What a farce for men to talk about maintaining the parity between the metals by means of legislation which directly tends to destroy the parity and drives gold to a premium! The legislation proposed will either pledge the Government to redeem all bonds in gold or it will discredit bonds already in existence. The probability is that the adoption of this resolution would be followed immediately by the demand from the holders of other bonds that they be put upon the same gold footing. I say probably, I may say that such a course is certain. No sooner had the President asked for authority to issue gold bonds than his faithful lieutenant in the Senate, Mr. Hill, offered a resolution pledging the Government to redeem all bonds in gold if gold goes to a premium. This remarkable resolution read as follows:

"Resolved (If the House of Representatives concurs), That it is the sense of Congress that the true policy of the Government requires that its efforts should be steadily directed to the establishment of a safe system of bimetallism, wherein gold and silver may be maintained at a parity, and every dollar coined may be the equal in value and power of every other dollar coined or issued by the United States; but if our efforts to establish or maintain such bimetallism shall not be wholly successful, and if for any other reason our silver coin shall not hereafter be at a parity with gold coin and the equal thereof in value and power in the market and in the payment of debts, then it is hereby declared that the bonds of the United States, now or hereafter issued, which by their terms are payable in coin, shall, nevertheless, be paid in standard gold dollars, it being the policy of the United States that its creditors shall at all times be paid in the best money in use."

This would not only pledge the Government to the previous issue in gold but would relieve the recent purchasers from the loss which they guarded against by an extortionate interest and yet leave them enjoy the fruits of their extortion. Thus does one vicious proposition tread upon the heels of another. Mr. Hill's plan is even worse than the President's, for under the plan of the latter the bondholder would bear whatever loss might arise if gold should happen to fall below silver, but Mr. Hill's plan burdens the Government with all the risks and guarantees to the bondholders all the chance of gain. Not only is Mr. Hill's plan directly antagonistic to the principle of bimetallism, but it offers a reward to the creditor if he can destroy the parity between the metals, whereas the creditor is interested in maintaining the parity when the option lies with the Government.

It is alarming to note the aggressiveness of the creditor classes, and humiliating to think that Congress should be asked to comply with their wishes regardless of consequences. The first effect of this government in the direction of gold contracts would be to reduce the amount of our primary money, and to build our entire credit system upon a narrow base of gold. Think of making an indebtedness public and private of $13,000,000,000 payable in gold, with only $600,-000,000 of gold in the country, and that is an estimate!

The government estimate of gold coin in the United States on the first of January, 1895, was about $600,000,000, and of that sum only about $214,000,000 was visible. About $100,000,000 was in the Treasury of the United States, and $114,000,000 was held by national banks. Beyond that no one knows the whereabouts of any large amount of this gold. We know that no large amount of gold is in circulation among the people or in hiding, and yet, with only $214,000,-000 of visible gold, the United States is expected to conduct a safe business on a gold basis. To make the attempt is to invite a panic—nay, more, it is to guarantee a disaster.

And yet, Mr. Speaker, if the immediate effect is bad, the ultimate effect of the proposed policy is infinitely worse. Every act of legislation discriminating against silver gives an impetus to the

Government in favor of a gold standard, and makes the restoration of bimetallism more difficult. No one act could, in my judgment, do more to obstruct the re-establishment of free bimetallic coinage as it existed prior to 1873 than the act which the President is attempting to force upon Congress. Are the gentlemen who are urging it deceived as to its purpose and necessary effect when they speak of it as an insignificant matter, or do they presume upon the credulity of their hearers? Believing that it is a long step in the direction of universal gold monometallism, and believing that universal gold monometallism would bring this country continuous and increasing financial distress beyond the power of language to exaggerate, we protest against the passage of this resolution. If we love our country and are interested in its welfare, no sacrifice on our part should be too great if necessary to prevent the adoption of such a policy by this the foremost nation upon the earth.

While the question immediately before us is whether we shall authorize the issue of gold bonds, I ask you to consider for a moment whether we need to issue bonds of any kind. Bonds have been issued to replenish the gold reserve, and the gold reserve has been drawn out because the holders of greenbacks and Treasury notes have been allowed to designate the coin of redemption. In other words, the option which belongs to the Government has been surrendered to the holders of the notes, and this has been done, not by the legislative enactment, but by an administrative policy. If the withdrawal of gold could be stopped, no bonds would be necessary. It becomes important, therefore, to know whether the Government has a legal right to protect itself from the gold-grabbing by redeeming greenbacks and Treasury notes in silver when silver is more convenient. On the 21st of January, 1895, Secretary Carlisle made a statement before the House Committee on Appropriations, and I quote the following question and answer from a printed report of his testimony:

" Mr. Sibley, I would like to ask you (perhaps not entirely connected with the matter under discussion) what objection there could be to having the option of redeeming either in silver or gold lie with the Treasury instead of the note-holder?

Secretary Carlisle.—If that policy had been adopted at the beginning of the resumption—and I am not saying this for the purpose of criticising the action of any of my predecessors or anybody else—but if the policy of reserving to the Government at the beginning of resumption the option of redeeming in gold or silver all its paper presented had been adopted, I believe it would have worked beneficially, and there would have been no trouble growing out of it ; but the Secretaries of the Treasury from the beginning of resumption have pursued a policy of redeeming in gold or silver at the option of the holder of the paper, and if any Secretary had afterwards attempted to change that policy and force silver upon a man who wanted gold, or gold upon a man who wanted silver, and especially if he had made that attempt upon such a critical period as we have had within the last two years, my judgment is it would have been very disastrous. There is a vast difference between establishing a policy at the beginning and reversing a policy after it has been long established, and especially after the situation has been changed."

This is sufficient proof that the Secretary has the legal right to redeem greenbacks and Treasury notes in silver, but is restrained by the fear that a different precedent having been established, an exercise of the legal right at this time would be "very disastrous." Senator Sherman, in March, 1878, in testimony given before a Senate Committee, also recognized the right of the Government to redeem greenbacks with silver. I quote from his testimony:

"Senator Bayard.—You speak of resumption upon a bimetallic basis being easier. Do you make that proposition irrespective of the readjustment of the relative values of the two metals as we have declared them?

"Senator Sherman.—I think so. Our mere right to pay in silver would deter a great many people from presenting notes for redemption who would readily do so if they could get the lighter and more portable coin in exchange. Besides, gold coin can be exported, while silver coin could not be exported, because its market value is much less than its coin value.

"Senator Bayard.—By the first of July next, or the first of January next, you have eighteen or twenty millions of silver dollars which are in circulation and payable for duties, and how long do you suppose this short supply of silver and your control of it by your coinage will keep it equivalent to gold when one is worth ten cents less than the other?

"Secretary Sherman.—Just so long as it can be used for any thing that gold is used for. It will be worth in this country the par of gold until it becomes so abundant and bulky that people will become tired of carrying it about; but in our country that can be avoided by depositing it for coin certificates."

No law has ever been passed surrendering the Government's rights to redeem in silver; and it is as valuable now as it was just after the passage of the Bland law in 1878, which restored silver as a part of our standard money. The testimony above quoted was given by Senator Sherman, then Secretary of the Treasury, soon after the passage of the Bland Act and before the resumption of specie payment.

Now, notwithstanding the fact that the Government has a legal right to redeem in silver, and thus protect the people from the gold hoarders and gold exporters, the President continues to pay in gold even when gold must be purchased by an issue of bonds, and we cannot authorize the issue of any bonds for the purpose of buying gold without endorsing the policy which permits the drain of gold, and thus gives an excuse for a bond issue. So far, the surrender to the note-holder of the right to designate the coin of payment is purely an act of the Executive, and has never received legislative approval.

If it is said that the President will issue bonds anyhow, and we ought, therefore, to authorize a bond drawing a low rate of interest, I reply that until we can restrain the President from further increasing our bonded indebtedness, and compel him to protect the Government by redeeming in silver when that is more convenient, we can better afford to allow him to bear the responsibility alone than by approving his course pledge the Government to a continuation of his policy. If the Secretary thinks that it would now be disastrous to depart from a precedent established by a former Secretary of the Treasury Capitol, how much more difficult it would be to change the policy after endorsing it by an act of Congress.

So long as the note holder has the option, bonds may be issued over and over again without avail. Gold will be withdrawn either directly or indirectly for the purpose of buying bonds, and an issue of bonds compelled again, whenever bond buyers have a surplus of money awaiting investment. This experiment has been tried but instead of convincing the President of the utility of bond issues it has simply led him to try a new experiment. By purchasing gold in Europe he may enlarge the circle around which the gold must pass, but the only remedy is the restoration of the bimetallic principle and the exercise of the option to redeem greenbacks and treasury notes in silver whenever silver is more convenient or whenever such a course is necessary to prevent a run upon the Treasury. To delay the remedy is to prolong our embarrassment; to authorize bonds of any kind is to rivet upon the country the policy which has brought our present troubles upon us; to authorize bonds payable specifically in gold is to invite new difficulties and to establish a still more dangerous precedent.

I am glad to hear some of our Republican friends denounce this gold bond proposition, but are they not in effect condemning a Republican policy. The gold bond is the legitimate result of the policy inaugurated and continued by Republican administrations. It was a Republican administration which first surrendered to the note holder the option to demand gold in redemption of greenbacks and treasury notes, and it was rumored that President Harrison was preparing to issue bonds to buy gold just before his term expired. The substitute for the Springer Bill, that is the substitute offered by the gentleman from Maine (Mr. Reed) authorized the issue of coin bonds to buy gold and yet the Republicans almost without exception voted for that substitute.

I offered an amendment to the Reed substitute, an amendment which reafirms the Matthews' resolution declaring all coin bonds payable in gold or silver, and yet less than twenty (I think thirteen) Republicans voted for my amendment. The great majority of the Republicans thus declared that coin bonds are gold bonds in fact. If coin bonds are really gold bonds there is less reason for agitation about the word gold in the bond. We who believe that greenbacks and treasury notes are redeemable in either gold or silver at the option of the Government—we, who believe in the rights of the Government to redeem its coin bond in either gold or silver, we, I say, can object to gold bonds as a violent change in our monetary policy, but those who insist that greenbacks, treasury notes and coin bonds are all payable in gold on demand have far less reason to criticise the precedent.

I repeat, the President is simply carrying a Republican policy to its logical conclusion. If the Republicans are in earnest in their opposition to gold bonds let them come with us and help to make all bonds unnecessary by restoring the bimetallic principle and exercising the option invested in the Government to redeem coin obligations in either gold or silver. The Government is helpless so long as it refuses to exercise this option.

Mr. Dunn.—Don't you want to make it more helpless?

Mr. Bryan.—No sir; I do not propose to make it more helpless. I propose the only policy which will help the Government. I propose the only policy which will stop the leak in the Treasury. I only ask that the Treasury department shall be administered in behalf of the American people and not in behalf of the Rothschilds and in behalf of the other foreign bankers.

But, Mr. Speaker, I desire, in conclusion, to call the attention of our eastern brethren to the fact that this controversy can be no longer delayed. The issue has come and it must be met. On these financial questions we find that the Democrats of the East and the Republicans of the East lock arms and proceed to carry out their policies, regardless of the interest and the wishes of the rest of the country. If they form this union offensive and defensive, they must expect that the rest of the people of the country will drop party lines, if necessary, and unite to preserve their homes and their welfare.

If this is sectionalism the East has set the

example. The demand of our eastern brethren, both Republicans and Democrats, is for a steadily appreciating monetary standard. They are creditors. They hold our bonds and our mortgages, and, as the dollars increase in purchasing power, our debts increase and the holders of our bonds and mortgages gather in an earned increment. They are seeking to reap where they did not sow; they are seeking to collect that to which they are not entitled; they favor spoliation under the forms of law. The necessary result of their policy is the building up of a plutocracy which will make servants of the rest of the people.

This effort has gone on steadily, and for the most part stealthily, during the past twenty years, and this gold bond proposition is but another step in the direction of financial bondage. But I warn them that no slavery was ever perpetual. It has often been attempted, it has even been successfully attempted for a time, but the shackles are always open at last. Bondage is ephemeral, freedom is eternal. "Weeping may endure for a night, but joy cometh in the morning."

The time will come when the unjust demands and the oppressive exactions of our eastern brethren will compel the South and West to unite in the restoration of an honest dollar—a dollar which will defraud neither debtor nor creditor, a dollar based upon two metals, "the gold and silver coinage of our Constitution." Thomas Jefferson still survives and his principles will yet triumph. He taught equality before the law, he taught that all citizens are equally entitled to consideration of Government, he taught that it is the highest duty of Government to protect each citizen from injury at the hands of any other citizen. We seek to apply his principles to-day to this great nation; we seek to protect the debtor from the greed of the creditor; we seek to protect society from avarice of the capitalist. We believe that in the restoration of bimetallism we shall secure the re-establishment of equity and restore prosperity to our country.

CHAPTER XXVI.

SPEECH OF HON. CLAUDE A. SWANSON

RETIREMENT OF THE TREASURY NOTES AND THE FREE COINAGE OF SILVER.

"Mr. Chairman : There are two propositions pending before us for acceptance or rejection. The first proposition is the one passed by this Republican House last December, authorizing the Secretary of the Treasury to sell $500,000,000 of three per cent. bonds, with which to redeem all the outstanding Treasury notes, impound them in the Treasury, and thus contract the currency of this country to that extent.

"When this proposal was first before the House I earnestly opposed it in a speech, and did my utmost to defeat it. I then pointed out that if this bill should ever become law, and the currency should be contracted to the extent designed, the actual money in circulation among the people would be less than half the annual taxes collected from them, less than half the annual interest paid, and would not be one-fortieth of the aggregate indebtedness of this country ; yet this House, with its immense Republican majority, by a large majority vote passed this bill to destroy this vast amount of money that had been preserved to the people by a Democratic House of Representatives.

"This bill went to the Senate and there the Democratic Senators, led by Senator Jones, of Arkansas, aided by a few Republican and Populist Senators, defeated that iniquitous measure and substituted in its place a free-coinage bill, which that sterling Democrat from Georgia, Judge Crisp, now proposes that this House shall adopt instead of the bill it formerly passed.

"Thus these two measures embody clearly and distinctly the two ideas struggling for supremacy in our financial system.

"The proposal to sell bonds and to retire the Treasury notes, or greenbacks, is the only relief offered by the gold monometallist to remedy the present distressed situation. I am unalterably opposed to this. In the last Democratic House, when the friends of the present Administration sought to have a bill similar to this passed and the vast amount of paper money destroyed, I earnestly spoke and voted against it. I am glad to say that the bill practically similar to this was defeated in the Democratic House by a large majority.

"This bill, indorsed nearly unanimously by the tremendous Republican majority in this House, commits this party in the future, without doubt and without question, to the maintenance of the gold standard in this country.

"The Republican majority in this House exceeds 100, and the proposal for free coinage will be defeated by a vote equal to that majority.

"The Republican party during the last canvass denounced the present Administration for selling bonds, and yet its first advent to power is marked by passing in this House, and insisting upon its enactment into law, a proposition to sell $500,000,000 of bonds and the retirement from circulation of that amount of money. The Republican policy, as here disclosed, shows a complete alliance with the gold monometallists of this country. It shows that the Republican party still adheres to the financial teachings of Senator John Sherman, who, in 1873, demonetized silver without cause, without excuse, and when it was at a premium over gold of three per cent. It shows that this party's policy is a contraction and not an expansion of the currency. It proves to the country what I have always known, that the party that wantonly destroyed silver will never consent to its rehabilitation.

"In the future no one need be deceived. If he believes in and desires the remonetization of silver, he must vote for and form alliances with a party different from the Republican party.

"I shall not go over the ground that I did in my former speeches and point out the great dis-

asters that must and will inevitably follow if this
Republican measure becomes law and one-third
of the legal-tender money of our country be destroyed without substituting anything in its place.
In them I have pointed out how this would be followed by further stagnation in business and by a
further fall in the prices of all products and
property.

" These two measures, as I have said, present
clearly the two methods existing for the settling
of our financial troubles. One is the solution offered by the single-standard gold man, and the
other is the solution offered by those who believe
in bimetallism. The solution of the gold man,
clearly stated, is: We have a currency of about
$500,000,000 of Treasury notes, about $210,000,-
000 of national bank notes, and about 425,000,000
of standard silver dollars, with only about $600,-
000,000 of gold. They claim that all this currency is kept in circulation and at par by being
practically redeemed in gold. They claim that
there is a 'want of confidence' in our ability to
redeem this in gold, and that 'to restore this confidence' we should destroy or retire all of our
Treasury notes. To retire these Treasury notes
they propose to sell bonds either for them or for
gold with which to redeem them. When redeemed they propose that the Treasury notes shall be
either destroyed or locked up in the Treasury and
kept out of circulation.

"That this is their solution is shown by the recent sale of bonds and by the present proposition. When the Treasury notes have been destroyed, they propose to destroy the 425,000,000 of standard silver dollars in circulation. They claim that this is only fiat money, and that all fiat money should be retired. Their determination to destroy this large amount in silver dollars is clearly shown by the veto of the bill directing the coinage of the silver bullion in the Treasury, and the refusal of this single gold standard Republican House to permit us ever to vote on that proposition.

"They are opposed to repealing the tax on State banks and giving us a local currency to supplement our national currency. This was disclosed when the vote was taken upon this question in the last Congress, when every single gold standard member, whether Democrat or Republican, voted against it.

"Their determination is to destroy all the legal-tender money in the country except gold and national bank notes redeemable in gold. They claim that when this is done, while the currency will be greatly contracted, yet confidence and credit will be restored. This is the entire relief offered by them to remove the present difficulties and bring back to the country the general diffusion of wealth and of prosperity.

"I believe these remedies will but intensify and

make greater the evils and distress which over-shadow us to-day.

"The 'want of confidence' in our country to-day is not a want of confidence in our currency, but a want of confidence in the solvency and ability of the producing classes to meet their obligations.

"I have yet to see a person who, when he refused another credit, debated in his mind whether the person would pay him in silver, gold or green-backs. The question in his mind is whether the person will be able to pay him at all. The want of confidence, if it exists, is because he is afraid the person could not pay in any kind of currency.

"This want of confidence in the ability of the debtor to pay will be greatly increased if the single gold standard men should succeed in reducing by more than half what can be used in payments. Activity in business, credit, confidence, and prosperity cannot be revived until the value of all products and property is restored. People will not trade nor buy on a declining market. A person will not buy goods on Monday when he expects they will be lower on Friday. A man will not purchase a lot, house, or farm this year when he sees them declining in value, as he expects to be able to do so for less the next year. Thus a declining market means losses, stagnation in business, and a paralysis of all activity.

"Falling prices also create distrust among creditors, and hence a collection of their debts. A creditor will not extend time to a debtor when he perceives the property upon which he depends for payment each year lessening in value. Thus failing prices necessarily create a liquidation of all debts.

"The aggregate minimum indebtedness of this country in 1890 amounted to $20,227,170,546. The collection of this vast indebtedness is proceeding not from any want of confidence in our currency, but from a want of confidence in the security and value of the property pledged for its payment. The truth of this is witnessed each day.

"A bank loans money to a man of large business and great property. At the time of the loan the value of the property was far in excess of the amount loaned. The bank, seeing the great depreciation in property, refuses to extend the loan, forces collection, sells the property at a greatly-reduced price, and the man who was rich finds himself bankrupt in the shrinkage of values.

"Let us trace business in its actual ramifications and see if the sources of the present troubles do not arise from the low price of all products and property.

"A bank in New York loans money to a country bank. That bank, at a greater rate of interest, loans it to merchants and business men. These buy or manufacture goods which they sell to farmers or the producing classes. The wheat, corn, oats, tobacco, hay, horses, and cattle raised by them sell so low that they are unable to pay the merchant or manufacturer. The merchants and manufacturers, not being paid, are unable to pay the bank from which they borrowed. This bank, not having its outstanding notes paid, is unable to meet its own notes with the New York bank. The bank in New York, knowing the conditions, becomes uneasy. It forces the country bank to settle. This in turn forces the merchants and manufacturers to settle, who in turn force the farmer. The farmer, having disposed of his crop for less than cost of production, is compelled to have his farm and other property sold to pay his indebtedness. The value of his crops having been greatly reduced, his land and property engaged in the business are correspondingly reduced. Thus the sale, when made, fails to pay the merchant; the merchant, being unpaid, cannot pay the home bank, and this bank cannot pay its depositors or the New York bank. Thus we have a bankrupt farmer, a failed merchant, a broken manufacturer, unemployed laborers, and a suspended bank, with all its evils and losses. Hundreds of cases like this have occurred and continue to occur.

"The single gold standard man is blind enough to tell you that all this arises from a lack of confidence in our currency, resulting from the greenbacks in circulation. His remedy is to contract the currency, and further lower the prices of all products and property. This remedy is as stupid as the old blood-letting process in medicine, which, when a patient was dying for want of blood, the ignorant doctors would bleed him. It is said that George Washington was killed by this remedy. It seems a strange fate that the country of which he was the father should now suffer from the same pernicious mistake.

"It is evident to any thoughtful and reasoning mind that these deplorable conditions arise from the great, unnatural fall in the prices of all products, and that if the prices of them continue to decline these evils will be greatly increased. Relief from these ruinous conditions will not come until we witness an advance in the prices of products and of property.

"David Hume, the noted philosopher and historian, long ago said:

'If prices rise everything takes a new face; labor and industry gain life; the merchant becomes more enterprising, the manufacturer more diligent and skillful, and even the farmer follows his plow with greater alacrity and attention. If prices fall the poverty, begging, and sloth that must ensue are easily foreseen.'

"What occasioned this present great fall in prices was the cause of our existing troubles. Whatever will restore these prices will remove debt, will revive credit and confidence, give em-

ployment to labor, bring back business activity
and enterprise, and bless the land with plenty and
prosperity.

"We who advocate bimetallism—that is, the
free and unlimited coinage of both gold and silver
at the mints at a fixed ratio—believe that the great
fall in prices results from the demonetization of
silver and the adoption of gold alone as the
standard of value. We believe that, this being
the cause, prices will be enhanced or restored
when we remonetize silver and let our standard
of value rest, as formerly, upon both gold and
silver. We claim that the value of everything is
regulated by the great law of supply and demand.
That this great and universal law of supply and
demand regulates the value of money when exchanged for commodities.

"We claim that as society has progressed,
wealth increased, commerce enlarged, and tremendous new enterprises been undertaken, taxes,
interest, and all fixed charges been augmented,
the demand for money has become greater; that
while the demand for money has greatly increased,
yet the supply of it has been reduced half since
1873, when silver was demonetized and gold made
the standard of value or money of final payment;
that the demand for money of final payment having increased and the supply lessened by half, the
value of things exchanged for it, or measured by
it, must necessarily be reduced correspondingly.

"Thus the natural result of destroying half the money of the world would be to greatly appreciate the value of the remaining half and reduce to that extent the value of all products and property exchanged for or measured by it.

" John Locke, the greatest of all English thinkers, many years ago said:

' For the value of money, in general, is the quantity of all the money in the world in proportion to all the trade.'

"This is a profund truth, and but emphasizes what I here insist upon, that as our trade has wonderfully increased since 1873, and as one-half of our primary money was then destroyed, the result has been to double the price of gold, and hence reduce by half the value of everything sold for gold.

" John Stuart Mill, the great thinker and writer upon this question, has well said:

' That an increase in the quantity of money raises prices and a diminution lowers them, is the most elementary proposition in the theory of coinage, and without it we should have no key to any of the others.'

·'This self-evident truth must show that the destruction of half of the money of the world must result in an equal reduction in the price of all commodities.

" This vital truth was recognized by the fathers of this Republic when our Government was organized.

"Alexander Hamilton in his famous report of 1791, said:

'To annul the use of either metal as money is to abridge the quantity of circulating medium and is liable to all the objections which arise from a comparison of the benefits of a full with a scanty circulation.'

"The immortal Jefferson, who had the interest of the people at heart more than any American leader and who was the father of the Democratic party, in February, 1792, said:

'I concur with you that the unit must stand on both metals.'

"I stand here to-day as a Democrat, receiving my inspiration from Jefferson and not from the latter-day saints of the party, and repeat that the 'unit of value must stand on both metals.' That is Democracy. That is bimetallism.

"In 1852, R. M. T. Hunter, one of the most talented and distinguished sons of Virginia, in a report made to the Senate as Chairman of the Committee on Finance, said:

'But the mischief would be great, indeed, if all the world were to adopt but one of the precious metals as the standard of value. To adopt gold alone would diminish the specie currency more than half, and the reduction the other way, should silver be taken as the only standard, would be large enough to prove highly disastrous to the human race. We require, then, for this reason, the double standard of gold and silver, but above all do we require both to counteract the tendency of the specie standard to contract under the vast increase of the value of the property of the world.'

"Thus forty-two years ago, when we had the double standard and were blessed with unexampled prosperity and progress, this wise statesman and sage of Virginia prophesied the great mischief and evils which would inevitably follow if we should ever adopt but one metal as our standard of value. The Republican party in 1873 did just what this wise Democrat had over twenty years before warned them against. The debt, the misery, the failures, the stagnation in business, the unemployed labor, the low price of all products and property, and the scarcity of money bear evidence to-day of a complete fulfilment of this prediction. Thus we can trace back clearly and distinctly, our present distress to the existence of the gold standard. Relief cannot and will not come until we abandon this and again put our standard of value upon both gold and silver. But I will not stop the investigation of this question here.

I have proven that the present ruinous conditions result from the prevalence of this great fall in the price of everything, and that relief will only come from a rise in prices.

"I will now investigate the history of the rise and fall in the price of commodities, so that we can also ascertain the cause of the present low prices by historical data.

"The London *Economist*, a paper of world-wide fame for ability and statistical knowledge, has

compiled the average prices of twenty-two leading commodities on the 1st of January of each
year from the year 1846, which is very instructive
and significant. This compilation shows that the
price of these twenty-two leading commodities
increased in value from 1845 to 1873, and that
from 1873 to the 1st of January, 1892, they had
fallen about 33 per cent.

"Augustus Sauerbeck, of the London Statistical Society, a man of eminence and ability, has
investigated the prices of forty-five leading and
representative commodities on the London market
with the same astounding results, that the average
price of these gradually increased until 1873,
when the increase ceased and a decline commenced, which amounted, with the forty-five commodities, to about 34 per cent. in 1892.

"Dr. Soetbeer, statistician for Hamburg, Germany, and a famous economic authority, compiled
the prices of 100 leading articles on the Hamburg
market and fourteen of British exports with the
same astounding result, that commencing with
1873 the average price of these had gradually
declined, until in 1891 their decline amounted to
22 per cent.

"In 1891 a committee of the United States
Senate investigated the prices in this country of
223 articles, and in a report to Congress shows
that since 1873 the average price of these has declined 28 per cent.

"In 1872 the price of wheat was $1.24 per bushel; in 1894 it was 49 cents per bushel. In 1873 the price of cotton was 20.14 cents per pound; in 1894 it was 6.94 cents per pound.

" Statistics will exhibit the same great fall in the price of tobacco, corn, oats, cattle and horses, as well as in other commodities. These statistics are undisputed even by the gold monometallists. They are gathered from sources so reliable, presented by men of such reputation and authority, so in accord with our own knowledge and experience, that they cannot and will not be denied. They all agree in one thing—that, commencing with the year 1873, the world over, prices have fearfully declined. Consequently it is evident that at that time something must have occurred to occasion a condition so world-wide.

" We examine and we find that in 1872 Norway and Sweden substituted the gold standard for the silver standard. We find that in 1873 the United States abandoned the double standard of gold and silver and adopted the single gold standard. We find that the same year Germany went from the silver standard to the single gold standard. We find that in a very short time after Germany does this France and the Latin Union suspend the free coinage of silver and substitute the gold standard. Thus about this time occurred a convulsion in the financial world surpassing any which ever transpired in the physical world. The great commercial nations of the world at this time went from the double standard of value to the single gold standard.

"It is impossible to point out anything else that happened at this time to precipitate a fall in prices.

"Why should prices be on an ascending plane until 1873 and then suddenly take a declining plane, which becomes greater each year? There were no great inventions in that year to cheapen production and hence to reduce prices. That year marked no overproduction so as to account for the sudden change.

"Any thoughtful mind, bent upon the ascertainment of the truth, must be convinced beyond doubt that the low prices the world over, commencing with the demonetization of silver, must have been caused by that and nothing else.

"I have proven that all the accepted authorities upon financial questions agree that when you lessen the amount of primary money you lower the price of everything exchanged for money. I have shown that the wisest of statesmen and thinkers years before prophesied that if the world should ever discard either of the two money metals and adopt only one lower prices would result and the very diastrous conditions that now confront us would inevitably come. I have traced from facts and statistics, undisputed by anyone, that the fall in prices commenced, as foretold, precisely at the time that the world destroyed silver as one of the money metals. Can arguments or facts be more conclusive? I have shown that this fall in prices commenced in 1873, and resulted from demonetizing silver and destroying its monetary functions. Thus the proper relief from the present distress is plain and unmistakable.

"The relief which will restore prices, revive business, encourage industries, inspire confidence, give employment to labor, and pay debts is the restoration of silver as one of the money metals, as it existed prior to 1873.

"We must right the crime of that year. We must leave the darkness in which we are now groping and return to the light and sunshine we then left.

"We do not know where this new departure on the gold standard will take us. We do not even know that prices have touched the bottom. We have no experience behind us to tell us what will be the ultimate effect of the gold standard. The world never tried the gold standard prior to 1873. Since its adoption, in falling prices, in the vast accumulation of debt, in the numerous and immense failures, in the frequent and great panics, in paralyzed business, in the mistrust and wretchedness which overshadow the country, we witness its ruinous effects.

"I am no alarmist, but thought and reflection teach me that if the gold standard is to be per-

manently maintained and the policies and designs
of its advocates, as here disclosed, to be carried
out that we will witness a yet greater fall in the
prices of all commodities, and a further shrinkage
in all values, with their attendant evils. It is inevitable.

"We have just completed a reassessment of
the land in my home county, Pittsylvania, and in
the city of Danville, situated therein. The lessons taught by it are significant. It presents how
frightfully the gold standard is shrinking the value
of lands. In 1890 the real estate in Pittsylvania
county was assessed at $4,012,464. In 1895 the
assessment amounted to only $3,115,938, being
$846,526 less in 1895 than in 1890. With all the
buildings and improvements put upon the lands
their value was reduced in five years over 20 per
cent. The supply of land did not increase during
the five years, while the demand did on account
of increased population. Thus, under natural conditions, we should have expected an increase instead of a decrease in its value from 1890 to 1895.
The lands there will now scarcely bring half as
much as they would prior to the demonetization
of silver.

"The assessment for the city of Danville presents the same remarkable conditions. In 1890
the real estate assessed in Danville amounted to
$5,170,928. In 1895 it amounted to only $4,650,-
406, being a reduction of $520,522. Here is a

city with great improvements and buildings during this time, with increased population; yet, including all these, a reduction in five years of over half a million of dollars in real estate values.

"When we ponder these startling figures, we can readily understand how farmers and business men who were formerly prosperous and rich find themselves bankrupt and impoverished. They have been ruined not by any fault of their own, but by the shrinkage in the value of their property. This shrinkage continues under this single gold standard, and no one knows when it will cease.

"The world's supply of gold is too small to give value to its immense amount of property. Each year witnesses a greater struggle for its possession, and hence a greater sacrifice of property to obtain it.

"The only way to remove the present evils and prevent the greater ones which await us is to again give silver the right of free and unlimited coinage at the mints.

"This is the relief proposed by us in opposition to the Republican measure to sell five hundred millions of bonds and retire that amount of paper money. We are prepared to appeal to the country upon the two methods of relief here presented.

"The gold monometallist cannot deceive the people by a pretended friendship for silver in advocating an international agreement. There is

not the remotest chance of an international agreement. The last hopes of one have disappeared.
We were told to wait only until Lord Salisbury
and the Tory party of England should come into
power and soon an agreement would be reached.
They have attained power by an immense majority and have distinctly stated that England has no
intention of changing her present gold standard
or entering into any international agreement for
the coinage of silver. France and Germany have
distinctly stated that they would be parties to no
agreement without England. Thus there is no
hope for any international agreement. It is useless to discuss an international agreement which
will never come. The people who advocate delay-
ing action upon the silver question until an international agreement can be reached are not friendly
to silver and only indulge in it to delay action by
creating hopes which will never be realized. The
people of the United States must continue the
present gold standard or must alone adopt the
double standard of gold and silver. This is plain
and clear. It is an issue which must be met, and
which politicians may try but they cannot dodge
nor deceive the people upon.

"If one favors the gold standard then he must
approve the recent sales of bonds, the present
Republican measure to sell $500,000,000 worth
of bonds to retire that amount of paper money,
and finally to destroy all the standard silver dol-

lars. If the gold standard is to be maintained all of this will inevitably follow. It cannot and will not be prevented. If one is opposed to all this and believes that it will bring disaster and not relief, then he should advocate that the United States should again reopen its mints to the free and un-limited coinage of silver and again make silver money of primary payment.

"I believe this. I am opposed to any sale of bonds. I am opposed to retiring the greenbacks and contracting the currency. I believe that the coin notes should be redeemed in either gold or silver, at the option of the Government and not of the holder. I believe that a continuance of the gold standard will precipitate a continued and a frightful fall in the prices of all commodities. I believe that it has more than doubled all debts, taxes, interest, and fixed charges. I believe that when our mints are opened to silver, prices will advance and the present troubles will disappear.

"Being convinced that there is no chance for an international agreement, I am prepared to vote for this country at once to resume the free and unlimited coinage of silver.

"No evils which the distorted imaginations of those who oppose this have presented can equal those which I am convinced will come if we con-tinue the single gold standard.

"I am convinced that the United States is able to do this and maintain all the silver coined at a parity with gold. I believe that when this is done silver bullion will rise in value until it is worth the coinage value. Every silver dollar coined to-day is at a par with gold. It is only the uncoined silver that is not at par. All that will be coined at our mints and made a legal tender will circulate at par with gold. We have experience in the past that should convince us that the United States is able to do this.

"France, from 1803 to 1873, by having her mints open to the free coinage of both gold and silver at the ratio of 15½ to 1, maintained that parity between them the world over. She was able to do this despite the great disparity existing during that time in the production and quantity of gold and silver. We to-day are more prepared to do this than was France when she maintained it.

"Statistics in 1870 show that France had about 10 per cent. of the imports and exports of the world. In 1889 the United States had nearly 10 per cent. of the imports and exports of the world. Mulhall, the world's greatest statistician, shows that the productive power of the United States is three times as great as was that of France in 1870 in proportion to the rest of the world. In 1870 France furnished less than 12 per cent. of the world's great agricultural products, while to-day we furnish about 20 per cent. of the world's supply. France in 1870 produced about 13 per cent. of the world's manufactures, and the United

States to-day furnishes almost 31 per cent. of the world's entire product. In 1870 France had about 7¾ per cent. of the world's railway mileage, while the United States now has about 44 per cent. of the world's entire mileage. In 1870 France's banking power in comparison with that of the world was 4 per cent, and the United States to-day has 32 per cent. of that of the world. In internal commerce and business we greatly exceed the proportion that was then possessed by France. Our wealth to-day in comparison with that of the world far exceeds what France's was in comparison with that of the world in 1870. Thus, by whatever test measured, the United States is able to do more than France did at that time. Yet from 1803 to 1873 France was able to maintain the parity between gold and silver the world over at the ratio of 15½ to 1. She did this despite the fact, that at that time the average number of ounces of silver in the world was thirty times as great as the average number of ounces of gold. To-day the number of ounces of silver in the world is about sixteen times as great as the number of ounces of gold—the ratio at which we propose to resume coinage. Thus to resume coinage as proposed in the United States, with all its greater ability and power, would only have to do half as much as France accomplished for seventy years. There should be no question that we can do this. We are safe in making the venture.

Success will crown our efforts. All we need is the courage and the resolution to establish our own financial system, suited to our wants and needs. I am convinced by thought and study that the United States is amply able to resume the coinage of silver and maintain parity. I am convinced that when this is done, prices will be restored and general prosperity and progress will return. I am convinced that the paths that the single gold standard men are trying to entice us into will but carry us further into the night of darkness and plunge us deeper into the abyss of sorrow and distress.

" Mr. Chairman, this great issue is now before the American people, and they are stirred upon it as they were never stirred before. They recognize the vast importance and the far-reaching consequences which will result from the proper settlement of this vital question.

" The coming great conflict, which will be fought to the finish, is the battle of the standards. The people have become tired of the miserable make-shifts and the temporary policies which the politicians have devised to avoid the settlement of this great question. The people can no longer be deceived.

"The great masses of the people are convinced that the continuance of the gold standard only benefits the capitalists and money lenders, and is destructive of the interests of the laborer, farmer, merchant and the business man. Politicians may try, but they cannot create false issues. Issues exist in the condition and in the minds of the people, and they must be met. This great problem cannot be brushed aside. Each year it rises into more and more importance.

"The intense struggle of the people for this reform is but a supreme effort on their part to release themselves from the greed, avarice and domination of the moneyed classes.

"The boast of the Democracy in all the years of its history has been that it is the party of the common people; that it is the champion of the rights of the toiling laboring masses. It has never espoused the cause of classes seeking to enrich themselves by depredation upon the masses. It is too late for it to do so now. It cannot climb upon the gold standard platform without trespassing upon ground long since occupied by and belonging to the Republican party.

"The issue is clear. The duty of Democracy is plain. It should make common cause with the people, remain true to its traditions and history, and carry the country back to that system and to those principles which our fathers founded and which gave us great prosperity and wealth, and the departure from which has brought us to our present woes and distresses." (Applause.)

CHAPTER XXVII.

THE FIRES STILL BURN.

The camp fires of patriotism still burn. The worm is not dead. The defeat of bimetallism is only temporary. It was not an ignominious one. All great causes and especially all great reforms in the interests of the masses have had set backs. The grand cause of free silver still has its able champions whose felicity it will soon be to see the consummation of the plans they are so earnestly advocating, and the application of the doctrine in which they believe.

The last presidential election was a close contest. Republicans and gold standard advocates made a grand blare of trumpets when the election of Major McKinley was established. They drew lessons and pointed morals from the results of the contest which were not warranted by the premises. Taking into consideration, as they did, the bare fact of McKinley's election without noting the circumstances leading up to it, and without considering the extremely large vote polled by the candidate of the bimetallic standard. Indicating the opinion of a very large body

(482)

of voters, they announced in flaring and exaggerated terms what they claimed as an overwhelming defeat of free silver. Frequently after the election of Nov. 4, '96, one heard in the public places and read in the press statements to the effect that a severe and impressive lesson had been administered to the Free Silver party, and that for years hence, after McKinley had given the country a magnificent administration, there would not be enough free silver men left to carry on a campaign. To use the expression William Bryan adopted with telling force so often, "Truth crushed to earth shall rise again." The six million voters for free silver have not changed their politics. If they live they'll be at the polls four years hence voting for the same principles they voted for last election, and they will bring thousands with them who will be brought to see the beauties and worth of the bimetallic standard and who will vote with them.

On November 6, two days after the election, and when enough of the figures were in to establish beyond dispute the election of Mr. McKinley. Mr. Bryan made the following announcement which was received with universal satisfaction all over the country and was given much favorable comment abroad. Mr. Bryan said:

"Conscious that millions of loyal hearts are saddened by temporary defeat, I beg to offer a word of hope and encouragement. No cause ever had supporters more brave, earnest, and devoted than those who have espoused the cause of bimetallism. They have fought from conviction, and have fought with all the zeal which conviction inspires. Events will prove whether they are right or wrong. Having done their duty as they saw it, they have nothing to regret.

"The Republican candidate has been heralded as the advance agent of prosperity. If his policies bring real prosperity to the American people, those who opposed him will share in that prosperity. If, on the other hand, his policies prove an injury to the people generally, those of his supporters who do not belong to the office-holding class, or to the privileged classes, will suffer in common with those who opposed him.

"The friends of bimetallism have not been vanquished; they have simply been overcome. They believe that the gold standard is a conspiracy of the money changers against the welfare of the human race, and until convinced of their error they will continue the warfare against it.

"The contest has been waged this year under great embarrassments and against great odds. For the first time during this generation public attention has been centered upon the money question as the paramount issue, and this has been done in spite of all attempts upon the part of our opponents to prevent it. The Republican Convention held out the delusive hope of international bimetallism, while Republican leaders labored secretly for gold monometallism. Gold-standard Democrats have publicly advocated the election of the Indianapolis ticket, while they labored secretly for the election of the Republican ticket. The trusts and corporations have tried to excite a fear of lawlessness, while they themselves have been defying the law, and American financiers have boasted that they were the custodians of National honor, while they were secretly bartering away the Nation's financial independence.

" But, in spite of the efforts of the Administration and its supporters, in spite of the threats of money loaners at home and abroad, in spite of the coercion practiced by corporate employers, in spite of trusts and syndicates, in spite of an enormous Republican campaign fund, and in spite of the influence of a hostile daily press, bimetallism has almost triumphed in its first great fight. The loss of a few States, and that, too, by very small pluralities, has defeated bimetallism for the present, but bimetallism emereges from the contest stronger than it was four months ago.

" I desire to commend the work of the three National Committees which have joined in the management of this campaign. Co-operation between the members of distinct political organizations is always difficult, but it has been less so this year than usual. Interest in a common cause of great importance has reduced friction to a minimum. I hereby express my personal gratitude to the individual members as well as the executive officers of the National Committee of the Democratic, Populist, and Silver Parties for their efficient, untiring, and unselfish labors. They have laid the foundation for future success, and will be remembered as pioneers when victory is at last secured.

" No personal or political friend need grieve because of my defeat. My ambition has been to secure immediate legislation, rather than to enjoy the honors of office, and, therefore, defeat brings to me no feeling of personal loss. Speaking for the wife who has shared my labors, as well as for myself, I desire to say that we have been amply repaid for all that we have done.

" In the love of millions of our fellow-citizens, so kindly expressed, in knowledge gained by personal contact with the people, and in broadened sympathies, we find full compensation for whatever efforts we have put forth. Our hearts have been touched by the devotion of friends, and our lives shall prove our appreciation of the affection of the plain people, an affection which we prize as the richest reward which this campaign has brought.

" In the face of an enemy rejoicing in its victory, let the roll be called for the next engagement, and urge all friends of bimetallism to renew their allegiance to the cause. If we are right, as I believe

we are; we shall yet triumph. Until convinced of
his error, let each advocate of bimetallism continue the work. Let all silver clubs retain their
organization, hold regular meetings, and circulate
literature. Our opponents have succeeded in
this campaign, and must now put their theories to
the test. Instead of talking mysteriously about
'sound money' and 'an honest dollar,' they must
now elaborate and defend a financial system.
Every step taken by them should be publicly considered by the silver clubs. Our cause has prospered most where the money question has been
longest discussed among the people. During the
next four years it will be studied all over this
nation even more than it has been studied in the
past.

"The year 1900 is not far away. Before that
year arrives, international bimetallism will cease
to deceive; before that year arrives, those who
have called themselves gold standard Democrats
will become bimetallists and be with us, or they
will become Republicans and be open enemies;
before that year arrives, trusts will have convinced still more people that a trust is a menace
to private welfare and public safety; before that
year arrives, the evil effects of a gold standard
will be even more evident than they are now, and
the people then ready to demand an American
financial policy for the American people will join
with us in the immediate restoration of the free

and unlimited coinage of gold and silver at the present legal ratio of 16 to 1, without waiting for the aid or consent of any other nation.

"W. J. BRYAN."

Overwhelming and all-pervading prosperity has not yet come. How true are the predictions of William J. Bryan we shall see. As he says, "The year 1900 is not far away."